RENÉ DESCARTES

was born in 1596. Probably because of
his delicate health in childhood, Descartes
early cultivated his enduring habit of
meditation. A proud, aloof, self-contained
man, Descartes achieved some fame even in his
youth. He lacked the patience with detail
that characterizes a scientist, and preferred
instead careful study and contemplation, which
led to the brilliant flashes of insight for
which he and his age are famous. Though
Descartes was considered by many to be an
atheist, he never actually swerved from the
path of his early religious training. He
devoutly believed that God was responsible for,
and guaranteed the truth of, his mathematics
and physics.

A BANTAM CLASSIC

ESSENTIAL WORKS

of

DESCARTES

TRANSLATED BY
LOWELL BAIR

WITH AN INTRODUCTION BY
DANIEL J. BRONSTEIN

BANTAM BOOKS / NEW YORK

ESSENTIAL WORKS OF DESCARTES

Published as a Bantam Classic / August 1961

CONTENTS

INTRODUCTION

I

Philosopher, scientist, mathematician, Descartes is none the less an engaging writer. Without the usual quotations from authorities, and with a minimum of technical jargon, his *Discourse on Method* tells about his schooling, his doubts, his travels and discoveries, and manages to convey the excitement and deep satisfaction which he himself experienced in applying a newly discovered method to problems in the sciences. Expressing the modest hope that some readers may find something of value in the *Discourse*, he invited all to send him their reactions so that he could benefit from their criticisms. (In the days before periodicals and timely reviews this was the only way an author could know how his work was received.) Now, three centuries later, the *Discourse* and the *Meditations* are still lucid, refreshing and stirring documents of the human mind seeking to understand itself and its surroundings by the unaided use of reason. This is not to say that there are no recondite passages in Descartes, or obscurities; there are, and even fallacious arguments and uncriticized dogmas, both philosophical and theological. But somehow they don't seem to loom large or detract seriously from his major achievements. To evaluate these achievements we must know something of his life and times.

Descartes was born in 1596 and died in 1650, when Newton was only eight years old. A contemporary of Galileo, he knew of the Italian's work but never met him. He admired Francis Bacon, and had contacts with Thomas Hobbes, William Harvey, and the great French mathematician Pierre de Fermat. The sciences of mechanics and medicine, which were then in their infancy, intrigued Descartes and he correctly anticipated a great future for them.

When he was eight years old, he was entered in the Royal

College of La Flèche which had just been established by the Jesuits at Anjou. The curriculum included Latin, literature, history, and of course theology and philosophy, not to mention tennis and fencing.* The last three years were devoted to philosophy, which at that time meant logic and ethics, mathematics, physics, and metaphysics. We can infer that Descartes was a pretty good student (although he refers to himself as only average) from the fact that he was given two special privileges: he was allowed to stay in bed late in the morning (a time he found ideal for concentrated thought) and was given access to books forbidden to other students; these included, perhaps, Raymond Lully and books on magic and the occult. Writing about his education in the *Discourse on Method* twenty-five years later, he confessed to a great disappointment. His schooling did not provide him with the wisdom which he had hoped to achieve; and since he regarded La Flèche as one of the most celebrated schools in Europe, and its teachers among the best, he could only conclude that there was no such wisdom in the world as he had been led to expect.

It was in Descartes' student days that Galileo made his brilliant discovery of the moons of Jupiter with the recently invented telescope. A special ceremony at La Flèche on June 6, 1611 which hailed this discovery by the celebrated mathematician of the Grand Duke of Florence, must have made a deep impression on the fifteen-year-old student at La Flèche. And it is not surprising that one of Descartes' earliest publications, his *Dioptrics*, was mainly concerned with the design and improvement of the telescope.

II

It has been the custom for a long time to reprint Descartes' *Discourse on Method* as if it were an independent work. Actually it was merely an introduction to three scientific treatises, which Descartes called "essays of this method." *Dioptrics*, the first of these, contains, in addition to suggested improvements in the telescope and microscope, an examination of the structure of the eye, a theory of vision and a statement of the law of refraction. The second, *Meteors*, discusses atmospheric phenomena and explains rainbows,

* According to his first biographer, Adrien Baillet (*La Vie de Monsieur Descartes*, 1691), Descartes wrote a little treatise, *On the Art of Fencing*, which has been lost.

while the third, the most famous of all Descartes' scientific works, his *Geometry*, offers many ingenious solutions to famous problems by his new method of applying algebra to geometry (analytic geometry). It also contains numerous contributions to the theory of equations and improvements in mathematical notation, some of which are still in use today. These scientific essays are not exactly easy reading, but the *Discourse* itself can be understood without them. It is worth noting, however, that when Descartes wrote about his Method of discovering truth in the sciences, he was not talking about a vision or a hope. He had already proved that his Method worked, and he was offering that proof to his readers.

The *Discourse on Method*, together with the *Dioptrics*, *Meteors*, and *Geometry*, published in Leyden in 1637, was actually the result of a compromise. As Descartes explains in Part V of the *Discourse*, he had been planning for some time to publish a somewhat different work to be called *The World*. "I had planned to include in it everything that I thought I had learned about the nature of material things." But he changed his mind when he heard (in 1633) that Galileo had been condemned and made to recant for holding that the earth moves and the sun stands still. The Inquisition at Rome even went so far as to declare this doctrine heretical. Since Descartes held similar views, he decided that to publish *The World* at such a time would only be to invite trouble and to court disaster for his philosophy, if not for himself personally. Anxious to have his ideas accepted and taught in the schools instead of the scholastic doctrines which he considered empty and inimical to scientific progress, he decided to withhold those of his views which might arouse the Church. *The World* was never published as he had originally planned it. Parts of it were incorporated in the *Discourse* and in the *Principles of Philosophy*; other parts were published posthumously; and some of it he never completed.

After 1633 Descartes wrote with one eye on Rome. His writings must be read, because they were written, with the condemnation of Galileo in mind. This is not to accuse him of insincerity or of cowardice. He believed that his philosophy harmonized with sacred doctrine as well as, if not better than, Aristotle's. His goal was to win over the theologians at the Sorbonne, at La Flèche, and at Rome, by first publishing his metaphysical views and then showing that the basic ideas of his physics are contained therein. With this in mind, his *Meditations on First Philosophy in Which the Existence of*

*God and the Immortality of the Soul** are Demonstrated* were dedicated *To the Most Wise and Illustrious the Dean and Doctors of the Sacred Faculty of Theology in Paris.* He addressed the Doctors in language of such extravagant flattery coupled with expressions not merely of humility but of self-abasement that an almost comic effect is produced.

"So high is the esteem in which your Faculty is held, and so authoritative is the name of the Sorbonne, that no other body, with the exception of the Sacred Councils, has ever been held in such great deference, not only in matters of faith, but also of human philosophy, for everyone acknowledges that it is impossible to find elsewhere greater perspicacity and soundness, or greater wisdom and integrity of judgment. Consequently I have no doubt that if you will deign to concern yourselves with this treatise, first by correcting it (for, being aware not only of my humanity but also of my ignorance, I would not dare to guarantee that it contains no errors), then by adding to it those things which are lacking, . . . I have no doubt . . . that all the errors and false opinions which have ever existed with regard to these two questions will soon be effaced from the minds of men."

Writing to his lifelong friend, Father Mersenne, Descartes adopted quite another tone: ". . . and I want to say, just *entre nous*, that these six *Meditations* contain all the fundamental ideas of my physics. But please keep this quiet, because if they knew it, the Aristotelians would be very reluctant to accept my views. What I am hoping is that they will become convinced by the very reasonableness of my doctrines before they realize that I am rejecting Aristotle's." Despite Descartes' blandishments, the learned Doctors at the Sorbonne never did lend their support to his *Meditations.* Father Mersenne distributed them to a number of theologians and philosophers —including Gassendi, Hobbes, Arnauld—who sent many criticisms of Descartes' views. These, together with his *Replies*, were published with the second edition of the *Meditations.* They occupied about six times as much space as the *Meditations* themselves. In his *Replies* Descartes corrected misinterpretations and expanded some of his ideas to produce greater clarification, but did not acknowledge that any of his critics had found an error in his writing.

* In the second and subsequent editions of the *Meditations* the phrase "Immortality of the Soul" was replaced by "the Real Distinction of the Soul and Body." Descartes explained in a letter that "I cannot prove that God cannot annihilate the soul, but only that it is of a nature entirely distinct from body and consequently that it is not by nature subject to perish with the body—which is all that is required to establish religion; and it is also all that I propose to prove."

III

Descartes is sometimes classified as a skeptic or as an advocate of universal doubt, as in this recent comment: "Like all men of his age, Descartes doubted everything including his own existence." Doubt does have an important role in his thinking; he used it to rid his mind of the errors that had crept into it since his earliest days. The method of doing this was similar, he thought, to that of removing the rotten specimens from a basket of apples. Wouldn't it be best to turn *all* the apples out of the basket, and then look them over one by one, returning the good apples and leaving out the rotten ones? In the same way, Descartes resolved to doubt all his beliefs for the purpose of reëxamining them and reinstating only those that were in conformity with reason. But he wanted it understood that he was not "imitating those skeptics who doubt for the sake of doubting and make a display of constant indecision; on the contrary," he said, "the sole object of my whole plan was to acquire certainty, to clear away the shifting soil and sand in order to find the rock or clay beneath it." (*Discourse*, Part III)

Descartes did not doubt because he was actually perplexed or uncertain of some of his beliefs, but because he wanted to discover whether there is anything that is certain (because it *cannot* be doubted). Even so, he specifically exempted several classes of belief from examination. These included the beliefs of his faith and the maxims of a code of morality which he adopted provisionally (see *Discourse*, Part III) while he was working out his philosophical beliefs. Replying to Gassendi's criticism, Descartes clarified this point as follows:

"But we must note the distinction emphasized by me in various passages, between the practical activities of our life and an enquiry into truth; for, when it is a case of regulating our life, it would assuredly be stupid not to trust the senses, and those skeptics were quite ridiculous who so neglected human affairs that they had to be preserved by their friends from tumbling down precipices. It was for this reason that somewhere I announced *that no one in his sound mind seriously doubted about such matters:** but when we raise an enquiry into what is the surest knowledge which the human mind can obtain, it is clearly unreasonable to refuse to treat them as doubtful, nay even to reject them as false, so as to allow us to become aware that certain other things, which cannot be thus

* In the synopsis of his *Meditations*, Descartes wrote that "no man of sound mind has ever doubted that there is a world, that men have bodies, and other such things."

rejected, are for this very reason more certain, and in actual truth better known by us." (*Reply to Objections* V)

The practical effect of Descartes' "universal" doubt emerges in connection with the first rule of his *Method*, "never to accept anything as true which I did not know to be evidently so, that is, carefully to avoid precipitancy and prejudice, and to include nothing in my judgments except what presented itself so clearly and distinctly* to my mind that I would have no occasion to doubt it." Not only must one remove prejudice from his mind (difficult enough) but he must rely strictly on the evidence as he sees it. It will no longer do to rely on Aristotle, St. Augustine, or St. Thomas. Science cannot rest on the method of authority, and it was a philosophy for the new science that Descartes was writing. He admitted that the undertaking to strip oneself of all former beliefs was not meant for everyone. Those with enough fortitude to attempt it would very likely have even more exalted plans of their own. Hence he declined the role of reformer of other men's beliefs and insisted he was merely relating his own intellectual biography.

Did Descartes succeed in setting aside all his former beliefs (with the exceptions noted)? Hardly. His writings contain many assumptions, implicit as well as explicit, that he never questioned. For example, there is the principle of causality, that there must be as much reality in the cause as in the effect, a principle he adopted from scholastic philosophy. Other assumptions are implicit in this one, for example, that ideas have "degrees of reality" which we can somehow measure and compare with one another. Descartes further assumed that we have an idea of God and that this idea has a very high degree of reality. Applying the principle of causality to his idea of God, he argued that such an idea could only have been produced by a cause having at least an equally high degree of reality, namely God himself. He was challenged on this by the authors of the *Second set of Objections*, who asked:

". . . how do you know that that idea would have come before your mind if you had not been nurtured among men of culture, but had

---

* Descartes' explanation of a clear and distinct idea is found in his *Principles of Philosophy*, Part I, Principle 45. "I term that *clear* which is present and apparent to an attentive mind, in the same way as we assert that we see objects clearly when, being present to the regarding eye, they operate on it with sufficient strength. But the *distinct* is that which is so precise and different from all other objects that it contains within itself nothing but what is clear."

passed all your life in some desert spot? Have you not derived it from reflections previously entertained, from books, from interchange of converse with your friends, etc., not from your own mind alone or from a supreme being who exists?"

Descartes' reply was that the argument would be the same with regard to the persons from whom he was supposed to have derived the idea of God. Where did they get it? The answer would always have to be the same. It was from God that the idea first originated.

Another proposition that seemed self-evident to Descartes is one that in these post-Freudian days no longer seems correct, let alone self-evident, namely "that nothing can exist in the mind, in so far as it is a thinking thing, of which it is not conscious." (*Meditation 3*; see also *Objections IV*, and Descartes' *Reply* to same.) Here also, there is an additional assumption, and probably an unconscious one at that, that the *mind* is an entity which contains thoughts even as a book contains pages. Another basic assumption of Descartes' metaphysics is his chosen criterion of truth itself, that "whatever I clearly and distinctly conceive, is true." The authors of *Objections II* pointed out that we have often seen a man deceived in those matters concerning which he believed he alone had clear knowledge, and they asked:

"What if your nature be such as to be continually, or at least very frequently deceived?"

Descartes' unskeptical reply was that we have a faculty of recognizing truth, given to us by God, and when we use this faculty properly, i.e. when we affirm what is clear and distinct, we cannot be mistaken, since otherwise God would be a deceiver. This reply opened him to the charge of circularity, since he used clear and distinct ideas to prove the existence of God, and then said that only God can guarantee the truth of our ideas. However that may be, his apparent need for a divine guarantee of philosophic and scientific truth may sound strange coming from "the father of modern philosophy" and one of the founders of scientific method. It is paradoxical that while Descartes was determined to rid physics of useless scholastic concepts like substantial forms and occult qualities, he found it necessary (or politic?) to assign a key role to God, who not only created the world, and recreates it at every moment, but is needed to support all truth claims in philosophy and science. It was because he felt that the truths of philosophy and science must be demonstrably certain, and proof against all possible doubt, that he needed the divine guarantee. There is, however, evidence from his letters to support the hypothesis that he anticipated attacks on his unorthodox physical theories by those who had condemned Galileo. He planned to defend himself by citing his proofs of the existence of God, and of the distinction of body and soul; also his view that the universe and its laws are dependent on God. Furthermore, he insisted that nothing in his philosophy was in opposition to established religion.

The reader will probably find other examples of propositions which Descartes took for granted. It is just too hard not to assume what really seems self-evident. Although Descartes employed doubt as a technique of rediscovery and evaluation of his beliefs, his approach to knowledge was quite the opposite of the skeptic's. For he believed that not only knowledge, but certainty, was attainable in philosophy and in science; he looked forward to the day when the implementation of his principles would make us "lords and masters of nature," and at one time he thought that two or three more discoveries would enable him to reach his goal.

IV

But how does one who has resolved to accept nothing as true except what can pass the most rigorous test of clarity and indubitability, find his first truth? Is there anything that is true beyond all possible doubt? Just as Archimedes, in order to move the earth, asked for a single fixed point, so Descartes needed one impregnable truth as a basis for reconstructing his beliefs. Where could he find it? Can't a confirmed skeptic doubt everything? In that case nothing at all will be certain, except perhaps this one proposition, that nothing is certain. Seeing, hearing, remembering—the usual ways of learning about the world, are sometimes subject to error and the skeptic cannot regard them as absolutely trustworthy. Even in reasoning, as in geometry, our mind is not infallible. As we read Descartes' description of his reflections, it becomes clear that he was determined to be as critical of his beliefs as possible, in order to show that skepticism breaks down as an ultimate philosophy. Next he considered the possibility that there is a God or other being who has placed these ideas in his mind. But he rejected this hypothesis* on the

* For the time being.

ground that he was perfectly capable of producing his ideas himself. But to produce ideas himself, wouldn't he have to exist? And is this, perhaps, the undeniable truth that he was hoping to find? To guard himself against overcredulity, Descartes pretended that an arch deceiver existed, very powerful and cunning, whose purpose was to lead him astray. Perhaps this creature had succeeded in deceiving him into falsely thinking that he existed. But would he not have to exist, even to be deceived? He could doubt that the past existed, or that the world exists, or that his body exists,* but he couldn't doubt that *he* existed while he doubted. This insight he formulated in his famous *Cogito, ergo sum,*† a truth which served Descartes as an escape from doubt and as the cornerstone of his metaphysics.

A great deal has been written about the *Cogito,* and many controversies have raged about its proper interpretation. Was it an original idea? Several contemporaries of Descartes lost no time in reminding him that St. Augustine used the very same method of establishing the existence of the self, but Descartes calmly and politely replied that the purpose which the *Cogito* served in his own system was quite different from the use made of it by Augustine; but his replies were so cagey that to this day we are not sure that he got the idea from Augustine,‡ although it seems unlikely that he had never read the passages in the Saint's writings. But what exactly had Descartes established in the *Cogito?* That he existed. But this needs clarification. Whose existence had he demonstrated? Was it that of René Descartes, *bon vivant* and *cavalier français,* or that of René Descartes, philosopher and scientist renowned in England as well as on the continent of Europe, "the intellectual Richelieu," as Paul Valery called him? Had he proved the existence of Descartes, pupil of the Jesuits and one-time soldier of fortune in the army of Prince Maurice of Nassau, or of Descartes, the lay spiritual adviser of Princess Elizabeth (niece of Charles I of England) and instructor in philosophy to Queen Christina of Sweden, to

---

* That is to say, these doubts would not involve him in any contradiction.
† *I think, hence I am.* Actually, since the *Discourse* was written in French, the first formulation of this celebrated proposition was: *Je pense, donc je suis.* In the *Meditations,* published four years after the *Discourse,* he wrote: "I must conclude that this proposition: *ego sum, ego existo* (I am, I exist) is necessarily true each time I state it or conceive it." Doubting, for Descartes, is a form of thinking; so is affirming, denying, understanding, imagining, perceiving, willing.
‡ See his letter to an anonymous correspondent, in this volume, p. 211 and his reply to Father Mesland, of May 2, 1644, on p. 221.

whom he dedicated his *Treatise on the Passions of the Soul?*
Not the first, because *that* Descartes lived many years before
his discovery of the *Cogito* and he was not thinking of *that*
Descartes when he affirmed: *Je pense, donc je suis;* nor the
second, because the Descartes there referred to did not yet
exist. The author of the *Cogito* tried to make it plain that
when he said "I think, hence I am" he meant by the "I"
nothing more than "a thing that thinks"; not a philosopher,
not a scientist, not even a man; but simply a *mind* (or *soul*).
Even here, in his first discovered truth, after doubt had ex-
pelled all his former beliefs, he was preparing his proof that the
world is divided into two parts (called substances*), mind (or
spirit), and matter; and that the two substances are totally
distinct from one another, the essence of mind being thought,
and the essence of matter, extension. Another question that
arose concerning the interpretation of the *Cogito,* was whether
it was meant as an argument from premise to conclusion,
as in: all thinking things exist, I am a thinking thing, hence
I exist. Descartes said it was not meant in this way, for when
he had doubted all that it was possible to doubt, he could
know nothing about other thinking things, and so could not
assert the premise of this argument, *all thinking things exist.*
The *Cogito,* Descartes insisted, is an *intuition,* something
grasped immediately,† not an inference.

V

Having found his first truth, how should he proceed?
While still at college it was mathematics that impressed him
more than his other courses "because of the certainty and
evidence of its reasoning." Determined to admit into his mind
only those beliefs whose certainty could be demonstrated, he
decided to prove all his beliefs rigorously as in mathematics,
starting from the existence of the thinking self, next demonstrating the existence of God, and finally the existence of the
external world. The scientist also, Descartes thought, should
adopt mathematics as his model while investigating natural
phenomena. Since the world can be described in mathematical terms, the laws of nature will be shown to be as certain
as the truths of geometry.‡ He thought of science as an

---

* By substance, was meant an independently existing entity.
† As he would say, by *the light of nature.*
‡ "That I do not accept or desire any other principle in Physics than in
geometry or abstract mathematics, because all the phenomena of nature may
be explained by their means, and sure demonstrations can be given of them."

ordered system of incorrigible truths derived deductively from indubitable first principles. This view is no longer held because we have come to see that if first principles are to be unquestionable, they will have to belong to logic or mathematics, and be what are called *analytic* truths, which say nothing about the world of fact, and imply no factual propositions; while if the first principles are to be fruitful sources of scientific knowledge, as Descartes required, they cannot be incorrigible or indubitable. Another reason scientists have abandoned Descartes' view is that their discoveries have not as a rule been made by deductions from first principles, but rather by intelligent guesses which were then experimentally confirmed.

Descartes did not exactly ignore experiments;* in fact, he criticized the scholastics for "neglecting experiments."

Among other things, he studied plant life, was one of the first to practice vivisection, and experimented with lenses of different curvature, hoping to find ways of improving optical instruments. But although he had a fondness for "experimentation," it didn't play an important role in his philosophy of science.

His own procedure, he said, was to start with general principles or "first causes" and to make deductions from them until he could go no further. Then "we would have to discover causes by their effects, and make use of many experiments." Descartes thought of the cause-effect relationship as a logical connection, and causality as a kind of physical necessity. The universe he regarded as an orderly mechanical system. Once we had grasped its basic principles, he thought, reasoning alone could yield an almost complete understanding of its laws and even of the relations of its parts to one another. For matters of detail, experiments would be needed.

One of the fundamental aims of the *Meditations* of Descartes was to establish the real distinction of the soul and the body.† This served the purposes of religion, because when the body dies, there is no need to assume that the soul, which is distinct from the body, must perish too. But it poses quite a problem, in fact a whole series of problems, for the philoso-

---

(*Principles of Philosophy*, Part I, LXIV) Elsewhere, Descartes said "my entire system of physics is nothing but geometry." (Letter to Mersenne). See also *Discourse on Method*, Part II.

* I am using the word "experiment" here as Descartes does, to include observations as well as controlled experiments.

† According to Descartes, two substances are said to be *really distinct*, provided that we can conceive the one clearly and distinctly without the other.

pher. How can two separate and distinct substances form an integrated human being? How can the soul, which is immaterial, influence and even direct the activities of the body, as it apparently does? And why is it that changes in the body make such a difference to the "passions of the soul"? Finally, how can the immaterial substance, mind, acquire any information concerning objects outside the mind? Descartes struggled with these problems (see his letters to Princess Elizabeth, and his treatise on the *Passions of the Soul* in this volume) but his basic presupposition of *dualism* made a satisfactory solution impossible.

VI

Descartes has been classified by historians of philosophy as a *rationalist*, a word that has meant many things to philosophers. By *rationalism*, the rationalists mean having a proper respect for the role of reason in science and philosophy. But empiricists mean by *rationalism*, relying on unexamined dogmas and attempting to deduce factual truths from them, while ignoring the need for experiment and observation. Since empiricism has been the dominant philosophy in the twentieth century, especially in America, when Descartes is called a "rationalist," it is usually meant as a reproach. In a slightly different sense, Descartes is also called a rationalist because he believed that man had a rational soul and consequently an affinity for the truth. An idea that appeared "clear and distinct," he thought, had to be true. On this ground he believed that a void, or vacuum is impossible,* that the blood circulates because the heart is a "warm organ,"† that the total amount of motion in the universe is always a constant,‡ tha the clouds could rain blood,§ that man's body was a machine, and that animals were automata. Traditional rationalism fell into disrepute when it was seen that not even a genius like Descartes could be protected from error by the doctrine of clear and distinct ideas.

Descartes' notion that beasts are machines, really just matter in motion, like a clock (the favorite example of a machine in the seventeenth century), is likely to interest the contemporary reader because of the current vogue of so-called

---

* Torricelli invented the barometer in 1643, and created an almost perfect vacuum with it.

† Descartes agreed with Harvey that the blood circulates, but stubbornly disagreed with Harvey's view that the heart acts like a pump.

‡ As we now know, motion is not conserved, but momentum is.

§ Quoted from Descartes' essay, *Meteors*, by H. Butterfield, *The Origins of Modern Science, 1300-1800*, p. 86.

"thinking machines." When Descartes said that animals are machines, he meant that they couldn't think. Only man can think. Of course, we have to define exactly what we mean by *thinking*. Descartes believed that the characteristic of thought, or rather the evidence of thought, was the use of language, that is, putting words together in a meaningful way. But now, we are asking whether machines can think. That a machine cannot think, was a clear and distinct idea for Descartes. Today we are no longer sure that machines cannot think. They can do some surprising things. Machines have been built that can learn by experience. Norbert Wiener, co-founder of *cybernetics*, the science of control and communication theory in the machine and in the animal, and co-inventor of the word,* maintains that machines can and do transcend some of the limitations of their designers. But I suppose Descartes would say that machines are made by men and man's mind was made by God, and certainly God's creation is superior to man's. But wouldn't a God who could create a mind, which in turn could create a thinking machine, be greater than a God who could not? And if, as St. Anselm said in his famous ontological argument, God is a being than whom no greater being can be conceived, would it not follow that God could create a being who could create a "thinking machine"? But whether He actually did, and whether man is that creature, we don't know.

Descartes' discussion of his animal-machine theory is in the *Discourse*, Part V, and in two letters, one to the Marquis of Newcastle and one to Henry More. Here is a brief quotation from the latter, written in 1649:

". . . although it has been shown, in my opinion, that there is no way to prove that animals have thoughts, I don't believe we can show that the contrary is false [that they have no thoughts], because the human mind cannot enter the heart to find out what goes on there. But, having weighed the pros and cons, I find no argument to prove that animals think, unless it be that since they have eyes, ears, a tongue, and other organs of sense like ours, it is likely that they have feelings like ours; and since, in our case, feelings are connected with thoughts, the same must be true for animals. This reasoning is easily understood by everyone; hence we have been influenced by it since childhood. But . . . it is more probable that we can make earthworms, flies, caterpillars, and the other animals move like machines, than that they are possessed of an immortal soul."

* Norbert Wiener, *Cybernetics*, John Wiley, 1948.

This argument is in accord with theology and also with the Principle of Parsimony—to make no unnecessary assumptions.

VII

Descartes' influence on philosophy would be difficult to exaggerate. Not only in France, but in Germany and England, whether they agreed or disagreed with him, philosophers tended to accept Descartes' fundamental orientation and his statement of philosophical problems. The main source of German and British idealism, which dominated philosophy for two centuries after Descartes, was his view that the Mind is known first and best, and that everything else must be understood and explained in terms of the mind's *ideas*. Although Descartes' writing had an unprecedented clarity, it cannot be claimed that his philosophy was free from inconsistencies. By ignoring some of his views and developing others, his successors were able to achieve greater consistency. Rationalism, mechanism, materialism, idealism, the doctrine of innate ideas, are all found in Descartes' writings. Like Descartes, whom he studied with great care, Spinoza developed a system of philosophy in geometrical fashion from a set of metaphysical postulates. His system also belongs to the tradition of rationalism, but he was more single-minded and more consistent than Descartes. A hundred years after Descartes' death LaMettrie wrote *Man, a Machine,* a more thoroughgoing mechanism than Descartes subscribed to. Similarly, Hobbes was a more consistent materialist, and Berkeley a more consistent idealist than Descartes.

This book contains Descartes' first two publications and his last (excluding the posthumous *The World*), all newly translated. The *Discourse* (1637) and the *Meditations* (1641) are two of his principal philosophical works. The *Passions of the Soul* (1649), which deals with questions of ethics and psychology, is the least technical and most practical of his writings. Some important works of Descartes not included in this volume are: *Principles of Philosophy, Objections* to the *Meditations* and Descartes' *Replies, Rules for the Direction of the Mind, The World,* and his *Geometry.* Descartes' correspondence (a very brief selection is included herein) contains much interesting material.

DANIEL J. BRONSTEIN

March 1961

DISCOURSE ON METHOD

❦

*Discourse on the Method of Rightly Conducting
the Reason and Seeking Truth in the Sciences.*

If this discourse seems too long to be read at one sitting,
it can be divided into six parts. In the first part will be found
various considerations concerning the sciences. In the second,
the principal rules of the method which the author has sought
to devise. In the third, some of the rules of the morality he
has drawn from this method. In the fourth, the reasons by
which he proves the existence of God and of the human soul,
which are the foundations of his metaphysics. In the fifth, the
order of the problems in physics which he has examined, and
in particular the explanation of the movement of the heart
and of certain other difficulties pertaining to medicine, then
also the difference between the human soul and the animal
soul. And in the last, the things he believes to be required in
order to advance further into the study of nature than he has
gone, and the reasons that have led him to write.

Part One

Good sense is the most equitably distributed thing in the world, for each man considers himself so well provided with it that even those who are most difficult to satisfy in everything else do not usually wish to have more of it than they have already. It is not likely that everyone is mistaken in this; it shows, rather, that the ability to judge rightly and separate the true from the false, which is essentially what is called good sense or reason, is by nature equal in all men, and thus that our opinions differ not because some men are better endowed with reason than others, but only because we direct our thoughts along different paths, and do not consider the same things. For it is not enough to have a good mind: what is most important is to apply it rightly. The greatest souls are capable of the greatest vices; and those who walk very slowly can advance much further, if they always keep to the direct road, than those who run and go astray.

For my part, I have never presumed my mind to be more perfect than average in any way; I have, in fact, often wished that my thoughts were as quick, or my imagination as precise and distinct, or my memory as capacious or prompt, as those of some other men. And I know of no other qualities than these which make for the perfection of the mind; for as to reason, or good sense, inasmuch as it alone makes us men and distinguishes us from the beasts, I am quite willing to believe that it is whole and entire in each of us, and to follow in this the common opinion of the philosophers who say that there are differences of more or less only among the accidents, and not among the forms, or natures, of the individuals of a single species.

But I am not afraid to say that I think I was very fortunate in my early youth to have entered upon certain paths that have led me to the considerations and maxims from which I have formed a method which, it seems to me, has given me a means of increasing my knowledge step by step, and gradually raising it to the highest point which the mediocrity of my mind and the short duration of my life will allow it to reach. For I have already gathered such fruits from this method that, although in the judgments I make of myself I always try to lean toward mistrust rather than presumption, and although, when I look with a philosophical eye upon the various actions and enterprises of all men, there are scarcely any which do not seem to me vain and futile, I nevertheless receive extreme satisfaction from the progress I think I have already made in the search for truth, and I conceive such hopes for the future that if, among the occupations of men who are purely and simply men, there is one which is of solid worth and importance, I venture to believe that it is the one I have chosen.

I may be mistaken, however, and what I take for gold and diamonds may be only a little copper and a few bits of glass. I know how subject we are to error in what concerns ourselves, and also how suspicious we ought to be of our friends' judgments when they are in our favor. But I shall be glad to point out, in this discourse, the paths I have followed, and to depict my life in it as though in a picture, in order that everyone may form his own judgment, and so that, in learning from common report the opinions that will be held with regard to what I have said, I shall have a new means of instructing myself which I shall add to those I am already accustomed to using.

Thus my intention is not to teach here the method which everyone ought to follow in order to conduct his reason correctly, but only to point out how I have tried to conduct my own. Those who take it upon themselves to give precepts ought to regard themselves as cleverer than those to whom they give them; and if they are lacking in the slightest thing, they must bear the blame for it. But in presenting this work only as a story, or, if you prefer, as a fable, in which, among some examples which may be followed, there may also be others which will be rightly avoided, I hope that it will be useful to some without being harmful to anyone, and that everyone will be grateful to me for my frankness.

I was nourished on books in my childhood, and since I had been persuaded that by means of them one could acquire clear and assured knowledge of everything that is useful in life, I was eager to learn from them. But as soon as I had completed that whole course of study at the end of which it is customary to be admitted into the ranks of the learned, I changed my opinion entirely, for I found myself entangled in so many doubts and errors that it seemed to me that the only benefit I had derived from my efforts to educate myself was a progressive discovery of my ignorance. And yet I had attended one of the most famous schools in Europe, where I thought there must be learned men if any were to be found on the face of the earth. I had learned there all that the others learned, and, not content with the sciences that had been taught to us, I had perused all the books dealing with those deemed to be rarest and strangest which happened to fall into my hands. Furthermore, I knew how others judged me, and it did not seem to me that I was regarded as inferior to my fellow students, even though some of them were already being prepared to replace our masters. And finally, the age in which we live seemed to me as flourishing, and as fertile in great minds, as any preceding age. I therefore took the liberty of judging all others by myself, and of deciding that there was no doctrine in the world which was such as I had been led to expect it to be.

I nevertheless continued to respect the training that is received in the schools. I knew that the languages learned there are necessary for the understanding of ancient books; that the graciousness of the fables awakens the mind; that it is exalted by the accounts of memorable deeds contained in books of history, and that, read with discretion, they help to form the judgment; that the reading of all good books is like a conversation with the finest men of the past who wrote them, a studied conversation, in fact, in which they reveal to us only the best of their thoughts; that eloquence has incomparable powers and beauties; that poetry has enchanting delicacy and sweetness; that mathematics has very subtle inventions which can be of great use in satisfying curious minds, as well as in furthering all the arts and crafts, and in diminishing the work of mankind; that moral treatises contain many teachings and exhortations to virtue which are very useful; that theology teaches us how to gain heaven; that philosophy enables us to speak plausibly of all things, and win the admiration of the least learned; that jurisprudence, medicine and the other sciences bring honors and wealth to those who cultivate them; and, finally, that it is good to have examined them all, even those most tainted with superstition and falsehood, in order to know their true worth and avoid being deceived by them.

But I thought I had already given enough time to the study of languages, and even to the reading of ancient books, with their histories and fables. For conversing with men of other centuries is almost the same as traveling. It is good to know something about the ways of various peoples, so that we can judge our own more soundly, and not think that anything contrary to our own customs is ridiculous and irrational, as is usually assumed by those who have seen nothing. But a man who spends too much time in traveling eventually becomes a foreigner in his own country; and a man who is too curious about what was done in the past usually remains extremely ignorant of what is being done in the present. Moreover, fables make us imagine many impossible events to be possible, and the most faithful histories, even if they do not change or enhance the value of the facts to make them worthier of being read, at least nearly always omit the basest and least glorious incidents and circumstances, so that what remains does not appear as it really was, and those who regulate their conduct by the examples they draw from it are prone to fall into the extravagances of the knights-errant in our romances, and to conceive designs which exceed their powers.

I held eloquence in high esteem, and I was in love with poetry, but I thought that both were gifts of the mind, rather than fruits of study. Those who have the strongest powers of reasoning, and who best digest their thoughts in order to make them clear and intelligible, are always best able to convince others of what they put forward, even if they speak only a Breton dialect and have never studied rhetoric. And those who have the most pleasing fancies, and know how to express themselves with the most grace and sweetness, will still be the best poets even if they are ignorant of the canons of poetry.

I took the greatest pleasure in mathematics, because of the certainty and clarity of its reasoning; but I was not yet aware of its true use, and, thinking that it served only the mechanical arts, I was surprised that no loftier edifice had been built on such a firm and solid foundation. On the other hand, I compared the moral treatises of the ancient pagans to splendid and magnificent palaces built only on sand and mud. They raise virtues to great heights and make them seem more worthy of esteem than anything else in the world, but they do not teach us enough about them, and often what they call by such a fine name is nothing but insensitivity, or pride, or despair, or parricide.

I revered our theology and was as desirous as anyone else of reaching heaven; but, having learned as a certainty that the way to heaven is open to the most ignorant no less than to the most learned, and that the revealed truths which lead us there are above our intelligence, I would not have dared to submit them to the weakness of my reasoning, and I thought that, in order for anyone to undertake to examine them, and to do so successfully, he would need some extraordinary aid from heaven, and would have to be more than a man.

I shall say nothing of philosophy except that, seeing that it had been cultivated by the most excellent minds in the world for many centuries, and that there was nevertheless nothing in it which was not in dispute and therefore doubtful, I was not presumptuous enough to hope that I might be more fortunate in it than others had been. And when I considered how many different opinions could be held by learned men with respect to a single topic, whereas only one of those opinions could ever be true, I regarded almost as false anything that was merely plausible.

As for the other sciences, inasmuch as they borrow their principles from philosophy, I judged that nothing solid could be built on such insecure foundations. And neither the honor nor the gain which they promise was enough to incite me to learn them, for I felt that, by the grace of God, my worldly situation was such that I was not obliged to make a trade of science in order to improve my fortune, and although I did not profess to despise glory in the manner of the Cynics, I cared very little for the kind of glory which I could hope to acquire only on false pretenses. And finally, I thought I already knew enough about unsound doctrines not to be deceived by the promises of an alchemist, the predictions of an astrologer, the impostures of a magician or the tricks and boasting of any of those who profess to know more than they do.

For these reasons, as soon as my age allowed me to free myself from subjection to my teachers, I entirely abandoned the study of letters. Resolving henceforth to seek no other knowledge than that which I might find within myself or in the great book of the world, I spent the rest of my youth in traveling, observing courts and armies, frequenting people of diverse character and rank, gathering various experiences, testing myself in the situations that chance brought my way, and everywhere reflecting on the things I encountered in such a way as to derive some benefit from them. For it seemed to me that I could find much more truth in the reasonings which each man makes with regard to matters that are important to him, and whose outcome will quickly punish him if he has judged badly, than in those made by a man of letters in his study, with regard to speculations which produce no effect, and which are of no consequence except insofar as he may draw all the more vanity from them the further they are removed from common sense, because he has had to employ all the more wit and ingenuity in making them appear plausible. And I always had a strong desire to learn to distinguish the true from the false, so that I could see my own actions clearly and walk with assurance in this life.

It is true that while I was doing nothing except considering the behavior of other men I found very little grounds for assurance in it, and that I observed almost as much diversity in it as I had previously observed in the opinions of philosophers. And so the greatest benefit I derived from this was that, seeing many things which, although they seem extremely immoderate and ridiculous to us, are nevertheless commonly accepted and approved by other great nations, I learned not to believe too firmly in anything whose validity rested only on example and custom; and thus I gradually freed myself from many of the errors which may obscure our natural light and make us less capable of listening to reason. But after I had spent several years in thus studying the book of the world and trying to acquire experience, I resolved one day to study within myself as well, and to use all the resources of my mind in choosing the paths I ought to follow. I succeeded much better in this, I believe, than I would have done if I had never left either my country or my books.

◄§ Part Two

I was then in Germany, where I had been drawn by the wars which are not yet ended. As I was on my way to rejoin the army after attending the Emperor's coronation, the beginning of winter detained me in a place where, finding no conversation to divert me, and fortunately having no cares or passions to trouble me, I remained alone all day in a stove-heated room where I was completely free to concern myself with my own thoughts. One of the first thoughts that came to me was that there is often less perfection in works composed of several pieces, and carried out by various hands, than in those carried out by a single man. Thus we see that buildings which a single architect has undertaken and completed are usually more beautiful and better designed than those which many have tried to restore by making use of old walls that were built for different purposes. The same is true of those ancient towns which, having originally been only villages, have in the course of time become great cities. They are usually badly laid out, compared to those orderly designs which an engineer can trace at will on a plain, and although their buildings considered separately often display as much art as those of other cities, or even more, when we see how they are arranged, with a big one here and a little one there, and how crooked and uneven they make the streets, we are inclined to say that these cities have been designed by chance, rather than by the will of men making use of reason. And if we consider that there have nevertheless always been officials responsible for making private edifices contribute to public beauty, we can easily understand how difficult it is to achieve any kind of perfection by working with what has already been done by others. Thus I reflected that nations that were once half savage and, having become civilized only little by little, have made their laws piecemeal as they were forced to do so by the ill effects of crimes and disputes, cannot be so well regulated as those which, from the time when they first assembled, have always observed the laws laid down by some wise legislator. Similarly, it is certain that the true religion, whose ordinances come from God alone, must be incomparably better ordered than any other. And to speak of human things, I think that Sparta flourished not because each of its laws was good in itself, for many of them were strange and even contrary to morality, but because, having been devised by one man, they all tended toward a single end. And so I thought that the teachings contained in books, at least those whose grounds are merely probable, and which have no demonstrations, having been composed by many different persons and gradually built up from their opinions, do not come so close to the truth as the simple reasonings of a man of good sense concerning the things he encounters. And finally I thought that, considering that we were all children before becoming men, that for a long time we were necessarily governed by our desires and our teachers, that they were often in opposition to each other, and that perhaps neither of them always advised us wisely, it was nearly impossible that our judgments should be as pure or sound as they would have been if we had had the full use of our reason from birth and had always been guided by it alone.

It is true that all the buildings in a city are never torn down for the sole purpose of rebuilding them in a different way and making the streets more beautiful, but it does happen that certain individuals tear down their own houses in order to rebuild them, and that sometimes they are even forced to do so, when their houses are in danger of collapsing and the foundations are insecure. From this example I concluded that it would be truly senseless for an individual to set out to reform a State by changing everything from the foundations upward and tearing it down in order to build it up again, or even to reform the body of the sciences or the established order of teaching them in the schools, but that, with regard to all the opinions I had hitherto accepted, I could no better than to undertake to reject them entirely in order to replace them with better ones later, or else accept the same ones again after bringing them to the level of reason. And I firmly believed that in this way I would succeed in conducting my life much better than if I built only on old foundations and relied only on the principles I had been persuaded to accept in my youth, without ever examining them to determine whether or not they were true. For although I saw rious difficulties in this, they were not without remedy, nor were they comparable to the difficulties involved in reforming anything concerning the public. Those great bodies are too difficult to lift when they have been brought down, or even to hold up when they have been shaken, and their falls cannot fail to be violent. As for their imperfections, if they have any—and their diversity alone is enough to ensure that many of them do—they have no doubt been softened by use, which has even imperceptibly avoided or corrected many of them which could not have been so easily remedied by prudence. And finally, these imperfections are always more bearable than their alternatives, just as the roads which wind their way among the mountains become so smooth and convenient from long use that it is much better to follow them than to try to take a more direct route by climbing over rocks and down precipices.

That is why I could in no way approve of those rash and

restless individuals who, having been called by neither birth nor fortune to the management of public affairs, are nevertheless constantly reforming them in their minds. And if I thought there was anything in what I have written that might make me be suspected of such madness, I would deeply regret its publication. My intentions have never gone beyond the attempt to reform my own thoughts, and to build on a foundation that is mine alone. If, since my work has pleased me well enough, I here present its pattern to you, that does not mean that I wish to advise anyone to copy it. Those on whom God has more lavishly bestowed His gifts will perhaps have loftier designs, although I fear that even mine will be too bold for many. The decision to rid oneself of all the opinions to which one has previously given credence is not an example that ought to be followed by everyone, and the world is made up almost entirely of two kinds of minds for whom it is thoroughly unsuitable. First there are those who, believing themselves to be cleverer than they are, cannot help making hasty judgments and do not have enough patience to conduct all their thoughts in an orderly manner, so that if they ever took the liberty of doubting the principles they have been taught, and of departing from the common path, they would never be able to keep to the road that would take them more directly toward their goal, and would remain lost for the rest of their lives. Then there are those who, having enough good sense or modesty to realize that they are less capable of distinguishing the true from the false than are certain others from whom they can learn, ought to content themselves with following the opinions of these others, rather than seeking better ones themselves.

As for myself, I would no doubt have been included among the latter if I had never had more than one teacher, or if I had not known the differences that have always existed among the opinions of the most learned. But I learned in school that one cannot imagine anything so strange and incredible that it has not been said by some philosopher, and later, in the course of my travels, I observed that all those who have sentiments strongly opposed to our own are not necessarily barbarians or savages, but that many of them use their reason as much as we do, or even more. And I considered the fact that if a man has been raised among Frenchmen or Germans, he becomes quite different from what he would have been, even with the same natural endowments, if he had always lived among Chinese or cannibals. I further considered that even in our fashions of dress, the same thing which pleased us ten years ago, and may please us again within another ten years, now seems excessive and ridiculous to us. From all this I concluded that we are swayed much more by custom and example than by certain knowledge, and that nevertheless a preponderance of opinion is worthless as a criterion for truths that are rather difficult to discover, since they are much more likely to be encountered by a single man than by a whole people. For these reasons, I could select no one whose opinions seemed preferable to those of others, and I found myself with little choice but to undertake to be my own guide.

But, like a man walking alone and in darkness, I decided to proceed so slowly, and with so much circumspection in all things, that while I might make little progress, I would at least avoid falling. I was even unwilling to begin entirely rejecting any of the opinions that might have slipped in among my beliefs, without having been placed there by my reason, before I had first spent enough time in planning the work I was undertaking, and in seeking the true method of attaining knowledge of everything within the capacity of my mind.

In my early youth I had made some study of logic (in philosophy) and of geometrical analysis and algebra (in mathematics), and it seemed to me that these three arts or sciences should contribute something to my design. But when I examined them I found that, in the case of logic, its syllogisms and most of its other teachings are useful not in acquiring knowledge, but in explaining to others what one knows already, or, as in the art of Lully, in speaking without judgment about things one does not know. And although logic does contain many true and good precepts, they are mingled with so many others which are either harmful or superfluous that it is as difficult to separate them as to draw a Diana or a Minerva from an unshaped block of marble. As for the geometrical analysis of the ancients and the algebras of the moderns, aside from the fact that they deal only with highly abstract matters which have no apparent practical use, the former is always so tightly bound to the consideration of figures that it cannot exercise the understanding without greatly tiring the imagination, and the latter is so subject to certain rules and notations that it has been made into a confused and obscure art which encumbers the mind, rather than into a science which cultivates it. I therefore decided that I must seek another method which would include the advantages of these three, yet be free of their defects. And just as a multiplicity of laws often provides excuses for vices, so that a State is much better governed if it has only a few laws and these are strictly observed, so, instead of the great number of precepts of which logic is composed, I believed that the four following ones would be enough for me, provided I maintained a firm and constant resolution never once to depart from them.

The first was never to accept anything as true which I did know to be manifestly so, that is, carefully to avoid precipitancy and bias, and to include nothing in my judgments except what presented itself so clearly and distinctly to my mind that I would never have occasion to doubt it.

The second, to divide each difficulty I examined into as many parts as possible, and as would be required in order to resolve it better.

The third, to conduct my thoughts in an orderly manner, beginning with those objects which are simplest and easiest to know, then rising little by little, as though by steps, to knowledge of the most complex, even assuming order to exist among those which have no natural order of precedence.

And the last, always to make such complete enumerations and comprehensive reviews that I could be sure I had overlooked nothing.

Those long chains of reasoning, each link of which is simple and easy, that geometers employ in reaching their most difficult demonstrations, had given me occasion to imagine that all things which may be known by men are interconnected in the same way, and that, provided we refrain from accepting any of them as true which are not so, and always maintain the order required for deducing them one from another, there can be none so remote that it cannot be eventually reached, or so hidden that it cannot be discovered. And I was not at a loss to decide with which to begin, for I knew already that I ought to begin with those that were simplest and easiest to know; and, considering that of all those who had hitherto sought truth in the sciences, only the mathematicians had been able to find any demonstrations, that is, certain and manifest reasons, I did not doubt that I ought to begin with the same things they had examined, although I expected no other use from them than that they would accustom my mind to nourishing itself on truth and refusing to content itself with false reasoning. But for this I had no intention of trying to learn all those particular sciences which are commonly called mathematics, and, seeing that although their objects are different, they nevertheless agree in attributing nothing to them except the various relations or proportions that are in them, I thought it would be better for me to examine only those proportions in general, assuming them only in subjects that would make it easier for me to know them, but without restricting them to those subjects, so that I could later apply them to all others to which they might be suited. Then, having noted that in order to know them I would sometimes need to consider each of them in particular, and sometimes only to remember them, or to take several of them together, I thought that, to consider them better in particular, I ought to suppose them to be in lines, because I could think of nothing simpler or capable of being represented more distinctly to my imagination and my senses, but that, to remember them or take several of them together, I ought to explain them by certain notations, as short as possible, and that in this way I would be borrowing the best from both geometrical analysis and algebra, and using one to correct all the defects of the other.

Indeed, I venture to say that scrupulous observance of the few precepts I had chosen made it so easy for me to clear up all the problems with which these two sciences are concerned that, within the two or three months I spent in examining them, having begun with the simplest and most general ones, and using each truth I discovered as a rule which later helped me to discover others, I not only solved many of them which I had previously regarded as very difficult, but it also seemed to me, toward the end, that even in the case of those I failed to solve, I was able to determine by what means and to what extent it was possible to solve them. In saying this, I shall perhaps not seem excessively vain to you if you consider that since there is only one truth about any given thing, whoever discovers it knows as much about it as can be known, and that, for example, when a child who has been taught arithmetic has done an addition according to the rules, he can be sure that he has discovered as much about the sum he has examined as the human mind can discover. For, after all, the method which teaches us to follow the true order, and to enumerate exactly every element of what we are seeking, contains everything that gives certainty to the rules of arithmetic.

But what pleased me most about this method was that it gave me the assurance of using my reason in everything, if not perfectly, at least as well as I possibly could. Furthermore, I felt that in making use of this method my mind was grad ually becoming accustomed to conceiving its objects more clearly and distinctly, and since I was restricted to no particular subject matter, I promised myself that I would apply it as usefully to the difficulties of the other sciences as I had done to those of algebra. Not that I dared to undertake an immediate examination of each science as it presented itself, for that would have been contrary to the order prescribed by the method. Having noted that their principles must all be borrowed from philosophy, in which I had not as yet found any that were certain, I thought that I must first try to establish such principles in it, and that since this was the most important thing in the world, and the one in which precipitancy and bias were most to be feared, I ought not to undertake it until I had reached a more mature age than twenty-three, which was my age at that time, and until I had first spent a great deal of time in preparing myself for it by uprooting from my mind all the unsound opinions I had hitherto accepted, by accumulating experiences that could later be the matter of my reasoning, and by constantly exercising myself in the method I had laid down for myself, in order to strengthen myself more and more in its use.

ৰ্গ *Part Three*

Before beginning to rebuild the house in which one lives, it is not enough to tear it down, supply oneself with building materials and engage architects, or become proficient in architecture and carefully draw up new plans; one must also have some other house in which one can live comfortably while the reconstruction is being carried out. Thus, in order that I might not remain irresolute in my actions while reason obliged me to be so in my judgments, and that I might continue to live as happily as I could, I formed a provisional morality for myself, consisting of only three or four maxims which I am quite willing to disclose.

The first was to obey the laws and customs of my country, constantly adhering to the religion in which, by God's grace, I had been instructed since my childhood, and governing myself in everything else in accordance with the most moderate and least excessive opinions that were commonly accepted in practice by the most sensible of those with whom I would have to live. For, having already begun to count my own opinions as nothing, since I was resolved to re-examine them all, I was sure that I could do no better than to follow those of the most sensible. And although there may be people among the Persians or the Chinese who are as sensible as any of us, it seemed to me that it would be more practical to regulate my behavior according to those with whom I would have to live, and that, in order to determine what their real opinions were, I ought to consider what they did, rather than what they said, not only because, in the corruption of our manners and morals, there are few people who are willing to say everything that they believe, but also because many do not even know what they believe, for the activity of thought by which we believe something is different from that by which we know that we believe it, and one often occurs without the other. And among several equally accepted opinions, I chose only the most moderate ones, not only because they are always the most convenient to put into practice, and are probably the best, since any excess is usually bad, but also in order to stray less far from the right path than I would do if I mistakenly chose one of two extremes when the other was the correct choice. In particular, I regarded as a form of excess all those promises by which we give up part of our freedom. Not that I disapproved of those laws which, to remedy the inconstancy of weak spirits, allow the making of binding vows or contracts when one has a good aim, or even, to safeguard commerce, when one has an aim that is morally neutral; but because I saw nothing in the world that always remained the same, and because, on my own account, I had promised myself that I would constantly improve my judgments, I would have considered it a crime against good sense if, because I approved of something at that time, I had obliged myself to give it my approval later, when it might have ceased to be good, or I might have ceased to regard it as such.

My second maxim was to be as firm and resolute in my actions as I could, and to follow the most dubious opinions, once I had decided to do so, no less constantly than if they were the most assured. In this I was guiding myself by the example of a traveler who, having lost his way in a forest, ought not to wander aimlessly in all directions, or still less stop in one place, but should walk as straight as he can in a single direction and not change it for any trivial reason, even though it was only chance that first made him choose it, for in so doing, while he may not go exactly where he wishes, he will at least eventually reach a place where he will no doubt be better off than in the middle of a forest. Thus, since the actions of life often allow of no delay, it is a very certain truth that when it is not in our power to distinguish the truest opinions, we ought to follow the most probable ones, and that when we can discern no more probability in one than in another, we must nevertheless decide on some of them and then no longer consider them as dubious, insofar as they relate to practice, but as true and certain, since our reason for deciding on them is true and certain. And this immediately freed me from all the repentance and remorse which usually agitates those weak and unsteady spirits who irresolutely allow themselves to practice as good what they later judge to be bad.

My third maxim was to try always to conquer myself rather than fortune, to change my desires rather than the order of the world, and, in general, to accustom myself to believing that there is nothing entirely within our control except our thoughts, so that after we have done our best with regard to things that are external to us, everything we fail to achieve is, for us, absolutely impossible. And this alone seemed to me sufficient to make me desire nothing I could not acquire, and so to make me content. For since our will naturally tends to desire only those things which our understanding represents to it as in some way possible, it is certain that if we consider all external goods as equally beyond our power, we shall no more regret the lack of those which seem to be our birthright, when we have been deprived of them through no fault of our own, than we regret not possessing the kingdom of China or Mexico, and that, making a virtue of necessity, as the saying goes, we shall no more desire to be healthy if we are ill, or to be free if we are in prison, than we now desire to have bodies made of a material as incorruptible as diamonds, or wings with which to fly like birds. But I admit that it takes long practice and repeated meditation to accustom oneself to looking at everything from this point of view, and I believe that this was the secret of those ancient philosophers who were able to withdraw themselves from the dominion of chance and, despite pain and poverty, to rival their gods in happiness. Constantly occupied in considering the limitations imposed on them by nature, they convinced themselves so thoroughly that nothing lay within their power except their thoughts that this alone was enough to prevent them from becoming attached to anything else, and they had such absolute control of their thoughts that they had some reason for considering themselves richer, more powerful, freer and happier than all other men who, not having this philosophy, could never thus control everything they wanted, however favored they might be by nature and fortune.

Finally, to conclude this moral code, I decided to review the occupations of men in this life in order to choose the best one of them; and, without wishing to say anything about the occupations of others, I thought that I could do no better than to continue the one in which I was already engaged, that is, to spend my whole life in cultivating my reason, and to advance as far as I could in the knowledge of truth, following the method I had laid down for myself. I had experienced such extreme satisfactions since beginning to use this method that I did not think it was possible to receive sweeter or more innocent ones in this life. Each day, by means of it, I discovered several truths which seemed to me rather important and generally unknown to other men, and the satisfaction I derived from this so filled my mind that nothing else affected me. Furthermore, the three preceding maxims were based only on my plan to go on instructing myself, for since God has given each of us some power of distinguishing the true from the false, I would not have thought for a moment that I ought to content myself with the opinions of others if I had not intended to use my own judgment in examining them when the time came, and I would not have been able to free myself from misgivings in following them if I had not hoped to lose no opportunity of finding better ones, if there were any. And finally, I would not have been able to limit my desires, or be content, if I had not been following a path which, I thought, would assure me of acquiring all the knowledge of which I was capable, as well as, by the same means, all the true goods that would ever lie within my reach, for inasmuch as our will does not tend to pursue or avoid anything unless our understanding represents it as good or bad, it is enough to judge well to do well, and to judge as well as we can in order to do our best, that is, to acquire all the virtues and all the other goods that we can acquire; and when we are certain that this is the case, we cannot fail to be happy.

Having thus assured myself of these maxims, and having set them apart with the truths of faith that have always ranked first in my belief, I judged that I could now safely undertake to rid myself of the rest of my opinions. And since I hoped to be able to accomplish this better by conversing with other men than by continuing to remain enclosed in the stove-

heated room were all these thoughts had come to me, I began
traveling again before winter was completely over. And for
the next nine years I did nothing but wander here and there
in the world, trying to be a spectator rather than an actor
in its comedies, and, by paying particular attention to those
aspects of each matter which might make it dubious and give
rise to misunderstanding, I meanwhile uprooted from my
mind all the errors that had previously slipped into it. Not
that I was imitating those skeptics who doubt for the sake of
doubting and make a display of constant indecision: on the
contrary, the sole object of my whole plan was to acquire
certainty, to clear away the shifting soil and sand in order to
find the rock or clay beneath it. In this I was rather successful,
it seems to me, for in trying to discover the falsity or uncertainty of the propositions I examined, not by feeble conjectures, but by clear and solid reasoning, I encountered none
that was so dubious that I could not draw a sufficiently certain
conclusion from it, if only that there was nothing certain
about it. And just as, when an old house is torn down, the
rubble is usually saved to be used in building a new one, so
in destroying all of my opinions which I judged to be ill
founded, I made various observations and acquired many
experiences which have since been of use to me in establishing
more certain opinions. Furthermore, I continued to practice
the method I had prescribed for myself. Besides being careful
to conduct all my thoughts in general according to its rules, I
reserved a few hours now and then for applying it to problems
in mathematics, or to other problems which I was able to
make closely similar to those of mathematics by detaching
them from all the principles of the other sciences, which I
found to be insufficiently firm, as you will see in the case of
those that are explained in this volume. And so, while appearing to live in the same manner as those who, having no other
occupation than to lead a pleasant and innocent life, take
pains to separate pleasures from vices and indulge in all decent
diversions in order to enjoy their leisure without boredom, I
continued to follow my plan and advance in knowledge of the
truth, more perhaps than if I had done nothing but read
books or frequent men of letters.

However, those nine years went by before I had taken any
definite stand with regard to the problems that are usually
debated among the learned, or had begun to seek the foundations of a philosophy more certain than the common one.
And the example of many excellent minds who had pre-

viously had such a plan, but seemed to me to have been unsuccessful, made me imagine such great difficulty in it that I would perhaps not have dared to undertake it so soon if I had not learned that certain people were circulating the report that I had already carried it out. I cannot say on what they based this opinion, and if I contributed anything to it by my words, it must have been by confessing my ignorance of some things more candidly than is usually done by those who have studied a little, and perhaps also by disclosing my reasons for doubting many things which others consider to be certain, rather than by boasting of having any particular knowledge. In any case, being honest enough not to want to be regarded as something I was not, I decided that I must try by every means to make myself worthy of the reputation that had been given to me. It was exactly eight years ago that this desire made me resolve to avoid all places where I had acquaintances and withdraw to this country,* where the long duration of the war has caused such discipline to be established that the sole purpose of the army maintained here seems to be to enable the population to enjoy the benefits of peace in greater security, and where, amid a multitude of busy people who are more concerned with their own affairs than curious about those of others, I have been able to lead as solitary and secluded a life as I could have led in the most remote of deserts, while at the same time lacking none of the conveniences to be found in the largest cities.

⋙ Part Four

I do not know whether I ought to tell you about the first meditations with which I concerned myself here, for they are so metaphysical and so far out of the ordinary that they may not be to everyone's taste. And yet, to make it possible for others to judge whether or not the foundations I have chosen are firm enough, I feel that I am more or less obliged to speak of them. I had long ago observed that in matters of custom and morality it is sometimes necessary to follow opinions that we know to be extremely uncertain as though they were unquestionably true, as I have already said; but since I now wished to occupy myself only with the search for truth, I thought I ought to do exactly the opposite and reject as

* Holland.

absolutely false anything in which I could imagine the slightest doubt, in order to see whether anything completely indubitable would afterward remain. And so, because our senses sometimes deceive us, I decided to assume that nothing in the world was such as they presented it to me. Having observed that some men went astray in their reasoning and made logical errors, even in the simplest geometrical matters, and having judged that I was as fallible as anyone else, I rejected as false all the reasonings I had previously accepted as demonstrations. And finally, considering that all the thoughts which come to us when we are awake can also come to us when we are asleep, without one of them then being true, I resolved to pretend that everything which had ever entered my mind was no more true than the illusions of my dreams. But then I immediately realized that while I was thinking of everything as false, I, who was so thinking, necessarily had to be something. Noting that this truth: *I think, therefore I am,* was so firm and assured that all of the most extravagant suppositions of the skeptics were incapable of shaking it, I judged that I could accept it without misgiving as the first principle of philosophy which I had been seeking.

Next I attentively examined what I was, and I saw that while I could pretend that I had no body and that there was no world or any place in which I was, I could not pretend that I did not exist; on the contrary, from the very fact that I was thinking of doubting the truth of other things, it followed manifestly and certainly that I existed, whereas if I had ceased to think, even though all the rest of what I had imagined were true, I had no reason to believe that I would have existed. From this I knew that I was a thinking substance, whose whole essence or nature was only to think, and which, in order to exist, had no need of any location and did not depend on any material thing. Thus the self, that is, the soul by which I am what I am, is entirely distinct from the body, is even easier to know than the body, and would still be all that it is if the body did not exist.

After this, I considered in general what is required of a proposition in order that it be true and certain, for since I had just discovered one which I knew to be such, I thought that I ought also to know in what its certainty consists. Having observed that there is nothing at all in the proposition, "*I think, therefore I am*" which assures me that I am speaking the truth, except that I see very clearly that, in order to think, it is necessary to be, I concluded that I could take it as a general rule that those things which we apprehend very clearly and distinctly are all true, but that there is some difficulty in determining which ones we apprehend distinctly.

Then, reflecting on the fact that I doubted, and that my being was therefore not entirely perfect, for I saw clearly that it was a greater perfection to know than to doubt, I decided to try to determine how I had learned to think of something more perfect than myself, and it became obvious to me that I must have learned it from some nature which was in fact more perfect. As for the thoughts I had of many other things outside myself, such as the sky, the earth, light, heat and countless others, I was less concerned to know from where they came, for since I saw nothing in them that seemed to make them superior to me, I could believe that, if they were true, they were dependencies of my nature, insofar as it had some perfection, and that, if they were not true, I had acquired them from nothing, that is, that I had them because of some deficiency in myself. But this could not be the case with the idea of a being more perfect than myself, for it was manifestly impossible that I should have acquired it from nothing, and since it is as contradictory to suppose that the more perfect follows from and is dependent upon the less perfect as it is to suppose that something comes from nothing, I could not have acquired it from myself. Thus it could only have been placed in me by a nature truly more perfect than myself, and possessing all the perfections of which I could have any idea; in short, it had been placed in me by God. I further reflected that, since I knew some perfections which I did not possess, I was not the only being in existence (here I shall, with your permission, freely use the terms of the School), but that there must necessarily be a more perfect being on which I depended and from which I had acquired everything I possessed. For if I had been alone and independent of any other being, so that I would have acquired from myself what little perfection I shared with the perfect being, I could also have given myself, by the same reasoning, all the other perfections which I knew to be lacking in me, and thus I myself could have been infinite, eternal, immutable, all-knowing and all-powerful; that is, I could have had all the perfections I could see in God. For, according to the reasoning I have just set forth, in order to know the nature of God insofar as my own nature was capable of doing so, I had only to consider, with regard to each thing of which I had any idea, whether or not it was a perfection to possess it, and

I could be sure that those which indicated any imperfection were not in Him, and that all the others were. I saw that doubt, inconstancy, sadness and other such things could not be in Him, for I myself would have been glad to be free of them. Furthermore, I had ideas of many perceptible and corporeal things, and even if I supposed that I was dreaming and that all the things I saw or imagined were false, I still could not deny that the ideas of them were really in my mind. But I had already seen very clearly, in examining myself, that intellectual nature is distinct from corporeal nature, and so, considering that all composition implies dependency, and that dependency is manifestly a defect, I concluded that it could not be a perfection in God to be composed of those two natures, and that consequently He was not so composed, but that if there were any bodies in the world, or any intelligences or other natures not entirely perfect, their existence must depend on His power in such a way that they could not subsist without Him for a single moment.

I next sought to discover other truths. Turning my attention to the object studied by geometers, which I conceived to be a continuous body, or a space indefinitely extended in length, breadth, and height or depth, divisible into various parts capable of having various shapes and sizes and being moved and transposed in all sorts of ways, for the geometers assume all this in the object of their study, I went through some of their simplest demonstrations. And having noted that the great certainty which everyone attributes to these demonstrations is based only on the fact that they are apprehended as manifestly true, in accordance with the rule I have stated above, I also noted that there was nothing in them which assured me of the existence of their object. I saw clearly that, given a triangle, for example, its three angles had to be equal to two right angles, but I saw nothing in this which gave me any assurance that there were any triangles in the world. But when I again began to examine the idea I had of a perfect being, I found that existence is included in it just as manifestly, or even more so, as having its three angles equal to two right angles is included in the idea of a triangle, or having all its parts equidistant from its center is included in the idea of a sphere, and that consequently it is at least as certain as any geometrical demonstration can be that God, who is this perfect being, is or exists.

But what causes many people to be convinced that it is difficult to know God, or even to know what their own souls

are, is that they never raise their minds above the objects of
their senses, and are so accustomed to considering nothing
without imagining it, which is a way of thinking used exclu-
sively for material things, that anything not imaginable seems
to them unintelligible. This is obvious from the fact that, in
the schools, the philosophers regard it as a maxim that there
is nothing in the understanding which was not first in the
senses, even though it is certain that the ideas of God and of
the soul have never been in the senses. And it seems to me
that those who try to understand them by means of their
imagination are doing exactly the same as if they tried to use
their eyes to hear sounds or smell odors, with this difference,
however, that the sense of sight gives us no less assurance of
the truth of its objects than do the senses of smell and
hearing, whereas neither our imagination nor our senses can
ever assure us of anything without the intervention of our
understanding.

Finally, if there are still some people who have not been
sufficiently convinced of the existence of God and the soul by
the reasons I have brought forward, I would like them to
know that all the other things which they may consider to be
more certain, such as that they have a body, that there are
stars and an earth, and so on, are actually less certain. For
while we have a moral assurance of these things which makes
it seem impossible to doubt them without being absurd, if we
are concerned with metaphysical certainty we cannot ration-
ally deny that we have sufficient grounds for not being entirely
certain of them when we have noted that we can, in the same
way, imagine while we are asleep that we have another body,
and that we see other stars and another earth, without this
actually being the case at all. For how do we know that the
thoughts which come to us in dreams are false rather than the
others, since they are no less vivid and definite? Let the
best minds study this as long as they please; I do not think
that they will ever be able to give any reason that will be
sufficient to remove this doubt, unless they presuppose the
existence of God. For, first of all, what I was taken as a rule,
namely, that the things which we apprehend very clearly and
distinctly are all true, is assured only by the fact that God is
or exists, that He is a perfect being, and that everything that
is in us comes from Him. Hence it follows that our ideas,
being real things which come from God, insofar as they are
clear and distinct, must be true. If we often have ideas which
contain falsity, they can only be those which are to some

extent confused and obscure because they partake of nothingness, that is, they are thus confused in us because we are not
entirely perfect. It is obvious that it would be as contradictory
for falsity or imperfection, as such, to come from God as it
would be for truth or perfection to come from nothing. But
if we do not know that everything real and true that is in us
comes from a perfect and infinite being, we shall have no
reason to be certain that our ideas have the perfection of
being true, no matter how clear and distinct they may be.

Now once the knowledge of God and the soul has made us
certain of this rule, it is quite easy to understand that the
dreams we have when we are asleep should in no way make us
doubt the truth of the thoughts we have when we are awake.
For if anyone should happen to have a very distinct idea even
while asleep—if, for example, a geometer should invent some
new demonstration—his sleep would not prevent it from
being true. As for the most common error of our dreams,
which consists in their representing various objects to us in the
same way as our external senses, it does not matter that it
gives us occasion to be suspicious of the truth of such ideas,
because they can deceive us rather often when we are awake,
as when those who have jaundice see everything as yellow, or
when stars and other distant objects appear to be much
smaller than they are. For whether we are awake or asleep, we
ought never to let ourselves be convinced of anything except
by the evidence of our reason. And I wish to stress that I am
speaking of our reason, not of our imagination or our senses.
Although we see the sun very clearly, we must not conclude
from this that its size is no greater than we see it to be; and
we can distinctly imagine the head of a lion grafted onto the
body of a goat without being forced to conclude that a
chimera exists. Reason does not tell us that everything we
thus see or imagine is true, but it does tell us that all our
ideas or notions must have some foundation of truth, for
otherwise it would not be possible that they had been placed
in us by God, who is completely perfect and veracious. And
because our reasonings are never so manifest or complete when
we are asleep as they are when we are awake, although sometimes in sleep our imaginings are even more vivid and definite,
reason also tells us that since our thoughts cannot all be true,
inasmuch as we are not entirely perfect, the truth that is in
them must necessarily be found in those we have when we are
awake, rather than in our dreams.

⤳ Part Five

I would be glad to go on and display here the whole chain of other truths which I have deduced from these first ones, but since this would require me to speak of many questions that are in dispute among the learned, with whom I have no desire to quarrel, I think it is better for me to refrain from doing so, and to say only in general what they are, leaving it to the wisest to decide whether it would be good for the public to be more fully informed about them. I am still firmly resolved never to adopt any other principle than the one I have just used in demonstrating the existence of God and the soul, and to accept nothing as true which does not seem clearer and more certain than geometrical demonstrations previously seemed to me. Nevertheless, I venture to say not only that I have found a means of satisfying myself within a short time with regard to all the principal difficulties that are usually dealt with in philosophy, but also that I have discerned certain laws which God has so established in nature, and whose notions He has so implanted in our souls, that after we have sufficiently reflected on them we cannot doubt that they are strictly observed in everything that is or happens in the world. Then, in considering the sequence of these laws, I seemed to have discovered many truths that were more useful and important than anything I had previously learned, or even hoped to learn.

But since I have tried to explain the principal ones in a treatise which certain considerations prevent me from publishing, I can give no better idea of them than by summarily indicating what this treatise contains. I had planned to include in it everything I thought I had learned, before writing it, about the nature of material things. But just as a painter, unable to represent all the sides of a solid object on his flat canvas, chooses one of the principal sides and places it in the light, shading the others to make them appear as they would seem if we were looking at the side facing the light, so, fearing that I might be unable to put into my discourse everything I had in my mind, I undertook only to expound fully what I understood about light, then, when the occasion arose, to add something about the sun and the fixed stars, since nearly all light comes from them; about the skies, since they transmit it; about the planets, comets and the earth, since they reflect it; and in particular about all terrestrial bodies, since they are colored, transparent or luminous; and finally about man, since he is the spectator of all this. Furthermore, in order to shade all these things a little, and be able to state my conclusions about them more freely, without being obliged either to follow or to refute the opinions that are accepted among the learned, I decided to abandon this whole world to their disputes, and to speak only of what would take place in a new world if God were now to create, somewhere in imaginary space, enough matter to compose it, and if He were to agitate the various parts of this matter in diverse fashions and without order, so as to make it into a chaos as confused as any poet could imagine, and if, after this, He were to do no more than lend His usual assistance to nature, leaving it to act in accordance with the laws He has established. And so, first of all, I described this matter and tried to represent it in such a way that there is nothing in the world, it seems to me, that is clearer or more intelligible, except what I have already said about God and the soul, for I expressly assumed that it had none of those forms or qualities which are debated in the Schools, and, in general, that there was nothing about it which was not so natural for our souls to know that we could not even pretend to be ignorant of it. Moreover, I showed what the laws of nature are, and, without basing my reasoning on any other principle than the infinite perfections of God, I tried to demonstrate all the laws of which there might be any doubt, and to show that they are such that, even if God had created many worlds, there could not be one in which these same laws were not observed. Then I showed that, as a result of these laws, the greatest part of the matter of this chaos had to dispose and arrange itself in a certain way which made it resemble our skies, and how some of its parts had to compose an earth, while others composed planets and comets, and still others composed a sun and fixed stars. And at this point I enlarged upon the subject of light, explaining at length the nature of the light that had to be found in the sun and the stars, how from them it traversed in an instant the vast spaces of the skies, and how it was reflected from the planets and comets toward the earth. I also added a number of things concerning the substance, location, movements and various qualities of these skies and heavenly bodies; and I believed that I had said enough about them to show that nothing could be observed in those of this world which should not, or at least could not, appear as exactly similar in those of the world

I was describing. I then went on to discuss the earth in particular. I explained how, even though I had expressly assumed that God had placed no heaviness in the matter of which it was composed, all its parts nevertheless tended exactly toward its center; how, with water and air on its surface, the disposition of the skies and the heavenly bodies, principally the moon, must cause an ebb and flow similar in all respects to that which we observe in our seas, as well as certain currents of water and air running from east to west, such as we observe in the tropics; how mountains, seas, springs and rivers could naturally be formed, and metals appear in mines, and plants grow in the fields, and, in general, how all those bodies which we call mixed or composite could be engendered. And among other things, since, aside from heavenly bodies, I know of nothing that produces light except fire, I endeavored to give a clear explanation of everything pertaining to its nature: how it comes into being and spreads; how it sometimes has only heat without light, and sometimes light without heat; how it introduces various colors and other qualities into different bodies; how its melts some and hardens others; how it can consume nearly all of them, or convert them into ashes and smoke; and finally how, solely by the violence of its action, it makes these ashes into glass; and since this transmutation of ashes into glass seemed to me as wonderful as any other transmutation that takes place in nature, I took particular pleasure in describing it.

However, I did not wish to infer from all these things that this world was created in the manner I was proposing, for it is much more likely that God made it as it is now from the beginning. But it is certain—and this is an opinion commonly accepted by theologians—that the action by which He now conserves it is the same as that by which He created it, so that if at first He gave it no other form than that of chaos, provided that, having established the laws of nature, He lent it His assistance to enable it to act as it normally does, we may believe, without detriment to the miracle of creation, that all purely material things could have eventually become as we now see them. And their nature is much easier to conceive when we see them thus developing little by little than when we consider them as fully formed.

From the description of inanimate bodies and plants, I went on to a description of animals, and particularly of men. But since I did not yet have enough knowledge to speak of the latter in the same way as of the rest, that is, in demon-

strating effects by their causes, and showing from what seeds
and in what manner nature must produce them, I contented
myself with assuming that God formed the body of a man
entirely similar to one of our own both in the outer shape
of its members and the inner conformation of its organs,
without composing it of any other matter than that which I
had described, and without placing in it, at the beginning,
any rational soul or anything else to serve as a vegetative or
sensitive soul, but that He kindled in its heart one of those
fires without light which I had already explained, and which
I regarded as being of the same kind as that which heats hay
when it is stored before it is dry, or causes new wine to boil
when it is allowed to ferment with the stems and stalks of the
grapes. For when I considered what functions there could
consequently be in such a body, I found all those which can
be in us without our thinking of them, and hence any contribution from our soul, that is, from the part of us which is
distinct from our body and whose whole nature, as I have
said above, is to think. I was unable to find any of those
functions which, being dependent on thought, are the only
ones which belong to us specifically as men, but I later
discovered them all when I assumed that God had created
a rational soul and joined it to this body in a manner which
I described.

But in order to show how I treated this matter in my
discourse, I wish here to explain the movement of the heart
and the arteries, for since this is the first and most general
movement we observe in animals, it will be easy to judge from
it what we ought to think of all the others. And in order that
my readers may have less difficulty in understanding what I
am going to say about it, I would like those who are not
versed in anatomy to take the trouble, before reading this, to
have the heart of some large animal dissected in front of
them, for it is in all respects quite similar to a human heart,
and to have the two chambers or cavities it contains pointed
out to them. First let them note the cavity in the right side,
to which two broad tubes are connected, namely, the vena
cava, which is the principal receptacle of the blood and is
like the trunk of a tree whose branches are all the other veins
of the body, and the pulmonary artery, which, starting from
the heart, is divided further on into many branches which
are spread throughout the lungs. Then there is the cavity in
the left side of the heart, to which are connected two tubes as
wide as the other two, or even wider, namely, the pulmonary

vein, which comes from the lungs, where it is divided into many branches interlaced with those of the pulmonary artery and those of what is known as the windpipe, through which we breathe, and the aorta, which, after leaving the heart, disperses its branches throughout the body. I would also like my readers to be carefully shown the eleven little membranes which, like so many little doors, open and close the entrances to the vena cava, where they are so disposed that they cannot prevent the blood it contains from flowing into the right-hand cavity of the heart, yet they effectively prevent it from flowing out; then there are three at the entrance to the pulmonary artery which, being disposed in the opposite manner, allow the blood in this cavity to flow into the lungs, but do not allow it to return; and similarly, there are two others at the entrance to the pulmonary vein which allow the blood to flow from the lungs to the left-hand cavity of the heart, but prevent its return; and finally, there are three at the entrance to the aorta which allow the blood to flow from the heart but not back into it. And there is no need to seek any other reason for the number of these membranes than the fact that the opening of the pulmonary vein, being oval because of its location, can conveniently be closed by two, whereas the others, being round, can better be closed by three. I would like my readers to observe, moreover, that the aorta and the pulmonary artery are of a much harder and firmer texture than the pulmonary vein and the vena cava; and that the latter two widen before entering the heart, where they form, as it were, two little pouches which are called the auricles and are composed of flesh similar to that of the heart itself; and that there is always more heat in the heart than in any other part of the body; and, finally, that this heat is capable of making any drop of blood that enters the heart promptly swell and dilate, just as liquids generally do when they are poured drop by drop into a hot container.

If these facts are borne in mind, to explain the movement of the heart I need say only that when its cavities are not filled, a certain amount of blood necessarily flows into its right-hand cavity from the vena cava and into its left-hand cavity from the pulmonary vein, since these two vessels are always full of blood and their openings, which face the heart, cannot then be blocked; and as soon as two drops of blood have thus entered the heart, one in each of its cavities, these drops, which must be very large because the openings through which they enter are very wide and the vessels from which they come are very full of blood, become rarefied and dilated because of the heat they encounter in the heart, and so, making the whole heart swell, they push against and close the five little doors that are at the entrances to the two vessels from which they have come, thus preventing any more blood from entering the heart; then, becoming more and more rarefied, they push against and open the six other little doors that are at the entrances to the two other vessels through which they flow out, thus making all the branches of the pulmonary artery and the aorta swell at almost the same moment as the heart, which, immediately afterward, deflates, as do these arteries also, because the blood that has entered them loses some of its heat, and their six little doors close again, and the five little doors of the vena cava and the pulmonary vein open again to admit two other drops of blood which, like the two preceding drops, make the heart and the arteries swell again. And because the blood which thus enters the heart passes through the two pouches known as the auricles, their movement is contrary to that of the heart: they deflate when the heart inflates. Moreover, so that this will not be denied without examination by those who are not familiar with the force of mathematical demonstrations, and are not accustomed to distinguishing true reasons from those which are merely plausible, I wish to inform them that the movement I have just explained follows as necessarily from the disposition of the organs that can be seen in the heart with the naked eye, from the heat that one can feel in it with the fingers, and from the nature of the blood, which can be known by experiment, as the movement of a clock follows from the force, arrangement and shape of its counterweights and gears.

But if one should ask why the blood from the veins, constantly flowing from the heart, is never exhausted, and why the arteries are never too full, since all the blood that passes through the heart flows into them, I need give no other answer than what has already been written by an English physician who must be praised for having broken the ice on this subject and being the first to teach that there are several little passages at the extremities of the arteries through which the blood they receive from the heart enters the little branches of the veins, from which it flows back to the heart, so that its course is an endless circulation. He proves this very well by referring to the common practice of surgeons who, having bound an arm rather tightly above the spot where they open the vein, cause the blood to flow out more abundantly than if they had not bound the arm at all, while the opposite would occur if they bound it further down, between the hand and the opening, or if they bound it very tightly above. For it is obvious that a moderately tight binding, though capable of preventing the blood that is already in the arm from returning to the heart through the veins, does not thereby prevent more blood from flowing through the arteries, because they are situated deeper than the veins and, being harder, are less easy to press shut, and also because the blood moves with greater force from the heart toward the hand, by way of the arteries, than it does when it flows back toward the heart through the veins. And since this blood flows out through an opening that has been made in one of the veins of the arm, there must necessarily be passages below the binding, that is, toward the extremities of the arm, through which it can flow from the arteries. He also proves very well what he says about the course of the blood by referring to certain small membranes which are so disposed in various places along the veins that they do not allow the blood to flow from the middle of the body toward the extremities, but only to return from the extremities to the heart, and, further, by pointing out that experience shows that all the blood in a body can flow out of it in a very short time through a single artery, even though it be tightly bound near the heart, if it is cut between the binding and the heart, so that there can be no reason to suppose that the blood is coming from anywhere else.

But there are a number of other things which indicate that the true cause of this movement of the blood is what I have said. First of all, the difference that is observed between the blood which comes from the veins and that which comes from the arteries can be explained only by the fact that, having been rarefied, and, as it were, distilled in passing through the heart, the blood is thinner, livelier and warmer immediately after leaving the heart, that is, when it is in the arteries, than it is shortly before entering the heart, that is, when it is in the veins. And careful observation will show that this difference is more apparent near the heart than in those parts of the body which are furthest away from it. And then the hardness of the walls of the pulmonary artery and the aorta shows clearly that the blood beats against them with greater force than against the walls of the veins. And why should the aorta and the left-hand cavity of the heart be broader and more capacious than the right-hand cavity and the pulmonary artery? The answer must be that the blood which comes from the pulmonary vein, having been only in the lungs after passing through the heart, is thinner and becomes rarefied more easily and to a greater extent than the blood which comes immediately from the vena cava. And what could a doctor learn from feeling the pulse if he did not know that, as the nature of the blood changes, it can be rarefied by the heat of the heart to a greater and lesser extent, and with more or less rapidity, than before? And if we inquire as to how this heat is communicated to the other parts of the body, must we not admit that it is by means of the blood, which is reheated as it passes through the heart, and then spreads throughout the body? It is for this reason that if we remove the blood from any part of the body, we also remove its warmth; and if the heart did not constantly send new blood to the hands and feet, it would not be able to warm them as it does, even if it were as hot as molten iron. And from this we know that the true function of breathing is to bring fresh air into the lungs to cause the blood which comes there from the right-hand cavity of the heart, where it has been rarefied and, as it were, changed into vapors, to thicken and become converted into blood again, before entering the left-hand cavity, for otherwise it would not be able to serve as fuel for the fire that is in the heart. This is confirmed by the fact that animals which have no lungs have only one cavity in their hearts, and that babies in the womb, who cannot use their lungs, have an opening through which blood flows from the vena cava into the left-hand cavity of the heart, and a passage by which it flows from the pulmonary artery into the aorta, without passing through the lungs. And how could digestion take place if the heart did not send heat into the stomach by way of the arteries, along with some of the most fluid parts of the blood, which help to dissolve the food? And is it not easy to understand the action which converts the juice of this food into blood, if we consider that it is distilled in passing through the heart perhaps one or two hundred times a day? And what else need we say to explain nutrition and the production of the various humors that are found in the body, except that the force with which the blood, as it becomes rarefied, flows toward the extremities of the arteries causes some of its parts to stop among those that are already present in a given portion of the body, and to drive out others and take their place, and that according to the location, shape and size of the pores they encounter, they go to certain places rather than others, just as different kinds of grain can be sorted out by using sieves with holes of different sizes? And what is most remarkable in all this is the generation of the animal spirits, which are like an extremely tenuous wind, or, rather, like an extremely pure and lively flame which, constantly rising in great abundance from the heart into the brain, goes from there, by way of the nerves, into the muscles, and gives movement to all the members of the body. And to explain why those parts of the blood which are the most agitated and penetrating, and are therefore best suited to compose the animal spirits, go to the brain rather than elsewhere, we need imagine no other reason than that the arteries which conduct them there are those which lead away from the heart in the straightest lines, and that, according to the rules of mechanics, which are the same as those of nature, whenever a number of things simultaneously tend to move toward a single place where there is not enough room for all of them, as in the case of the parts of the blood which come from the left-hand cavity of the heart and tend to move toward the brain, the weaker and less agitated ones are turned aside by the stronger ones, so that only the latter reach the end of their original course.

I explained all these things in rather great detail in the treatise I once intended to publish. And next I showed what the structure of the nerves and muscles of the human body must be in order that the animal spirits within should have the power to move its members, as is seen in the case of heads which, for a short time after being severed, go on moving, and bite the ground, even though they are no longer animate. I then showed what changes must take place in the brain in order to cause wakefulness, sleep and dreams; how light, sounds, odors, tastes, heat and all the other qualities of external objects can imprint various ideas in the brain by means of the senses; how hunger, thirst and the other internal passions can also send their ideas to it; what must be regarded in it as common sense, in which these ideas are received, as memory, which preserves them, and as imagination, which can change them in various ways and compose new ones, and which, distributing the animal spirits into the muscles, can move the members of this body in as many different ways, according to the objects that are presented to its senses and the internal passions that are in it, as our bodies can move without being directed by the will. This will not seem at all strange to those who, knowing how many different kinds of *automata,* or moving machines, can be made by human ingenuity with the use of very few parts in comparison with the great multitude of bones, muscles, nerves, arteries, veins and all the other parts that are in the body of any animal, will consider this body as a machine which, having been made by the hands of God, is incomparably better ordered, and has more wonderful movements, than any machine that man can invent.

At this point in my treatise I showed that if there were such machines which had the organs and appearance of a monkey or some other animal without reason, we would have no way of recognizing that they were not of the same nature as those animals in every respect, whereas if there were machines which resembled our bodies and imitated our actions as much as possible, we would still have two very certain ways of recognizing that they were not real men. The first is that they would not be able to use words or signs as we do in order to make known our thoughts to others. For we can conceive of a machine so made that it can utter words, even words that are related to bodily actions which cause some change in its organs: for example, if we touch it in a certain spot it may ask us what we want to say to it, if we touch it in another spot it may cry out that we are hurting it, and so on; but we cannot conceive of a machine capable of arranging words in various ways so as to be relevant to the meaning of anything that is said in its presence, as the stupidest of men can do. And the second is that, although these machines might do many things as well as any of us, or even better, they would inevitably fail in others which would reveal to us that they acted not from knowledge, but from the disposition of their organs. For whereas reason is a universal instrument which can be used in all sorts of circumstances, these organs need some particular disposition for each particular action; hence it is not practically possible for a machine to have a sufficient number of differently disposed organs to make it act in all the circumstances of life in the same ways as our reason makes us act.

These two considerations also make it possible for us to know the difference between men and animals. For it is a remarkable fact that there are no men, not even the least intelligent, who are so dull-witted and stupid that they are incapable of putting words together in such a way as to express their thoughts, and that, on the other hand, there is no animal, however perfect and fortunately born, that can do the same. This is not due to lack of proper organs, for we see that magpies and parrots can utter words as we do, and yet they cannot speak as we do, that is, they cannot show that their words express their thoughts, whereas men who are born deaf and dumb, and may be even more seriously lacking than animals in the organs that other men use for speaking, usually invent signs by which they can express themselves to those who are often with them and therefore have time to learn their language. And this shows not only that animals have less reason than men: it shows that they have none at all. For we can all observe that it takes very little reason to learn to speak; and since there is as much inequality among animals of the same species as there is among men, so that some are easier to train than others, it is incredible that a monkey or a parrot that is one of the most perfect of its species should not be able to equal in this respect the stupidest child, or at least a child with a defective brain, if its soul were not of an entirely different nature from our own. And we must not confuse speech with those natural movements which bear witness to the passions and can be imitated by machines as well as by animals, nor should we think, as some of the ancients did, that animals speak although we do not understand their language, for if this were so, since they have many organs that are quite similar to ours, they would be able to make themselves understood by us as well as by their fellow animals. It is also remarkable that while many animals show greater ingenuity than we do in some actions, they show none at all in many others, so that what they do better than we do does not prove that they have any intelligence—for in that respect they would have more of it than any of us and would do better in everything—but, rather, that they have none, and that it is nature which acts in them, according to the disposition of their organs. Similarly, despite all our wisdom, we cannot count the hours and measure time as accurately as a clock which is composed only of gears and springs.

After establishing these points in my treatise, I described the rational soul and showed that, unlike the other things I had discussed, it cannot be derived from the power of matter, but must necessarily have been expressly created. I then showed how it is not sufficient for it to be lodged in the human body like a pilot in his ship, except perhaps for the purpose of moving its members, but that it must be more closely joined and united with it in order also to have feelings and appetites like ours, and thus compose a real man. Moreover, at this point I dwelt at some length on the subject of the soul, because it is one of the most important, since, aside from the error of denying God, which I think I have already sufficiently refuted, there is no error more likely to lead weak minds from the path of virtue than the idea that the souls of animals are of the same nature as our own, and that consequently we have no more to fear or hope for after this life than do flies and ants. But when we know how great the difference is, we understand much better the reasons which prove that our soul is by nature entirely independent of the body, and is therefore not subject to dying with it; and then, when we see that there is nothing else which might destroy the soul, we are naturally led to conclude that it is immortal.

◈§ Part Six

It has now been three years since I completed the treatise which contains all these things, and I had just begun to go over it again before placing it in the hands of a printer when I learned that certain persons to whom I defer, and whose authority has no less power over my actions than my reason over my thoughts, had disapproved of a theory in physics which had been published by someone a short time before. I do not mean to say that I accepted this theory, but I will say that, before their censure, I had seen nothing in it which I could imagine to be detrimental to religion or the State, and nothing, therefore, which would have prevented me from writing it myself, if reason had convinced me of its validity. This made me fear that among my own views there might be some in which I was mistaken, despite the great care I have always taken never to write anything that might be harmful to anyone. These considerations were enough to make me change my decision to publish my treatise. For although the reasons which had led me to that decision were very strong, my own inclination, which has always been to hate the whole business of publishing books, immediately supplied me with others that made me change my mind. And these reasons on both sides of the matter are such that it is somewhat to my own interest to state them here, and also perhaps to the interest of the public to know them.

I have never attached any great importance to the things

that came from my mind, and so long as the only fruit of the method I employ was my own satisfaction in solving certain problems pertaining to the speculative sciences, and in trying to regulate my conduct in accordance with what it taught me, I felt under no obligation to write anything. For with regard to matters of conduct, everyone is so firmly convinced of his own opinions that there might be as many reformers as there are heads if anyone other than those whom God has established as the rulers of His peoples, or to whom He has given enough grace and zeal to be prophets, were allowed to set about making any changes in the ways and customs of mankind. And so, although my speculations pleased me greatly, I assumed that others had their own which pleased them perhaps even more. But as soon as I had acquired a few general notions in physics and had seen, after beginning to test them in various specific problems, how far they could lead and how different they were from the principles hitherto in use, I felt that I could no longer keep them hidden without gravely sinning against the law which obliges us to further the general welfare of all men as much as we can. For they have made me see that it is possible to obtain knowledge which is extremely useful in life, and that in place of the speculative philosophy which is taught in the schools, we can find a practical one which, by teaching us to know the force and action of fire, air, the heavenly bodies, the skies and all the other bodies that surround us, as distinctly as we know the various trades of our artisans, will enable us to use them in the same way for all purposes to which they are suited, thus making ourselves, as it were, the masters and possessors of nature. And this is desirable not only for the invention of countless devices by means of which we could, without toil, enjoy the fruits of the earth and all the good things it contains, but also, and chiefly, for the preservation of health, which is no doubt the first good and the foundation of all the others in this life; for even the mind is so dependent on the temperament and the dispositions of the organs of the body that if it is possible to find some way to make men wiser and cleverer than they have been so far, I think it must be sought in medicine. It is true that medicine as it is now practiced contains few things of any remarkable usefulness, and, while I have no desire to deprecate it, I am sure that there is no one, even among those who have made it their profession, who would not admit that everything now known in it is almost nothing compared to what still remains to be known,

and that we might be freed from countless maladies, of both
the body and the mind, and perhaps also from the debility of
old age, if we knew enough about their causes and all the
remedies which nature has provided. Now, intending to spend
the rest of my life in search of this highly necessary knowledge, and having come upon a path which, iit seems to me,
must infallibly lead one to find it unless one is prevented from
reaching the end of the path by the shortness of life or lack
of empirical data, I decided that there was no better way to
overcome these two obstacles than to give the public a complete and faithful account of the little I had found, and to
urge all men of intelligence and good will to go further by
contributing, each according to his inclination and ability, to
the observations and experiments required, and by informing
the public of everything they learned, in order that the latest
ones might begin where their predecessors had left off, and
that in thus joining the lives and labors of many, we might all
go forward together much further than any of us would have
been able to do alone.

With regard to observations and experiments, I noted that
they become all the more necessary as one's knowledge
becomes more advanced. For in the beginning it is better to
use only those which present themselves spontaneously to the
senses, and which we cannot fail to understand if we reflect
on them to any extent, rather than to see rarer and more
complex ones. The reason for this is that these rarer ones often
deceive us when we do not yet know the commonest causes,
and that the circumstances on which they depend are nearly
always so special and so minute that it is very difficult to
distinguish them. The order I maintained in this is the following: first, I tried to discover in general the principles, or first
causes, of everything that is or may be in the world, without
considering, for this purpose, anything but God, who created
the world, and without drawing them from anything but
certain seeds of truth which are naturally in our minds. After
this, I sought to determine the first and commonest effects
that could be deduced from these causes, and it seems to me
that in so doing I found skies, heavenly bodies, an earth, and
even, on the earth, water, air, fire, minerals and a number of
other things which are the commonest and simplest of all, and
therefore the easiest to know. Then, when I decided to turn
to those that were more special, I encountered so many different ones that I did not think it possible for the human mind
to distinguish the forms or species that are on the earth from

an infinite number of others which might be on it if it were God's will to place them there, or, consequently, to make them useful to us, unless we seek causes from effects and make use of many special observations and experiments. And I venture to state that when I went over in my mind all the objects that had ever presented themselves to my senses, I found nothing that I could not conveniently explain by means of the principles I had discovered. But I must also confess that the power of nature is so plentiful and vast, and these principles are so simple and general, that I now scarcely ever observe a particular effect without seeing immediately that it can be deduced from them in several different ways, so that my greatest difficulty is usually to determine in which one of these ways it depends on them. I know of no other expedient for the purpose than to try several more experiments which are such that their results will vary according to which one of these ways is the correct explanation. Moreover, it seems to me that I have now reached the point where I can see well enough how to go about most of these experiments, but I also see that they are of such a nature, and so numerous, that neither my abilities nor my income, even if I had a thousand times more than I have now, would be enough for all of them; in the future, therefore, the degree of my progress in the knowledge of nature will depend on my opportunities to make experiments. It was this knowledge that I intended to disclose in my treatise, and I also intended to show its potential usefulness to the public so clearly that I would oblige all those who desire the general welfare of mankind, that is, all those who are truly virtuous, not virtuous merely in appearance and by reputation, to inform me of the experiments they had already made, and to aid me in seeking out those which still remained to be made.

Since then, however, other reasons have made me change my mind and decide that I really ought to go on writing down everything I judge to be of any importance, as I discover the truth about it, and to devote as much care to my work as if I were going to have it printed, in order to have all the more opportunity to examine it, since we no doubt always look more closely at something we believe will be seen by many other people than at something we do only for ourselves, and since things which seemed true to me when I first conceived them have often seemed false when I began putting them down on paper. Also, I want to lose no opportunity to benefit the public if I am capable of doing so. If my writings are worth anything, those who will have them after my death can use them in whatever way seems best. I decided not to let them be published during my lifetime, lest the opposition and controversies to which they might give rise, or even any reputation they might bring me, should give me occasion to waste some of the time I intend to devote to my own instruction. For although it is true that each man has a duty to further the welfare of others insofar as he is able, and that to be of no use to anyone is, strictly speaking, to be worthless, it is also true that our efforts ought to be directed beyond the present, and that it is right not to do things which might be of some benefit to our contemporaries when our intention in refraining from doing them is to do other things which will be of still greater benefit to posterity. I am quite willing for everyone to know that the little I have learned so far is almost nothing in comparison with what I do not know, but do not despair of being able to learn; for it is the same with those who gradually discover truth as with those who, once they have begun to become rich, have less difficulty in making great acquisitions than they had previously, when they were poorer, in making much smaller ones. Or they can be compared to military leaders, whose forces usually grow in proportion to their victories, and who need greater skill to maintain their position after losing a battle than they do to capture cities and provinces after winning one. For it is truly fighting a battle to try to overcome all the difficulties and errors which prevent us from reaching knowledge of the truth, and it is losing one to accept a false opinion with regard to some general and important matter; we then require more skill to recover our previous position than we need for making great progress when we already have principles that are assured. As for myself, if I have already discovered a few truths in the sciences (and I hope that the things contained in this volume will show that I have), I can say that they have followed from and depended upon my overcoming five or six principal difficulties, which I consider as so many battles in which luck was on my side. I shall even venture to say that I believe I now need to win only two or three more similar battles in order to achieve my goal entirely, and that my age is not so far advanced, in relation to the normal course of nature, that I cannot still have enough time to do so. But I consider myself all the more obliged to be careful as to how I spend my time now that I have more hope of being able to put it to good use, and I would no doubt have many opportunities to waste it if I published the foundations of my physics, for although they are nearly all so manifestly true that they need only to be understood in order to be believed, and although there is not one which I do not think I can demonstrate, nevertheless, because it is impossible that they should be in accord with all the diverse opinions of other men, I foresee that I would often be distracted by the opposition they would arouse.

It may be said that this opposition would be useful because it would make me recognize my mistakes, and because, if I had anything worth while, others would thereby come to know more about it and, beginning to make use of it immediately, would also help me with their own discoveries, for many men can see more than one. But although I acknowledge that I am extremely subject to error and almost never trust the first thoughts that come into my mind, my experience of the objections that can be made against me prevents me from expecting any benefit from them, for I have often been made aware of the judgments of those I regarded as my friends, of certain others whom I thought to be indifferent to me, and even of some whose malice and envy would, I knew, try to discover things which affection would conceal from my friends, but it has seldom happened that anyone has raised an objection that I had totally failed to foresee, unless it was far removed from my subject, so I have almost never encountered a censor of my opinions who has not seemed to me either less rigorous or less equitable than myself. And I have never observed that the controversies which are carried on in the schools have ever led to the discovery of any previously unknown truth, for while each contestant strives for victory, he makes much greater efforts to render his arguments plausible than to weigh the reasons brought forward on both sides of the question; and those who have for a long time been good lawyers do not necessarily make the best judges.

As for the usefulness of my thoughts to others, it could not be very great, since I have not carried them so far that many things would not have to be added to them before they could be put into practice. And I think I may say without vanity that if there is anyone capable of doing so, it must be myself rather than anyone else—not that there may not be in the world many minds incomparably better than mine, but because one cannot understand a thing as well, and make it one's own, when one learns it from someone else as when one discovers it oneself. This is so true of the matter I am discussing that, although I have often explained some of my opinions to people who had very good minds, and who seemed to understand them very well while I was speaking to them, when they later repeated them I nearly always saw that they had changed them in such a way that I could no longer accept them as my own. And in this connection I would like to ask those who will come after me never to believe anything attributed to me unless I have said it myself. I am not surprised by the extravagant ideas attributed to all those ancient philosophers whose writings have not come down to us, and since they were the best minds of their time, I do not judge that their thoughts were extremely irrational, but only that they have been badly reported to us. We see also that they have almost never been surpassed by any of their disciples, and I am sure that the most passionately devoted of those who now follow Aristotle would consider themselves fortunate if they knew as much about nature as he did, even on condition that they would never know more. They are like ivy, which never seeks to climb higher than the tree that supports it, and often even turns downward after it has reached the top, for it seems to me that they also turn downward, that is, make themselves less learned, in a sense, than if they had refrained from studying, when, not content with knowing everything that is intelligibly explained in their author's works, they also try to find in them the solutions of many problems which he said nothing about, and which may never even have occurred to him. However, their way of philosophizing is extremely convenient for those who have only mediocre minds, because the obscurity of the distinctions and principles they use enables them to speak about all things as boldly as if they knew them, and to maintain everything they say about them against the ablest and most subtle minds, without there being any means of convincing them that they are wrong. In this they are, it seems to me, like a blind man who, in order to fight on equal terms with a man who can see, makes him descend into the depths of a dark cellar; and I may say that it is to their interest that I should refrain from publishing the principles of philosophy which I employ, for since these principles are quite simple and manifestly true, if I published them it would be almost the same as if I had opened a few windows and let some light into the cellar into which they have descended to fight. But even the best minds have no reason to wish to know my principles. If they want to know how to speak about everything and acquire a reputation for erudition, they will succeed more easily by contending themselves with plausibility, which can be found without great difficulty in all sorts of matters, than by seeking truth, which can be discovered only little by little in a few, and which, when we are called upon to speak about the others, obliges us frankly to confess our ignorance. If, however, they prefer the knowledge of a few truths to the vanity of appearing to be ignorant of nothing, as they no doubt should, and if they wish to follow a plan similar to mine, they have no need to be told anything more than what I have already said in this discourse, for if they are capable of going beyond what I have done, they will surely be capable of discovering for themselves everything I think I have discovered. And inasmuch as I have always examined things only in proper order, it is certain that what still remains for me to discover is inherently more difficult and recondite than what I have hitherto been able to encounter, and they would have much less pleasure in learning it from me than in learning it for themselves. Furthermore, the habit they will acquire of first seeking easy things, then going on gradually and step by step to others that are more difficult, will be of greater use to them than all my instructions could ever be. As for myself, I am convinced that if I had been taught in my youth all the truths I have since sought to demonstrate, and had had no difficulty in learning them, I might never have known any others, and that I would at least never have acquired the habit and facility I now have of always finding new ones in proportion to my efforts to seek them. In short, if there has ever been an undertaking which could not be completed as well by anyone other than the man who began it, it is the one in which I am now engaged.

It is true that one man could not perform all the experiments and observations required, but it is also true that he could not usefully employ any other hands than his own, except for those of artisans or such people as he could pay, and who would be moved by the hope of gain, which is a very effective means, to do exactly everything he prescribed. As for those volunteers who might offer to help them out of curiosity or a desire to learn, aside from the fact that they usually promise more than they accomplish and do nothing but make fine proposals which never come to anything, they would want to be paid by an explanation of certain difficulties, or at least by compliments and useless conversations which could not take up so little of his time that he would not be the loser in the exchange. As for experiments and observations that have already been performed by others, even if they were willing to communicate them to him, which those who call them secrets never do, most of them are composed of so many superfluous circumstances and elements that it would be very difficult for him to decipher the truth contained in them. Furthermore, he would find them nearly all so badly explained, or even so false, because those who performed them tried to make them appear to be in conformity with their principles, that even if there were some of them which might be useful to him, they would not be worth the time it would take to select them. Therefore, if there were someone in the world who was known with certainty to be capable of discovering the greatest and most useful things possible, so that other men did everything in their power to help him achieve his goal, I do not see that they could do anything for him except to defray the costs of the experiments he would need, and to prevent anyone's importunity from taking up his time. But, besides the fact that I am not so presumptuous as to wish to promise anything extraordinary, and that I do not indulge in such vain thoughts as to imagine that the public ought to take a great interest in my projects, my soul is not so base that I would accept from anyone any favor which I might be thought not to have deserved.

All these considerations, taken together, led me to decide, three years ago, not to publish the treatise I had completed, and even not to disclose any other, during my lifetime, which would be equally general or capable of giving an understanding of the foundations of my physics. Since then, however, there have been two other reasons which have obliged me to publish a few particular essays in this volume, and to give the public some account of my actions and projects. The first reason is that if I failed to do so, many of those who were aware of my former intention to publish some of my writings might imagine that my reasons for not publishing them were less to my credit than they actually are. For although I have no excessive love for glory, and may even say that I hate it, insofar as I judge it to be inimical to my tranquillity, which I value above all else, I have never tried to conceal my actions as if they were crimes, nor have I ever taken a great many precautions to remain unknown, both because I would have felt that I was doing myself an injustice, and because it would have given me a certain anxiety that would also have been inimical to the perfect tranquillity of mind which I seek. And since, being thus indifferent as to whether I was known or not, I was not able to prevent myself from acquiring some sort of reputation, I thought I ought at least to do my best to avoid acquiring a bad one. The other reason why I have written this is that I see more clearly every day that my plan to instruct myself is being delayed by countless experiments and observations which I need but which I cannot perform without the help of others, and that, although I do not flatter myself so much as to expect the public to be greatly concerned with my interests, I do not wish to fail in my duty to myself by giving those who will live after me any grounds for complaining some day that I could have left them many much better things if I had not been too negligent in letting them know how they could have contributed to my projects.

And I thought that it would be easy for me to choose a few subjects which, while not giving rise to a great deal of controversy or forcing me to declare more of my principles than I wished to do, would nevertheless show clearly enough what I can or cannot do in the sciences. I cannot say whether or not I have succeeded in this, and I do not wish to influence anyone's judgment in advance by speaking about my own writings; but I shall be glad if others will examine them carefully, and, in order to provide greater opportunity for doing so, I beg all those who have any objections to make to be so kind as to send them to my publisher, and after he has forwarded them to me I shall try to have them published with my replies, so that, seeing them together, my readers may more easily judge the truth for themselves. I do not promise to make any long replies, but only to confess my errors frankly, if I perceive them, or, if I do not, to say simply what I believe to be required for the defense of the things I have written, without adding an explanation of any new matter, in order not to become involved in endless discussions.

If some of the things I have said at the beginning of my essays on Dioptrics and on Meteors are at first displeasing to the reader because I call them suppositions and seem to have no desire to prove them, let him have the patience to read attentively to the end, and I hope he will be satisfied, for it seems to me that the reasons contained therein follow one another in such a way that the last ones are demonstrated by the first ones, which are their causes, while these first ones are in turn demonstrated by the last ones, which are their effects. And it must not be imagined that in this I am committing the error which logicians call reasoning in a circle, for since experience makes most of these effects quite certain, the causes from which I deduce them serve not so much to prove them as to explain them; on the contrary, it is the causes which are proved by the effects. And I have called them suppositions only to make it known that I think I can deduce them from the primary truths I have explained above, but that I have deliberately refrained from doing so in order to prevent people with a certain type of mind, who imagine that they know in one day everything it has taken someone else twenty years to think out, as soon as he has said only two or three words to them about it, and who are all the more subject to error, and less capable of truth, to the extent that they are shrewd and quick-witted, from taking the opportunity to build some extravagant philosophy which would be based on what they considered to be my principles, and for which I would be blamed. As for those opinions which are wholly mine, I do not defend them as being new, for if the reasons for them are carefully considered, I am sure that they will be found to be so simple and so thoroughly in accord with common sense that they will seem less extraordinary and strange than any other opinions that one might have on the same subjects. I do not boast of having been the first to discover any of them, but of having accepted them neither because they had already been stated by others nor because they had never been stated before, but only because reason has convinced me of their truth.

If artisans cannot immediately carry out the invention explained in my essay on Dioptrics, I do not think it can be said for this reason to be bad, for since it requires skill and practice to construct and adjust the devices I have described, so that no detail is missing, I would be as surprised to hear that they had succeeded on the first attempt as I would be to hear that someone had learned to play the lute excellently in one day by merely being given a good musical score. And if I write in French, which is the language of my country, rather than in Latin, which is that of my teachers, it is because I hope that those who use only their pure, natural reason will judge my opinions better than those who believe only in ancient books. As for those who combine good sense with learning, and who are the only judges I desire, I am sure that they will not be so partial to Latin that they will refuse to understand my reasonings because I have explained them in the language of the people.

Finally, I do not wish to speak here, in detail, about the

progress I hope to make in the sciences in the future, or to make any promises to the public which I am not sure of being able to keep. I shall say only that I am resolved to spend the rest of my life in trying to acquire such knowledge of nature as will make it possible to establish rules in medicine which will be more firmly assured than any we have had so far, and that my inclination is so far removed from all other pursuits, particularly those which cannot be useful to some without being harmful to others, that if circumstances were to force me to undertake one of them, I do not think I would be capable of succeeding in it. In making this statement, I am well aware that it cannot be of service in making me a man of consequence in the world, but I have no desire to be one; and I shall always consider myself more obliged to those by whose favor I am able to enjoy my leisure without hindrance than to anyone who might offer me the most distinguished positions on earth.

MEDITATIONS

❧❦❧

❧ To the Most Wise and Illustrious, the
Dean and Doctors of the Sacred Faculty
of Theology in Paris

My motive in presenting this work to you is so worthy,
and I am so confident that you will have so worthy a motive
for giving it your patronage when you have become acquainted
with its aim, that I feel I can best commend it to you by
stating in a few words what I have set out to do.

I have always considered that the two questions of God and
of the soul were the chief of those which ought to be demonstrated by means of philosophy rather than theology, for
while it is sufficient for us, the faithful, to believe on faith
that the human soul does not perish with the body, and that
God exists, it certainly does not seem possible ever to convince infidels of any religion, or of almost any moral virtue,
unless these two things have first been proved to them by
natural reason; and since, in this life, greater rewards are
often offered for vices than for virtues, few people would
prefer the right to the useful if they were restrained by
neither the fear of God nor the expectation of another life.
It is absolutely true that we must believe that there is a God
because we are so taught by the Holy Scriptures, and that we
must believe the Holy Scriptures because they come from
God, the reason for this being that, since faith is a gift of
God, He who gives us the grace which enables us to believe
other things can also give us the grace which enables us to
believe that He exists. However, this argument cannot be proposed to infidels, for they might judge us to be reasoning in
a circle. And I have observed that you and all other theologians affirm not only that the existence of God can be proved
by natural reason, but also that the Holy Scriptures teach us
that knowledge of God is much easier for us to acquire than

that of many created things, so easy, in fact, that those who do not have it are blameable. This is shown by the following words in *The Wisdom of Solomon*, Chapter 13: "Howbeit neither are they to be pardoned. For if they were able to know so much that they could aim* at the world, how did they not sooner find out the Lord thereof?" And in *Romans*, Chapter 1, it is said that they are "without excuse"; and again, in the same chapter, from these words: "That which may be known of God is manifest in them," it appears that we are admonished that everything which can be known about God can be established by reasons obtained solely from our own minds.

As for the soul, although many have judged that its nature cannot easily be determined, and some have even ventured to say that human reasoning leads to the conclusion that it dies with the body, and that only faith can make us believe that it does not, nevertheless, since the eighth session of the Lateran Council held under Leo X condemns these opinions and expressly calls upon Christian philosophers to refute the arguments on which they are based, and to use all their powers in making known the truth, I have ventured to do so in this treatise.

Moreover, I am aware that the principal reason given by many impious persons for not believing that there is a God, and that the human soul is distinct from the body, is that no one has yet been able to demonstrate these two facts. While I am not of their opinion, but maintain, on the contrary, that nearly all the reasons which so many great men have brought forward concerning these two matters are demonstrations when they are rightly understood, and that it is nearly impossible to discover new ones, I nevertheless believe that nothing more useful could be done in philosophy than to seek out the best of these reasons with great care, once and for all, and to present them so clearly and precisely that it will henceforth be obvious to everyone that they are genuine demonstrations. And finally, having been urged to do this by a number of people who knew that I had been practicing a certain method for resolving all sorts of difficulties in the sciences—a method which is not really new, since nothing is more ancient than truth, but which they knew I had used rather successfully in other matters—I decided that it was my duty to try to apply it to this matter also.

---

* The translation of this passage is taken from the Authorized (King James) Version of the Apocrypha. The word "aim," in the sense in which it is used here, means "to guess at," or "to estimate."—L. B.

This treatise contains all that I have been able to accomplish. Not that I have compiled in it all the different reasons which might be adduced as proofs with regard to this subject, for I consider that necessary only in cases where no single proof is certain; but I have dealt with the first and principal ones in such a way that I feel justified in presenting them as manifest and certain demonstrations. And I will say further that they are of such a nature that I do not think there is any way for the human mind to discover better ones, for the importance of the subject, and the glory of God to which all this relates, force me to speak here a little more freely about myself than I am wont to do. But no matter how certain and evident I consider them to be, I cannot convince myself that everyone will be able to understand them. In geometry, many of the demonstrations left to us by Archimedes, Apollonius, Pappus, and others, are accepted by everyone as being certain and evident because they contain nothing which, considered separately, is not easy to understand, and no consequences which do not follow perfectly from their antecedents; and yet, because they are rather lengthy and demand the reader's entire attention, they are understood by only a few. Similarly, although I consider the demonstrations which I have here employed to be equal or even superior in certainty and evidence to those of geometry, I nevertheless fear that there will not be many who can adequately understand them, because they are also rather lengthy and interdependent, and particularly because they require the mind to be totally free of prejudice and readily able to detach itself from the affairs of the senses. And fewer people have an aptitude for metaphysics than for geometry. There is also this difference, that everyone approaches geometry with the belief that, as a general rule, nothing is advanced in it which cannot be demonstrated with certainty, so that those who are not entirely proficient in it err more often by assenting to what is false, in order to appear to understand it, than by rejecting what is true, whereas in philosophy, where everything is believed to be open to dispute, there are few who search for truth, and many, wishing to be known as bold thinkers, arrogantly oppose the most obvious truths.

Therefore, since my reasonings are within the realm of philosophy, however forceful they may be, I cannot expect them to have any great effect on the minds of others unless you support them with your patronage. So high is the esteem in which your Faculty is held, and so authoritative is the

name of the Sorbonne, that no other body, with the exception
of the Sacred Councils, has ever been held in such great
deference, not only in matters of faith, but also of human
philosophy, for everyone acknowledges that it is impossible
to find elsewhere greater perspicacity and soundness, or greater
wisdom and integrity of judgment. Consequently I have no
doubt that if you will deign to concern yourselves with this
treatise, first by correcting it (for, being aware not only of
my humanity but also of my ignorance, I would not dare to
guarantee that it contains no errors), then by adding to it
those things which are lacking, finishing those which are incomplete, and personally taking the trouble to give me a fuller
explanation of those which require it, or at least pointing
them out to me so that I may work on them myself, and
finally, after the reasonings by which I prove that there is a
God, and that the human soul is distinct from the body, have
been made so compelling, as I am sure they can be made,
that they must be regarded as flawless demonstrations, if you
will declare this to be so and testify to it publicly, I have
no doubt, I say, that all the errors and false opinions which
have ever existed with regard to these two questions will soon
be effaced from the minds of men. Truth itself will make all
men of learning and intelligence subscribe to your judgment,
and your authority will cause atheists, who are usually more
arrogant than learned and judicious, to discard their spirit
of contradiction, and perhaps they themselves will lend their
support to the reasonings which they will see accepted as
demonstrations by all intelligent men, lest they appear not
to understand them. Finally, all other men will readily yield
to so much testimony, and there will no longer be anyone
who dares to doubt the existence of God or the real distinction between the human soul and the body. It is now for you,
who see the disorders produced by doubt of this belief, to
judge, in your singular wisdom, the importance of its establish-
ment. It would not here become me to say more in support
of God and religion to you who have always been the firmest
pillars of the Catholic Church.

In my *Discourse of the Method of Rightly Conducting the Reason and Seeking Truth in the Sciences,* published in French in 1637, I have already touched briefly on the questions of God and the human soul. It was not then my intention to deal with them thoroughly, but only, so to speak, in passing, in order to learn from the judgment of my readers how I ought to deal with them in the future. For these questions seemed so important to me that I judged it best to speak of them more than once; and the path I follow in explaining them is so little trodden, and so far from the common road, that I did not think it advisable to reveal it in a French discourse that might be read by everyone, lest weak minds believe that they too might follow the same path.

In my *Discourse on Method* I asked all those who might find anything censurable in my writings to do me the favor of informing me of it. No noteworthy objections have been brought to my attention except two things concerning what I wrote on those two questions, and I will briefly reply to them here, before going on to a more detailed explanation.

The first objection is that from the fact that, when the human mind reflects upon itself, it is not aware of itself as being anything except a thinking thing, it does not follow that its nature or essence is only to think, so that the word "only" excludes all the other things which might also be sa to belong to the nature of the soul. To this I reply that was not there my intention to exclude them in accor with the order required by the truth in this matter which I was not then dealing), but only in accordance the order of my thinking; my meaning was that I was awar of nothing which I knew to belong to my essence except tha was a thinking thing, or a thing that had within itself the faculty of thinking. I shall later show that, from the fact that I am aware of nothing else which belongs to my nature, it follows that there is nothing else which actually does belong to it.

The second objection is that, from the fact that I have within me the idea of something more perfect than myself, it does not follow that this idea is more perfect than I am, and still less that what is represented by this idea exists. I reply that the word "idea" is here used equivocally, for it may be taken materially as being an operation of my understanding, in which sense it cannot be said to be more perfect than myself, or it may be taken objectively as being what is represented by this operation, and even though this thing is not regarded as existing outside of my understanding, it may nevertheless be more perfect than I am, by reason of its essence. Later in this treatise I shall show more fully how, from the sole fact that I have within me the idea of a thing more perfect than myself, it follows that this thing actually exists.

In addition to these two objections, I have seen two rather lengthy works on this matter, but they challenged not so much my reasoning as my conclusions, and this by arguments drawn from the commonplaces of the atheists. But since arguments of this kind can make no impression on those who understand my reasoning, and since there are many men who have such weak and irrational judgment that they are much more often convinced by the first opinions they have received, however false and unreasonable they be, than by a true and sound, but subsequently heard, refutation of those opinions, I will not reply to these objections, lest I first be obliged to state them. I will say only in general that everything the aethists say to disprove the existence of God depends either on imputing human feelings to God, or on attributing such power and wisdom to our own minds that we may presume to determine and understand what God can and ought to do. Therefore, nothing they say need give us any difficulty, provided we recall that our minds must be regarded as finite, and God as infinite and incomprehensible.

Now that I have given sufficient attention to the opinions of men, I shall again take up the questions of God and the human soul, and in so doing I shall deal with the foundations of all first philosophy, but without expecting any acclaim from the multitude, or any great number of readers. I invite no one to read my work, in fact, except those who are willing and able to meditate seriously with me, and detach their minds from the senses and all prejudices; and I know all too well that such men are rare. As for those who, without caring to understand the order and connections of my reasonings, will criticize only isolated portions of this treatise, as many are wont to do, they will not benefit greatly from reading it; and although they may find occasion to quibble here and there, it is unlikely that they will be able to make any serious objections or say anything that deserves a reply.

Since I do not promise others that I shall satisfy them at once, and since I am not so presumptuous as to believe that I can foresee everything which may be a source of difficulty for each one of my readers, I shall first set forth in these *Meditations* the same thoughts which I believe to have led me to certain and evident knowledge of the truth, in order to learn whether the same reasonings which have convinced me are also capable of convincing others. Then I shall answer the objections that have been made by certain men of great intelligence and learning to whom these *Meditations* were sent for examination before being printed. Their objections are so numerous and varied that I venture to think it unlikely that anyone will be able to suggest others of any consequence that have not been touched upon. I therefore beg my readers not to pass judgment on these *Meditations* until they have read all the objections and the replies I have made to them.

In the first Meditation I set forth the reasons for which we may doubt all things in general, and material things in particular—at least so long as we have no other foundations for the sciences than those we have had heretofore. Although the utility of such a general doubt may not be immediately apparent, it is nevertheless very great, for it delivers us from all kinds of prejudice, offers a very easy way for the mind to detach it self from the senses, and, finally, makes it impossible for us to have any further doubts with regard to what we later conclude to be true.

In the second Meditation, the mind, making use of the freedom that is proper to it, assumes that nothing exists whose existence can in any way be doubted, but is forced to recognize that, in so doing, it must itself exist. This is also of great utility, for it enables the mind to distinguish easily between those things which pertain to it, that is, to intellectual nature, and those which pertain to the body. Since there may be some who will expect me at this point to state reasons in proof of the immortality of the soul, I feel that I must now inform them that, having tried to write nothing in this treatise for which I could not give an exact demonstration, I have found myself obliged to follow an order similar to that which is used by geometers, namely, to state all the premises on which the proposition in question depends, before making any conclusion with respect to it. Now the first and principal prerequisite for knowing the immortality of the soul is to form a conception of it that is as clear as possible and is entirely distinct from any conception of the body; and this has been done in the second Meditation. In addition, we must know that all things which we conceive clearly and distinctly are true, just as we conceive them, and I was not able to prove this until the fourth Meditation. Furthermore, we must have a distinct conception of corporeal nature, which is given partly in the second and partly in the fifth and sixth Meditations. And finally, we must conclude from all this that things which are conceived clearly and distinctly as being different substances, as are mind and body, actually are different substances, distinct from one another; and this conclusion is drawn in the sixth Meditation. This is also confirmed in the same Meditation by the fact that we can conceive body only as divisible, and mind only as indivisible, for we cannot conceive half of a mind, as we can half of a body, however small; thus we see not only that their natures are different, but also that they are to some extent contrary to each other. I have not, however, undertaken to pursue the matter any further in this treatise, because these considerations are sufficient to show that the extinction of the mind, or soul, does not follow from the decay of the body, and thus to give men the hope of life after death, and also because the premises from which we may infer the immortality of the soul depend on an exposition of the entire science of physics, for it would first have to be established that, in general, all substances, that is, those things which cannot exist without having been created by God, are by nature incorruptible, and can never cease to be unless God withdraws His support from them, thereby reducing them to nothing; and then it would have to be established that body in general is a substance, and therefore cannot perish, but that the human body, insofar as it differs from other particular bodies, is composed only of a certain configuration of members, and other similar accidents, whereas the human soul is not composed of any accidents, but is a pure substance. For even though all these accidents change, even though, for example, it thinks, wills and senses other things, it is nevertheless always the same soul, while the human body is no longer the same if the structure or form of any of its parts is changed. From this it follows that the human body may easily perish, but that the mind, or soul,*

* Descartes here uses the single Latin word *"mens."* The French version renders it by *"l'esprit, ou l'âme"* and adds the parenthetical statement that he makes no distinction between the two. This was presumably done either by Descartes himself or with his approval, because he examined the French version before its publication and made a number of revisions in it. Furthermore, he sometimes uses the Latin *"mens"* and *"anima"* interchangeably. I have therefore used either "mind" or "soul," or both, according to cont[...] And in several other passages I have included explanatory remarks or phr[...] that were added to the French version.—L.B.

(I make no distinction between them), is by nature immortal.

In the third Meditation, I have explained at sufficient length, it seems to me, my principal argument in proof of the existence of God. However, wishing to make it easier for the reader to detach his mind from the senses, I decided that I would not here make use of any comparisons drawn from corporeal things, and so there may still be many obscurities, which, I hope, will be entirely cleared up by the replies I have made to certain objections. Thus, for example, it is rather difficult to understand how the idea, which we have within us, of a supremely perfect being contains so much objective reality, that is, participates by representation in so many degrees of being and perfection, that it must necessarily proceed from a supremely perfect cause. But I have made this clear in my replies to objections by using the comparison of a perfectly contrived machine, the idea of which is in the mind of a workman. Just as the objective artifice of this idea must have a cause, namely, either the knowledge of the workman or of someone else from whom he has learned it, so the idea of God which is in us must have God Himself as its cause.

In the fourth Meditation, it is proved that whatever we apprehend clearly and distinctly is true, and, at the same time, the nature of error is explained. It is necessary to know this both in order to confirm the preceding truth and in order better to understand those that follow. (It should be noted, however, that I do not here deal with sin, that is, error committed in the pursuit of good and evil, but only with error which arises in distinguishing between the true and the false. And I do not discuss matters which pertain to faith or the conduct of life, but only those speculative truths which can be known by means of the natural light.)

In the fifth Meditation, corporeal nature is explained in a general sense, and the existence of God is demonstrated by a new proof. Certain difficulties may also be encountered in this proof, but they will be resolved in my replies to objections. It is further shown in what sense it is true that the certainty even of geometrical demonstrations depends on our knowing that there is a God.

Finally, in the sixth Meditation, I distinguish the action of the understanding from that of the imagination and describe the marks of this distinction. I prove that the mind is really distinct from the body, yet so closely conjoined with it as to form a single entity. I indicate all the errors which may proceed from the senses, and show how to avoid them. And lastly I bring forward all the reasons from which we infer the existence of material things, not because I regard them as very useful for proving what they prove, namely, that there is a world, that men have bodies, and other such things which no one of sound mind has ever doubted, but because when we consider them closely we see that they are not so firm or evident as those which lead to knowledge of our soul and of God, so that these latter are the most certain and evident of all things which can be known by the human mind. Proving this has been my sole aim in these Meditations. I have therefore made no mention here of many other questions which are discussed incidentally.

MEDITATIONS ON FIRST PHILOSOPHY

&ξ&

*In Which the Existence of God and the Distinction
between Soul and Body Are Demonstrated.*

MEDITATION I

Concerning Things Which May Be Doubted

Many years ago I realized how many false opinions I had been accepting as true ever since my childhood, and how doubtful everything I had based on them must be. I therefore decided that if I wanted to establish anything solid and lasting in the sciences, I must deliberately rid myself of all the opinions I had hitherto accepted, and begin building again from the foundations. But since this seemed to me an enormous undertaking, I waited until I had reached such a mature age that I could no longer expect to be able to carry it out at any later time. This has made me delay so long that I would now consider it wrong to go on consuming in deliberation the time that is left to me for action. Today, then, having freed my mind of all care and assured myself of untroubled leisure in peaceful solitude, I shall apply myself earnestly and freely to the general overthrow of all my former opinions.

It will not be necessary, for this purpose, to show that they are all false, a task which I might never finish; but since reason has already persuaded me that I ought to withhold belief no less carefully from things which are not entirely certain and indubitable than from those which appear to be manifestly false, the slightest grounds for doubt will be enough to make me reject any of my opinions. And for this I have no need to examine each one of them in particular, which would be an endless labor, but, since the destruction of the foundations brings about the collapse of the entire structure, I shall first attack the principles on which all my former beliefs were based.

Everything that I have hitherto accepted as truest and most certain has been learned either from the senses or through them. Now I have sometimes found the senses to be deceptive, and it is prudent never to place complete confidence in those who have once deceived us.

But although the senses sometimes deceive us with regard to very small or distant objects, there may be many other things which, even though they are known by means of the senses, cannot possibly be doubted, such as the fact that I am here, sitting by the fire, wearing a dressing gown, with this paper in my hands, and so on. How could I deny that these hands and this body are mine? To do so would be to liken myself to those madmen whose brains are so disturbed and clouded by dark bilious vapors that they persist in assuring us that they are kings when they are poverty-stricken, that they are dressed in purple when they are naked, that they have clay heads, that they are gourds, or that they are made of glass; but they are insane, and I would be no less demented if I were to follow their example.

However, I must bear in mind that I am a man, and therefore in the habit of sleeping, and that I imagine the same things in my dreams as these madmen imagine when they are awake, or sometimes even more absurd things. How often have I dreamed that I was here, fully dressed and sitting by the fire, when I was actually undressed and lying in bed! At this moment it certainly seems to me that my eyes are awake as I look at this paper, that the head I move is not asleep, that I am intentionally and deliberately extending this hand and feeling it. What happens in my dreams is not so distinct as all this. But I recall having been often deceived by similar illusions while I was asleep. When I reflect on this at greater length I see clearly that there are no certain indications which distinguish waking from sleeping, and I am so amazed by this that I can almost believe myself to be asleep.

Let us suppose, then, that we are asleep, that all these particulars—namely, that we have our eyes open, move our heads, stretch out our hands, etc.—are illusions, and that our hands or our entire bodies may not be what we see them to be. Nevertheless we must at least admit that the things we see in sleep are like pictures which can be formed only in the likeness of something real and true, and that at least these general things—namely, eyes, heads, hands and all the rest of the body—are not imaginary, but true and existent. For when painters endeavor to represent sirens and satyrs by the most unusual and fantastic forms, they cannot give them entirely new natures, but only make a mixture of members from various animals; and even if they should succeed in devising something so novel that nothing like it has ever been seen before, so that their work represents something entirely fictitious and false, at least the colors they use in composing it must be real. And by the same reasoning, even though these general things—eyes, heads, hands, etc.—might be imaginary, it must nevertheless be admitted that there are still simpler and more universal things which are true and existent, and from the intermixture of which, as with the intermixture of certain colors, all the images of things which are present in our mind, whether they be true or false, are formed. To this class of things belong corporeal nature in general and its extension, the shape of extended things, their quantity or size, and their number, and also the location in which they are, the time through which they endure, and so on.

It is therefore, perhaps, not unreasonable to conclude that physics, astronomy, medicine and all the other sciences which depend on the consideration of composite things are doubtful, while arithmetic, geometry, etc., which deal only with the simplest and most general things, with little concern as to whether or not they actually exist in nature, contain something that is certain and indubitable. For whether I am asleep or awake, 2 and 3 are 5, and a square has no more than four sides; and it does not seem possible that such obvious truths could ever be suspected of falsity.

And yet, although I have long believed in the existence of an all-powerful God who created me such as I am, how can I be sure that He had not arranged matters in such a way that there is no earth, sky, extended bodies, shape, size or location, but that all these things appear to me to exist exactly as they do now? And, just as I sometimes judge that others are mistaken, even in those things which they believe they know best, may it not be that I am mistaken whenever I add 2 and 3, or count the sides of a square, or make some even simpler judgment, if anything simpler can be imagined? But perhaps it is not God's will that I should be thus deceived, for He is said to be supremely good; but if it is contrary to His goodness that I should always be mistaken, it would also seem to be contrary to it that I should sometimes be mistaken, and it cannot be said that this does not happen.

There may be some who will prefer to deny the existence of such a powerful God, rather than believe that all other things are uncertain. Let us not oppose them for the moment: let us assume that everything that has been said about God is a fable. Nevertheless, in whatever way they suppose that I have come to be what I am, whether by fate, by chance, by a continual succession and connection of things, or by some other means, since to be deceived and to err is an imperfection, the less power they attribute to the author of my being, the more likely it is that I am so imperfect that I am always mistaken. I have nothing to reply to such an argument, and I am forced to admit that, of all the opinions I once accepted as true, there is not one which I cannot now doubt, not from lack of reflection or seriousness, but for strong and thoroughly considered reasons. Therefore, if I want to discover something certain, I must henceforth give no more credence to these opinions than to things which are obviously false.

But it is not enough to have made these observations: I must also be careful to remember them, for those old, accustomed opinions constantly recur, and long, familiar usage has given them the right to occupy my mind and almost dominate my belief against my will. And I shall never lose the habit of assenting to them and trusting them as long as I regard them as what they actually are, namely, in some way doubtful, as I have shown, and yet highly probable, so that there is much more reason to accept them than to reject them. I therefore think that I shall be acting wisely if I take an opposite course and deliberately set out to deceive myself, pretending that all these opinions are false and imaginary, until my prejudices have so balanced one another that they cannot incline me in either direction, and my judgment is no longer dominated by bad habits and turned aside from the road to truth. I am convinced that there can be no danger or error in this course, and that, for the moment, I cannot be too skeptical, since I am not now concerned with action, but solely with knowledge.

And so I will now suppose, not a supremely good God who is the source of truth, but an evil spirit, as powerful as he is cunning and deceitful, who has employed all his powers to deceive me; I will suppose that the sky, the air, the earth, colors, shapes, sounds, and all the other external things that ve perceive, are only illusions which he uses to snare my credulity; I will consider myself as having no hands, eyes, flesh, blood or senses, but as falsely believing that I have all these things. I will stubbornly cling to this idea, and if by this means I am not able to reach knowledge of any truth, it is at least within my power to suspend judgment. I will therefore take care not to give credence to anything that is false, and I will so arm my mind against this deceiver that he will never be able to impose anything on me, however powerful and cunning he may be. But this undertaking is arduous, and a certain indolence draws me back into the ordinary course of my life. Just as a captive, enjoying an imaginary freedom in his sleep, dreads to awaken when he begins to suspect that it is only a dream, and conspires with his pleasant illusions to prolong the deception, so do I willingly fall back into my old opinions, and dread to rouse myself from my peaceful slumber, lest it be succeeded by an arduous vigil spent not in the light of truth, but in the dark shadows of the difficulties that have just been raised.

MEDITATION II

Concerning the Nature of the Human Mind: That It Is More Easily Known than the Body.

Yesterday's Meditation has filled me with so many doubts that it is no longer in my power to forget them, yet I do not see how they can be resolved. I am like someone who, having unexpectedly fallen into deep water, is so disconcerted that he can neither gain a foothold on the bottom nor swim on the surface. But I shall not cease my efforts; I shall follow the same path I took yesterday, rejecting anything which I can doubt in any way as though it were absolutely false, and I shall continue along this path until I have reached something certain, or, failing that, until I at least know with certainty that nothing is certain. In order to move the entire earth, Archimedes asked only for one firm and immovable point; similarly, I shall be entitled to entertain high hopes if I am fort͟ te enough to find one thing which is certain and in͟ able.

shall assume, therefore, that everything I see is false, that one of the things presented to me by my deceptive memory has ever existed, that I have no senses, and that body, shape, extension, movement and location are only fictions. What is there, then, which can be regarded as true? Perhaps only this, that nothing is certain.

But how do I know that there is not something which is different from all the things I have just mentioned, and which cannot give rise to the slightest doubt? Is there not some God or other being, by whatever name we call Him, who has placed these thoughts in me? Yet why should we assume this? Perhaps I am capable of producing them myself. Is it not at least true, then, that I am something? But I have already denied that I have a body and senses. I am now perplexed, however, for what follows from this? Am I so bound up with my body and my senses that I cannot exist without them? In persuading myself that there is nothing at all in the world, no sky, earth, minds or bodies, have I not also persuaded myself that I do not exist? No, for in persuading myself of something, I must exist. But what if there is an extremely powerful and cunning deceiver who is deliberately and constantly deceiving me? Again, there can be no doubt that, if he is deceiving me, I exist. Let him deceive me as much as he can, he will never cause me to be nothing as long as I am thinking that I am something. And so, after careful reflection, I must conclude that this proposition, I *am*, I *exist*, is necessarily true each time I state it or conceive it.

However, I still do not know well enough what I am, I who am certain that I am; I must be careful not to mistake something else for myself, and so go astray in this knowledge I maintain to be the most certain and evident of all. I shall therefore consider what I believed myself to be before I ventured upon these thoughts. I shall reject all those beliefs which can be invalidated to any extent by the reasons I have cited, so that only what is certain and indubitable will remain.

What, then, did I previously believe myself to be? A man, of course. But what is a man? Shall I say he is a rational animal? No, for I would then have to inquire what is meant by an "animal" and by "rational"; this one question would thus lead me to others still more difficult, and I have no time to waste on such subtleties. Instead, I shall dwell upon those things which spontaneously and naturally sprang into my mind when I considered my own being. I considered myself, first, as having a face, hands, arms, and all the other parts of that structure which can be seen in a corpse, and which I called my body. I considered, furthermore, that I ate, walked, felt and thought, and I referred all these actions to the soul. But either I did not stop to consider what this soul was, or else I imagined it as something subtle, like a kind of wind, flame, or ether, that was diffused throughout my grosser parts. As to the nature of body, I was not troubled by any doubts, for I thought I knew it quite distinctly, and if I had wished to describe the manner in which I then conceived it, I would have explained it as follows: By body I understand whatever can be determined by a certain shape, be comprised in a certain location, and fill a space in such a way that any other body is excluded from it; whatever can be perceived by touch, sight, hearing, taste or smell; and whatever can be moved in various ways, not by itself, but by something foreign to it which touches it. For I did not believe that the powers of self-movement, sensation and thought could be attributed to the nature of body; on the contrary, I marveled that such faculties should be found in certain bodies.

But now that I am assuming that there is a supremely powerful and, if I may say so, malignant being who employs all his power and skill in deceiving me, what shall I say that I am? Can I assert that I possess any of those things which I have attributed to the nature of body? When I think about them all and review them carefully, I find none which I can claim to possess; it would be useless and tiresome to repeat them. Let us now consider those which I have attributed to the soul. What of eating and walking, for example? If I have no body, I cannot eat or walk. Sensation? Nothing can be sensed without the body; and besides, in sleep it has often seemed to me that I was sensing things which I later realized I had not sensed at all. Thought? Here I find what belongs to me: it alone cannot be separated from me. *I am, I exist:* that is certain. For how long? As long as I continue to think, for it might be that if I ceased to think, I would also cease to exist. I am not now admitting anything which is not necessarily true; I am therefore regarding myself only as a thinking thing, that is, a mind, soul, understanding or reason—terms whose meaning has hitherto been unknown to me. I am, then, a real thing, one that truly exists. But what kind of thing? I have already said it: a thinking thing.

What else am I? I call upon my imagination. I am not that assemblage of members which is known as the human body. Nor am I a tenuous air diffused throughout those members, nor a wind, fire, vapor, breath or anything else I can form; for I am assuming that all those things are nothing.

And yet, in so doing, I find that it is still true that I am
something. But may it not be that these very things, whose
existence I have denied because they are not known to me,
are actually no different from myself, whom I do know? I
cannot say, and I shall not now discuss it; I can judge only
things that are known to me. Having acquired the knowledge
that I am, I now wish to learn what I am. Now it is certain
that this knowledge, taken in this precise sense, does not
depend on things whose existence is not yet known to me,
and consequently it does not depend on anything invented
by my imagination. Indeed, the very word "invent" warns me
of my error, for I would in fact be inventing if I were to
imagine myself as being something, since imagining is nothing
else than contemplating the shape or image of a corporeal
thing. I know with certainty that I exist, and that all those
images and, in general, everything relating to the nature of
body, may be nothing but dreams or illusions. I therefore see
clearly that it is no more reasonable to say, "I will now make
use of my imagination to learn more distinctly what I am"
than to say, "I am now awake and I see something real, but
since I do not yet see it clearly enough, I will deliberately
go to sleep in order that I may see it with greater truth and
evidence in my dreams." Thus I know that nothing I can
comprehend by means of my imagination pertains to this
knowledge of myself, and that the mind must be turned away
from the workings of the imagination if it is to know its own
nature with perfect distinctness.

What am I? A thinking thing. What is a thinking thing?
A thing that doubts, understands, affirms, denies, wills,
refuses, and also imagines and senses.

All this is a great deal to belong to my nature. But why
should it not? Am I not the same being who doubts nearly
everything, who nevertheless understands some things, who
affirms that only one is true and denies the others, who desires
to know more, who refuses to be deceived, who imagines many
things, even unwillingly, and who perceives many things
which seem to come to him by way of his sense organs? Even
if I am always dreaming and the being who created me
employs all his powers in deceiving me, is there anything in
what I have just said which is not as true as that I am, that
I exist? Can any of those attributes be distinguished from
my thinking? Can any of them be said to be separate from
me? It is so obvious that it is I who doubt, understand,
desire, that there is no need to add anything to make it

required to make me certain of anything? In this first piece of knowledge there is nothing but a clear and distinct apprehension of what I am affirming, and this would not be sufficient to make me certain of its truth if it could ever happen that anything I apprehend clearly and distinctly should prove to be false. It therefore seems to me that I can now lay down the general rule that whatever I apprehend very clearly and distinctly is true.

In the past, however, I have accepted as completely certain and manifest many things which I later recognized as doubtful. What were those things? The earth, the sky, the stars and all the other things I apprehended by means of my senses. But what was there about them that I apprehended clearly? Nothing except that the ideas or thoughts of those things presented themselves to my mind. Even now I do not deny that such ideas are within me. But there was something else which I affirmed, and which, because I was accustomed to believing it, I thought I apprehended clearly, although actually I did not, namely, that there were things outside of me from which these ideas proceeded, and which they exactly resembled. Either I was mistaken in this, or else, if I was not, the correctness of my judgment was not based on the nature of my apprehensions.

But when I considered something very simple in arithmetic or geometry, for example that 2 plus 3 is 5, and other things of this sort, did I not apprehend them, at least, clearly enough to affirm their truth? If I later judged that they could be doubted, it was only because it occurred to me that some God might have given me a nature such that I was mistaken even with regard to those things which seemed most obvious to me, and whenever this supposition of God's omnipotence presents itself to me, I am forced to admit that it is easy for Him, if He so wishes, to make me err even in what I believe to be most evident. And yet, when I consider something which I think I apprehend very clearly, I am so firmly convinced of its truth that I cannot help saying, "Let anyone deceive me who can, he will never be able to bring it about that I am nothing while I am thinking that I am something; or, at some future time, that I have never existed, it being true that I now exist; or that 2 plus 3 is more or less than 5; or that anything else is true in which I see a manifest contradiction." And certainly since I have no reason to believe that there is a God who deceives me, or even, so far, that there is any God at all, the reason for doubt which depends entirely on this

supposition is very slight and, so to speak, metaphysical. But
in order to eliminate it, I must at the earliest opportunity
consider whether there is a God, and, if so, whether He can
be a deceiver, for until I know the answers to these two
questions I do not see how I can be certain of anything.

In order to examine them without interrupting the order of
meditation that I have laid down for myself, which is to
proceed step by step from the first notions I find in my mind
to those which I later find there, I must here divide all my
thoughts into certain categories and consider in which of these
categories truth and error are properly to be found. Some of
my thoughts are, as it were, images of things, and it is to them
alone that we may properly give the name of "ideas": as when
I represent to myself a man, a chimera, heaven, an angel, or
even God. Other thoughts have other forms, as when I will,
fear, affirm or deny; in so doing, I am apprehending something
as the subject of my thoughts, but I am also adding something to my idea of it. Of the thoughts in this category, some
are called volitions or emotions, while others are called
judgments.

If ideas are considered in themselves, and not in relation
to anything else, they cannot, strictly speaking, be false; for
whether I imagine a goat or a chimera, it is as true that I am
imagining the latter as that I am imagining the former. Nor is
there any need to fear falsity in volitions or emotions, for
although I may desire something bad, or even something that
has never existed, it is none the less true that I do desire it.
Thus there remain only judgments in which I must take care
not to be mistaken. The chief and most frequent error that
occurs in them consists in judging that the ideas that are in
me resemble or correspond to things which are outside of me;
for certainly if I considered these ideas as merely certain
modes of my thinking, they could scarcely give me any
occasion for error.

Some ideas seem to be innate, others seem to come to me
from outside of myself, and still others seem to have been
made or invented by me. For my ability to understand what
a thing is, or a truth, or a thought, does not seem to come
from anything except my own nature; and when I hear a
sound, or see the sun, or feel heat, I have hitherto judged
that this is due to something outside of myself; and finally, it
seems to me that sirens, hippogriffs, and so on, are inventions
of my own mind. But I may yet decide that all these ideas
come to me from outside of myself, or that they are all innate,

on all invented by me, for I have not yet clearly discerned their true origin.

My principal task is now to consider those ideas which seem to come to me from outside of myself, and to examine the reasons that lead me to believe that they resemble those things. The first reason is that I seem to be so taught by nature. The second is that my experience tells me that they are independent of my will, for they often present themselves to me in spite of myself. I now feel heat, for example, whether I will to feel it or not, and I therefore assume that this sensation or idea of heat is produced in me by something other than myself, namely, by the heat of the fire near which I am sitting. And what could be more natural than to conclude that this external thing is impressing its likeness upon me, rather than something different?

I must now consider whether these reasons are sufficiently sound. When I say that I am so taught by nature, I understand by the word "nature" only a certain spontaneous impulse which inclines me toward this belief, and not a natural light which shows me that it is true. These two things are quite different. I cannot doubt what the natural light shows me to be true (such as, for example, that from the fact that I doubt, it follows that I exist), for I have no other faculty which can be trusted as much as the natural light, and which can show me that its teachings are false. As for my natural impulses, however, I have observed that they often mislead me when I must choose between right and wrong, so I do not see why I should rely on them to distinguish what is true from what is false.

And although these ideas are independent of my will, it does not follow that they must necessarily proceed from things outside of me. For just as the impulses of which I have been speaking are in me even though they are not always in accordance with my will, so it may be that there is in me some faculty, still unknown to me, which is capable of producing these ideas; it has always seemed to me, in fact, that when I am dreaming, such ideas actually are formed in me without the help of any external things.

Finally, even if these ideas do proceed from things that are outside of me, it does not follow that they may resemble them. I have often observed great disparities among various ideas which supposedly represent the same object. I find, for example, that there are in me two different ideas of the sun. One of them seems to be drawn from the senses, and to belong to that category of ideas w I have described as coming from outside of me: it ma e sun appear quite small to me. The other is derive he reasonings of astronomy, that is, from certain no re innate in me, or have been somehow produce represents the sun as being many times larger . Now both these ideas cannot resemble the sa ason convinces me that the one which bears t. lance to it is the one which seems to have come d.

All this shows clearly enough that hitherto m the existence of external things which implant their idea or images in me by means of the sense organs, or in some other way, has not been based on any sound judgment, but only on blind impulse.

But it occurs to me that there is another way of seeking to determine whether any of the ideas that are in me represent things that exist outside of me. If these ideas are taken only as ways of thinking, I can discern no inequality among them, and they all seem to proceed from me in the same manner. If, however, we consider them as images, each representing some particular thing, then it is obvious that they may differ greatly from one another. Those which represent substances are without doubt something more, and, so to speak, contain more objective reality, that is, participate by representation in more degrees of being or perfection, than those which represent only modes or accidents. Furthermore, the idea by which I conceive of a sovereign, eternal, infinite, omniscient and omnipotent God, who has created all things external to Himself, surely has more objective reality in it than those ideas by which finite substances are represented.

Now it is manifest by the natural light that there must be at least as much reality in the efficient and total cause as in its effect. For whence can the effect draw its reality if not from its cause? And how could the cause impart this reality if it did not have it? From this it follows that something cannot proceed from nothing, and that what is more perfect, that is, contains more reality, cannot proceed from what is less perfect. And this is obviously true not only of those effects whose reality is called actual or formal by the philosophers, but also of those ideas whose reality is considered to be only what they call objective. For example, a stone which has not yet existed cannot now begin to exist unless it is produced by something which has within it, either formally or eminently, everything that enters into the composition of the stone, that is, something which contains either the same things as those that are in the stone, or others that are more excellent; and heat can be produced in something devoid of it only by a cause of an order at least as perfect as that of heat; and so on. Furthermore, the idea of heat or of a stone cannot be in me unless it has been placed in me by a cause which contains at least as much reality as I conceive to be in heat or in a stone. For although the cause transmits none of its actual or formal reality to the idea, I must not consider the cause to be less real. I must recognize that an idea requires for itself no formal reality other than that which it borrows from thought, or the mind, for it is merely a mode or manner of thinking. If, however, an idea is to contain one objective reality rather than another, it must undoubtedly receive it from a cause whose formal reality is at least as great as the objective reality contained in the idea. For if I suppose that there is something in the idea which is not in its cause, then the idea must have received that something from nothing. But however imperfect that mode of being may be, by which a thing exists objectively, or by representation, in the understanding through its idea, we cannot say that it is nothing, or that the idea has come from nothing.

Nor must I suspect that since the reality I consider in my ideas is only objective, it need not be formally present in their causes, but that it suffices for it to be present in them only objectively. Just as the objective mode of being belongs to ideas by their very nature, so the formal mode of being belongs to their causes, at least to their first and principal causes, by the very nature of those causes. And although it may be that one idea gives birth to another, this process cannot be carried back in an infinite series; we must eventually reach a first idea whose cause is, as it were, the archetype in which all the reality or perfection that is in the idea only objectively, or by representation, is contained formally, or actually. Thus the natural light makes it evident to me that ideas are present in me like pictures or images which, although they may certainly fall short of the perfection of the things from which they are derived, can never contain anything greater or more perfect.

The longer and more carefully I examine all these things, the more clearly and distinctly I recognize that they are true. But what am I to conclude from all this? That if the objective reality of any one of my ideas is so great that I am certain it cannot be in me either formally or eminently, and that consequently I myself cannot be its cause, it necessarily follows that I am not alone in the world, that something else also eixsts which is the cause of this idea. If, however, there is no such idea in me, I shall have no argument that can make me certain of the existence of anything except myself, for I have carefully examined all the arguments and have so far found no other.

Among my ideas, in addition to the one which represents me to myself, about which there can here be no difficulty, there is one which represents God, and others which represent corporeal and inanimate things, angels, animals, and, finally, men similar to myself.

As for those which represent other men, or animals, or angels, I can easily conceive that they may have been compounded from ideas of myself, of corporeal things, and of God, even if there are, outside of me, no men, animals or angels in the world.

As for my ideas of corporeal things, there does not seem to be anything in them so great that it could not have originated in myself. If I consider them more closely and examine them as I examined the idea of wax yesterday, I find that there is little in them which I apprehend clearly and distinctly, namely, size, or extension in length, breadth and depth; shape, which results from the limits of this extension; the location which differently shaped bodies have in relation to one another; motion, or change of location; and, finally, substance, duration and number. As for other things such as light, colors, sounds, odors, tastes, heat, cold and the other tactual qualities, they present themselves to me so confusedly and obscurely that I do not know whether they are true or false, that is, whether my ideas of them are ideas of real things or not. For although, as I have already observed, falsity properly so called, or formal falsity, can be found only in judgments, there can nevertheless be a certain material falsity in ideas, namely, when they represent what is nothing as though it were something. For example, the ideas I have of heat and cold are so far from clear and distinct that I cannot determine from them whether cold is merely an absence of heat, or heat an absence of cold, or whether either or neither is a real quality. Now since ideas are like images, there cannot be any which do not seem to represent something; therefore, if it is true that cold is nothing but an absence of heat, then the idea which represents it to me as something real and positive may deservedly be called false; and the same is true of other similar cases.

It is not necessary for me to assign any author to these ideas other than myself. For if they are false, that is, if they represent nothing, the natural light shows me that they proceed from nothing, that is, that they are in me only because of some lack or imperfection in my nature. And if they are true, they exhibit so little reality to me that I cannot distinguish it from non-being, so I do not see why they may not have been produced by myself.

As for the clear and distinct ideas I have of corporeal things, there are some which, it seems to me, I may have drawn from the idea I have of myself, such as those of substance, duration, number, and the like. When I think that a stone is a substance, or a thing capable of existing in itself, and that I, too, am a substance, in so doing I conceive of myself as a thinking, non-extended thing, and of the stone as an extended, non-thinking thing, so that there is a notable difference between the two conceptions, and yet they agree in that they both seem to represent substances. Similarly, when I think that I exist now, and recall that I have existed in the past, and have various other thoughts whose number I know, I acquire the ideas of duration and number, which I can later transfer to other things. It is true that the other qualities composing the ideas of corporeal things—namely, extension, shape, location and motion—are not formally in me, since I am nothing other than a thinking thing; but because they are merely certain modes of substance, the garments, as it were, in which corporeal substances appears to us, and because I, too, am a substance, it seems that they may be contained in me eminently.

Thus there remains only the idea of God in which I must consider whether there is anything that could not have come from me. By the word "God" I mean a substance that is infinite, eternal, immutable, independent, all-knowing and all-powerful, by which I and anything else that may exist have been created. All these attributes are so great and eminent that the more attentively I consider them, the less it seems possible that my idea of them could have come from myself alone. Thus, from all that has been said, it must be concluded that God necessarily exists. For although the idea of substance may be in me by the very fact that I myself am a substance, I could not have the idea of an infinite substance, since I am finite, unless it came from the infinite substance itself.

I must not suppose that I apprehend the infinite, not by a

true idea, but only by a negation of what is finite, as I apprehend rest and darkness by a negation of motion and light. On the contrary, I see that there is obviously more reality in an infinite substance than in a finite one, so that my apprehension of the infinite is, in a sense, prior to my apprehension of the finite, that is, my apprehension of God is prior to my apprehension of myself. For how could I know that I doubt and desire, that is, that something is lacking in me and that I am not wholly perfect, if there were not in me the idea of a being more perfect than myself, by comparison with which I recognize my deficiencies?

And it cannot be said that this idea of God may be materially false, and that consequently it may come from nothing, that is, that it may be in me only because of some lack or imperfection in my nature, as I have already said with regard to the ideas of cold, heat and other similar things. On the contrary, since this idea is entirely clear and distinct, and contains more objective reality than any other, there is none which is truer in itself, or less open to the suspicion of falsity. This idea of a supremely perfect and infinite being is, I maintain, entirely true, for although it may be possible to make the supposition that no such being exists, it cannot be supposed that my idea of it exhibits nothing real to me, as I have said of the idea of cold. The idea of God is entirely clear and distinct for the further reason that whatever I apprehend clearly and distinctly as being real and true, and as having any perfection, is contained wholly within it. This is true even though I cannot comprehend the infinite, and even though there may be in God countless things which I cannot comprehend or attain by thought in any way, for it is of the nature of the infinite that I, who am finite, cannot comprehend it. If I understand this, and judge that everything I apprehend clearly and know to have some perfection, and perhaps also countless other perfections of which I know nothing, is in God formally and eminently, my idea of Him must be the truest, clearest and most distinct of all the ideas that are in me.

But perhaps I am something more than I take myself to be; perhaps all the perfections I am attributing to God are somehow in me potentially, although they have not yet been realized and do not manifest themselves in action. Indeed, I already know from experience that my knowledge has been gradually increasing, and I see no reason why it should not increase to infinity; or why, once it has thus increased to infinity, I should not be able by means of it to acquire all the other perfections of God; or, finally, why the power of acquiring these perfections, if it is already in me, should not be sufficient to produce the ideas of them.

When I examine this more closely, however, I see that it cannot be true. First of all, while it may be true that my knowledge has been increasing by degrees, and that there are many things in me potentially which have not yet become actual, all this has no relation to my idea of God, in which nothing is potential and everything is actual, and the fact that my knowledge increases by degrees is undeniable evidence of its imperfection. Furthermore, even if my knowledge should continue to increase, I know that it can never be actually infinite, for it can never become so great that it cannot increase still more; but I judge God to be actually infinite, so that nothing can be added to His perfection. And finally, I see that the objective being of an idea cannot be produced by a merely potential being, which, strictly speaking, is nothing, but only by an actual or formal being.

Surely there is nothing in all this which is not made manifest by the natural light to anyone who considers it attentively; but when I relax my attention and my mind is, as it were, blinded by the images of sensible things, it is not easy for me to remember why the idea of a being more perfect than myself must necessarily have come from such a being. I therefore wish to inquire, further, whether I, who have this idea, could exist if there were no such being.

What could be the source of my existence? Myself, perhaps, or my parents, or something else less perfect than God, for it is impossible to conceive of anything more perfect than God, or even of anything equally perfect.

But if I were the author of my own being, and were therefore independent of anything else, I would have no doubts or desires, and nothing would be lacking in me; I would have given myself all those perfections of which I have any idea, and I would thus be God. And it must not be thought that what is lacking in me is more difficult to acquire than what I already possess. On the contrary, it would obviously be much more difficult for me, a thinking thing or substance, to emerge from nothingness than it would be for me to acquire knowledge of many things of which I am ignorant, and which are only accidents of that substance. If I had given myself existence, I would certainly not have deprived myself of what is easier to acquire, namely, the knowledge which I now lack;

nor would I have deprived myself of any of the things contained in my idea of God, for none of them seems to me more difficult to acquire. And if one of them were more difficult, it would certainly appear to me as such (assuming that I had given myself all the other things I possess), because I would experience it as a limitation of my power.

Nor can I escape the force of this reasoning by supposing that I have always existed as I am now, so that there is no need to seek any author of my being. The entire duration of my life can be divided into innumerable parts, none of which depends in any way on the others. Thus, because I was in existence a short time ago, it does not follow that I must exist now, unless there be some cause which, as it were, creates me anew at this moment, that is, preserves me. If we carefully consider the nature of time, it is obvious that for a thing to be preserved at each of the moments in which it endures, it requires the same force and action that would be required in order to create it if it did not yet exist. That the difference between preservation and creation resides only in our way of thinking is one of the things made manifest by the natural light.

I must now ask myself whether I have any power which is capable of bringing it about that I, who now exist, shall still exist in the immediate future. Since I am nothing but a thinking thing, or at least since that is the only part of myself which is now under consideration, if such a power were in me, I would undoubtedly be conscious of it. But I am aware of no such power, and this makes it obvious to me that I am dependent on some being different from myself.

Perhaps, however, the being on which I am dependent is not the being I call God; perhaps I am produced by my parents, or by some other cause less perfect than God. But this cannot be true, for, as I have already said, it is obvious that there must be at least as much reality in the cause as in the effect, and since I am a thinking thing and have in me an idea of God, any cause that may be assigned to my nature must also be a thinking thing, and have in it the idea of all the perfections I attribute to God. It may be asked whether this cause derives its existence from itself or from some other cause. If it derives its existence from itself, it follows from what has been said above that it is God, for, having the power to exist of itself, it must also have the power to possess actually all the perfections of which it has an idea, that is, all those which I conceive as being in God. If, however, it derives its existence from a cause other than itself, we may ask whether this second cause exists of itself or through some other cause, and this inquiry may be continued until we eventually reach an ultimate cause, which will be God. And it is obvious that there can here be no infinite regression, for we are concerned less with the cause which produced me in the past than with that which now preserves me.

Nor can it be objected that I may have been produced by the concurrence of several partial causes, and that from one of them I have received the idea of one of the perfections I attribute to God, and from another the idea of some other, so that, while all these perfections are indeed to be found somewhere in the universe, they are not conjoined in a single being which is God. On the contrary, the unity, simplicity or inseparability of all the things that are in God is one of the principal perfections which I conceive to be in Him, and certainly this idea of the unity of all His perfections could not have been placed in me by any cause from which I had not also received the ideas of all His other perfections, for it could not have made me aware that they were conjoined and inseparable without also making me aware of what they were.

As for my parents, even if everything I have ever believed about them is true, it does not follow that it is they who now preserve me, or that it was they who brought me into existence insofar as I am a thinking thing, for all they did was to implant certain dispositions in that matter in which I (that is, my mind, which is all I now consider myself to be) now judge myself to be. Thus there can be no difficulty with regard to them; and from the fact that I exist and have in me the idea of a supremely perfect being, that is, of God, it must be concluded that the existence of God is demonstrated in the most evident manner.

It remains for me only to examine how I have acquired this idea. I have not acquired it through the senses, and it has never come to me unexpectedly, as the ideas of sensible things do when those things present themselves, or seem to present themselves, to the external organs of the senses. Nor is it my own invention, for it is not in my power to add anything to it or take anything away from it. Consequently, it can only be innate in me, like the idea of myself.

And certainly I ought not to find it strange that God, in creating me, has placed this idea in me to be, as it were, the mark of the workman imprinted on his work. Nor need the mark be different from the work itself. From the sole fact that

God has created me, it is highly credible that He has in some
fashion made me in His own image and resemblance, and that
I perceive this resemblance, in which the idea of God is contained, by the same faculty by which I perceive myself; that
is, when I consider myself attentively, I know not only that I
am an incomplete, dependent thing, indefinitely aspiring to
something greater than myself, but also that He on whom I
depend has in Himself all those great things to which I
aspire, and that He has them, not indefinitely or potentially,
but actually and infinitely, and that He is thus God. The
whole force of the argument which I am here using to prove
the existence of God consists in this, that I recognize that
my nature could not be as it is, that is, that I could not have
in me the idea of God, if God did not truly exist, that same
God whose idea is in me, who possesses all the perfections
which I can in some way reach by thought, although I cannot
fully comprehend them, and who is subject to no defect. From
this it is evident that He cannot be a deceiver, for the natural
light shows us clearly that all fraud and deceit proceeds from
some defect.

But before I examine this conclusion more carefully and
go on to consider other truths that may be drawn from it, it
seems good that I should pause for a time to contemplate this
all-perfect God, to ponder at leisure His marvelous attributes,
to consider, admire and worship the incomparable beauty of
that immeasurable light insofar as it is within the power of
my dazzled mind to do so. For, as faith teaches that the
supreme bliss in the life to come consists solely in the contemplation of the divine majesty, so do we now experience
that a similar contemplation, though much less perfect, can
give us the greatest joy we are capable of feeling in this life.

MEDITATION IV

Concerning Truth and Falsity

In these past few days I have become so accustomed to
detaching my mind from the senses, and so fully aware of
how little we know with certainty about corporeal things,
whereas we can know much more about the human mind, and
still more about God, that it is now easy for me to turn my
thoughts away from what belongs to the senses and the

magination, and direct them toward things which, being free of all matter, are purely intelligible. Certainly the idea I have of the human mind, insofar as it is a thinking thing, not extended in length, breadth or depth, and having nothing which appertains to body, is much more distinct than the idea of any corporeal thing. And when I consider that I doubt, that is, that I am an incomplete and dependent thing, the idea of a complete and independent being, that is, of God, presents itself to me with such clarity and distinctness, and from the sole fact that this idea is in me, or that I, who have this idea, exist, I am so convinced that God exists and that my existence depends entirely on Him at every moment of my life, that I am confident that nothing more manifest or certain can be known by the human mind. Thus it already seems to me that I have found a path that will lead me from this contemplation of the true God, in whom all the treasures of knowledge and wisdom are contained, to knowledge of all other things.

For I recognize, first of all, that it is impossible that He should ever deceive me, since all fraud or deceit involves a certain imperfection. Although the ability to deceive may seem to be a sign of cunning or power, the will to deceive unquestionably shows malice and weakness, and therefore cannot be present in God.

Furthermore, I experience in myself a certain power of judging, which, like everything else I possess, I have undoubtedly received from God; and since He does not wish to deceive me, it is certain that this power cannot lead me into error if I use it rightly.

There would be no remaining doubt of this fact if it did not seem to imply that I could never err; for if everything I have comes from God, and if He has given me no faculty for error, it would seem that I could never be mistaken. And indeed, when I think only of God, I am aware of no cause of error or falsity; but when I turn back to myself, I recognize that I am subject to countless errors. In seeking to determine their cause, I note that there is in me not only the real and positive idea of God, that is, of a supremely perfect being, but also a negative idea, so to speak, of nothingness, or that which is infinitely far removed from all perfection. Thus I see that I am something midway between God and nothingness, between the supreme being and non-being, so that while it is true that, inasmuch as I have been created by the supreme being, there is nothing in me that can lead me into error, it is also true that, inasmuch as there is in me some element of nothingness or non-being, that is, inasmuch as I am not myself the supreme being, I am subject to countless deficiencies, and it is therefore not surprising that I should be capable of error. Hence I know with certainty that error, as such, is not something real which depends on God, but only a deficiency. In order to fall into error, therefore, I have no need of any power given to me by God for that particular purpose; I do so only because the power of distinguishing truth from falsity, which I have received from God, is not infinite in me.

However, this does not yet satisfy me completely, for error is not a pure negation, that is, the mere absence of some perfection which is my due: it is, rather, the lack of some knowledge which I apparently ought to possess. And when I consider the nature of God, it does not seem possible to me that He should have given me any faculty which is not perfect of its kind, that is, which lacks any perfection that it ought to have. For if it is true that the more skilled the artisan the better his work, how can we suppose the sovereign Creator of all things to have produced something which is not perfect in every respect? It is certain that God could have created me such as to be incapable of error, for it is equally certain that He always wills what is best. Is it then better that I should err than that I should not?

As I ponder this more attentively, the first thought that occurs to me is that there is no reason for me to be surprised if I do not understand why God does what He does, and that therefore I ought not to doubt His existence merely because I may see other things without being able to understand how or why He made them. Since I already know that my nature is extremely weak and limited, and that His nature is boundless, incomprehensible and infinite, I now recognize that there are in His power countless things whose causes are beyond my understanding. This alone is enough to convince me that what are called final causes are of no use in the study of physical things, for it seems to me that it is rash and foolish to seek to discover God's purposes.

It also occurs to me that, in inquiring as to whether the works of God are perfect, we ought not to consider one creature separately, but the universe and everything in it as a whole. For something which may with some reason be regarded as highly imperfect when it is taken by itself will be seen to be quite perfect when it is considered as part of the universe. So far, since resolving to doubt all things, I have come to know nothing with certainty except my own existence and that of God. In so doing, however, I have come to recognize God's infinite power, and I cannot deny that He may have created many other things, or at least that He is capable of creating them, so that I exist as part of the totality of things.

Next, when I consider myself more closely and examine my errors (which are the only indication that there is any imperfection in me), I find that they depend on two concurrent causes: on my power of knowing, and on my power of choosing, or my free will; in short, they depend on both my understanding and my will. By my understanding alone I neither affirm nor deny anything: I merely apprehend the ideas of things which I can affirm or deny. If the understanding is considered thus precisely, it may be said that no errors, properly so called, are ever to be found in it. And although countless things may exist without my having any ideas of them, it cannot be said that I am deprived of those ideas, but only that I do not have them, for there is no reason to assume that God ought to have given me a greater power of knowing than He has. However skilled an artisan I conceive Him to be, I have no grounds for thinking that He ought to place in each one of His works as much perfection as He can place in some of them. Nor can I complain that He has not given me a sufficiently far-reaching and perfect will, that is, genuine free will, for I experience it as being without limits. And what seems to me particularly noteworthy is that, of all the other things that are in me, there is none so great or perfect that I do not recognize that it could be greater or more perfect than it is. If, for example, I consider my faculty of understanding, I see that it is small and extremely limited; at the same time, I also have the idea of another such faculty which is much greater and even infinite, and from the sole fact that I can form the idea of it, I know that it belongs to the nature of God. Similarly, if I examine my memory, my imagination or any of my other faculties, I find none which is not small and circumscribed in me, and infinite in God. My free will is the only faculty which I find to be so great in me that I cannot conceive of it as being greater than it is, so that it is chiefly this faculty which enables me to know that I bear the image and resemblance of God. God's will is incomparably greater than mine, insofar as the knowledge and power that are joined with it make it stronger and more efficacious, and

insofar as it can take so many more things as its object;
nevertheless, it does not seem greater to me if I consider it
formally and precisely in itself, for the power of will consists
only in this, that we can either do or not do something (that
is, affirm or deny it, pursue or avoid it), or rather only in
this, that when we affirm or deny, pursue or avoid the things
that are presented to us by the understanding, we do so
without feeling that our choice is imposed upon us by any
external force. In order to be free, it is not necessary that I
should be indifferent to the choice between alternatives; on
the contrary, the more inclined I am toward one of them,
whether because I know it is good and true or because God
has so disposed my innermost thoughts, the more freely I
choose it. Divine grace and natural knowledge, far from
diminishing my freedom, increase and strengthen it. Indeed,
the indifference I feel when there is no reason which inclines
me toward one alternative rather than another is the lowest
degree of freedom, and indicates a deficiency of knowledge
rather than a perfection of the will, for if the true and the
good were always clearly apparent to me, I would never have
to deliberate as to what I ought to judge or choose, and I
would thus be entirely free, without ever being indifferent.

From all this I perceive that the power of will, which I
have received from God, is not in itself the cause of my
errors, for it is ample and perfect of its kind. Nor are they
caused by my power of understanding, for since I understand
only by means of this power which God has given me, I must
understand rightly anything that I understand at all, and in
this I cannot be mistaken. What, then, is the source of my
errors? This alone, that I do not restrain my will within the
same limits as my understanding, which is of narrower scope,
but extend it also to things I do not understand. Since the
will is of itself indifferent to them, it easily turns away from
the true and the good, and thus it is that I fall into error
and sin.

For example, when, in the course of my recent attempts
to determine whether anything at all existed in the world, I
saw that, from the very fact that I was examining the question, it manifestly followed that I myself existed, I could not
help judging that what I understood so clearly was true, not
because I was compelled to do so by any external force, but
because the great light in my understanding was followed by
a strong inclination of my will, and thus I believed all the
more freely as I was less indifferent. Now, however, not only

do I know that I exist insofar as I am a thinking thing, but I also have a certain idea of corporeal nature which makes me wonder whether the thinking nature which is in me, or rather by which I am what I am, is different from this corporeal nature, or whether they are both the same. I am assuming that I am not now aware of any consideration which could make one view seem more likely to me than the other. Certainly in this case I am indifferent as to whether I affirm or deny, or even as to whether or not I make any judgment at all.

And this indifference extends not only to things of which the understanding has no knowledge, but also, in general, to all things which are not known quite clearly while the will is deliberating with regard to them; for however probable the conjectures which draw me toward one view, the mere awareness that they are only conjectures, and not certain and indubitable reasons, is enough to drive me toward the opposite view. I experienced this recently when, simply because I had observed that it was possible to doubt them in one way or another, I rejected as false all the things I had previously accepted as true.

If I suspend judgment with regard to something which I do not apprehend clearly and distinctly enough, it is obvious that I am acting rightly and that I am not mistaken. If, however, I affirm or deny it, I am not using my free will rightly. If my assertion is false, I am obviously mistaken; but even if it should happen to be true, I am nevertheless at fault, because the natural light shows clearly that apprehension by the understanding should always precede determination of the will. It is in this misuse of free will that the privation which constitutes the form of error resides. The privation is in the operation insofar as it proceeds from me, but not in the power I have received from God, or even in the operation insofar as it depends on Him.

I have no reason to complain about God's not having given me a greater power of understanding or a greater natural light, for it is in the very nature of a finite understanding that it does not understand many things, and of a created understanding that it is finite. But I have every reason to thank God, who has never owed me anything, for what He has given me, and I must not think that I have been unjustly deprived of what He has not given me.

Nor have I any reason to complain about His having given me a will whose scope is wider than that of my understanding, for since the will consists of a single thing and is, so to speak, indivisible, its nature appears to be such that nothing can be taken from it. Indeed, the wider its scope, the more I should be grateful to Him who has given it to me.

Finally, I must not complain that God concurs with me in bringing about those acts of will, or judgments, in which I am mistaken. Those acts are entirely true and good insofar as they depend on God, and, in a sense, there is greater perfection in me because I can bring them about than there would be if I could not. As for the privation in which alone the formal reason of error and sin consists, it has no need of God's concurrence because it is not an entity; and if it is related to God as its cause, it must be called not privation, but only negation, in accordance with the meanings given to these words in the School. For it is certainly not an imperfection in God that He has given me the freedom of assenting or not assenting to things of which He has not placed a clear and distinct apprehension in my understanding; but it is undoubtedly an imperfection in me that I misuse this freedom by passing judgment on things which I do not apprehend rightly. Nevertheless, I recognize that God could easily have created me in such a way that, despite my freedom and my limited knowledge, I would never fall into error. He could have done this either by giving my understanding a clear and distinct apprehension of everything on which I would ever have to deliberate, or by impressing so deeply in my memory the resolution never to judge anything without this clear and distinct apprehension that I could never forget it. And I easily understand that insofar as I consider myself alone, as though there were only myself in the world, I would have been much more perfect than I am if God had created me in that fashion. But I cannot deny that, in a sense, it is a greater perfection in the universe as a whole that some of its parts should not be free from defect while others are, than that they should all be exactly alike. And I have no right to complain because God has not willed to place me among the most excellent and perfect things in the world.

Furthermore, while it is not possible for me to avoid all error by the first means mentioned above, which depends on a clear and distinct apprehension of everything on which I must deliberate, it is at least possible for me to employ the second means, which is to remember always to withhold my judgment with regard to things whose truth is not clearly apparent to me. For although I am well aware of the weakness which prevents me from keeping the same thought always in my mind, by careful and repeated meditation I can make it recur to me whenever I need it, and thus I can acquire the habit of avoiding error.

Since it is in this that the greatest and foremost perfection of man consists, I consider that I have gained more than a little from today's Meditation in discovering the cause of falsity and error. And surely there can be no other cause than the one I have explained, for if I always restrain my will in such a way that it makes judgments concerning only those things which are clearly and distinctly apprehended by the understanding, I can never be mistaken, because every clear and distinct apprehension must be something, and consequently cannot proceed from nothing, but must necessarily have been produced by God, who, being supremely perfect, can never be the cause of any error; consequently, every clear and distinct apprehension must be true. And I have learned today not only what I must avoid in order not to fall into error, but also what I must do in order to acquire knowledge of the truth. I shall surely acquire it if I am sufficiently attentive to those things which I understand perfectly, and separate them from those which I apprehend only confusedly and obscurely. Henceforth I shall diligently devote myself to this task.

MEDITATION V

◄§ Concerning the Essence of Material Things; and Again, Concerning God: That He Exists.

I still have many things to examine with regard to the attributes of God and my own nature, that is, the nature of my mind, and I shall perhaps return to them later. But now that I have discovered what must be done and what must be avoided in order to acquire knowledge of the truth, my chief concern is to try to extricate myself from the doubts into which I have recently fallen, and to see whether anything certain can be known about material things.

But before I seek to determine whether such things exist outside of me, I must consider the ideas I have of them and see which are distinct and which are confused.

First, I have a distinct image of that quantity which

philosophers commonly call continuous, or of the extension in length, breadth and depth which is in that quantity, or rather in the thing to which it is attributed. Further, I can distinguish several parts in it, and attribute various sizes, shapes, locations and movements to each one of them. And finally I can attribute various durations to each one of these movements.

Not only do I know these things distinctly when I consider them in general, but also, when I apply my attention to them more closely, I become aware of countless particulars regarding numbers, shapes, movements, and other such things, whose truth is so evident and so accordant with my nature that it does not seem to me that I am discovering anything new, but rather that I am remembering something I already knew, or taking note of something that was already in my mind, although I had not yet directed my attention to it.

What seems to me most noteworthy here is that I find in me countless ideas of things which, although they may not exist outside of me, cannot be regarded as nothing, and which, although I am free to think them or not, as I choose, are not invented by me, but have their own true and immutable natures. When, for example, I imagine a triangle, even though it may be true that there is not and never has been any such figure in existence outside of my mind, it nevertheless has a determinate nature, or essence, or form, which is immutable and eternal, which I have not invented, and which does not depend on my mind. This is evident from the fact that it is possible to demonstrate various properties of the triangle—that its three angles are equal to two right angles, that its greatest angle is subtended by its longest side, etc.—which, whether I wish to or not, I now clearly recognize as belonging to it, even though I had in no way thought of them when I first imagined a triangle; consequently, they were not invented by me.

Nor can it be objected that since I have sometimes seen bodies that are triangular in shape, the idea of a triangle has perhaps come to me from external things by way of the sense organs. I can conceive countless other shapes which cannot be suspected of having ever been conveyed to me by my senses, and of which I can demonstrate various properties, as I can in the case of the triangle. Now they must all be true, since I apprehend them clearly, and they are therefore something, not nothing, for it is obvious that whatever is true is something, and I have already fully demonstrated that whatever I apprehend clearly is true. And even if I had not demonstrated it, the nature of my mind is such that, as long as I apprehend something clearly, I must accept it as true. Furthermore, I recall that even when I was most firmly attached to the objects of the senses, I recognized as the most certain and evident of all truths those which related to shape, number and everything else pertaining to arithmetic and geometry.

Now if, from the sole fact that I can form an idea of a thing in my mind, it follows that whatever I recognize clearly and distinctly as belonging to that thing actually does belong to it, may I not draw from this an argument that will prove the existence of God? Certainly the idea of God, that is, of a supremely perfect being, is no less present in me than the idea of any shape or number, and I know no less clearly and distinctly that actual and external existence belongs to His nature than I know that whatever can be demonstrated of a shape or number belongs to the nature of that shape or number. Therefore, even if it were shown that not all of what I have concluded in these Meditations is true, I would still have to consider the existence of God to be at least as certain as I have hitherto considered mathematical truths to be.

However, this is not entirely evident at first sight, and even seems to be something of a sophism, for, being accustomed in all other things to distinguishing between existence and essence, I readily believe that existence can be separated from the essence of God, and thus that I can think of God as not actually existing. But on closer consideration it becomes manifest to me that existence can no more be separated from the essence of God than the fact that its three angles are equal to two right angles can be separated from the essence of a triangle, or than the idea of a mountain can be separated from the idea of a valley. Therefore, to think of God (that is, a supremely perfect being) without existence (that is, without a particular perfection) is as contradictory as to think of a mountain without a valley.

But although I cannot think of God without existence any more than I can think of a mountain without a valley, from the fact that I think of a mountain with a valley it does not follow that there is a mountain anywhere in the world, and it might seem that, similarly, from the fact that I think of God as existing it does not follow that He exists, for my thinking imposes no necessity on things. It might be said that, just as I can imagine a winged horse even though no horse has wings, so I might be attributing existence to God even though no God exists.

This objection rests on a hidden fallacy. It is true that from the fact that I cannot think of a mountain without a valley it does not follow that any mountains and valleys exist, but only that the mountain and the valley, whether they exist or not, cannot be separated from each other. But from the fact that I cannot think of God without existence it follows that existence is inseparable from Him, and therefore that He actually exists. Not that my thinking makes it so or imposes any necessity on things—on the contrary, the necessity of the thing itself, namely, the existence of God, determines me to think in this way, for I am not free to think of a God without existence (that is, of a supremely perfect being without supreme perfection), as I am free to imagine a horse with or without wings.

Nor can it be objected that, while it is indeed necessary to grant that God exists if the assumption is made that He has all perfections, including existence, the assumption itself is not necessary, just as it is not necessary to assume that all four-sided figures can be inscribed in a circle, although once the assumption has been made it is necessary to conclude that a rhombus can be inscribed in a circle, which is clearly false. This objection does not hold, for while it is not necessary that I should ever think of God, nevertheless, whenever I do think of a first and supreme being, drawing the idea of such a being, so to speak, from the storehouse of my mind, I must necessarily attribute all perfections to Him, even though I do not enumerate them all, or direct my attention to any of them in particular. And this necessity is sufficient, once I have recognized that existence is a perfection, to make me conclude that this first and supreme being exists; just as, while it is not necessary that I should ever imagine a triangle, whenever I consider a rectilinear figure having only three angles, I must necessarily attribute to it all those properties from which it can be correctly concluded that its three angles are not greater than two right angles, even though I may not take note of that particular conclusion at the time. But when I consider what figures can be inscribed in a circle, it is not at all necessary for me to think that all four-sided figures are included among them; on the contrary, I cannot even pretend that this is so, as long as I refuse to accept anything except what I apprehend clearly and distinctly. Consequently there is a great difference between such false suppositions and the true ideas that have been placed in me, the first and chief of which is the idea of God. There are a number of considerations which show me that this idea is not something fictitious which depends solely on my thinking, but is the image of a true and immutable nature. First, I can think of nothing except God to whose essence existence belongs. And then it is impossible to conceive of two or more Gods of this kind. And, given that there is a God who now exists, I see clearly that He must have existed from all eternity and must continue to exist eternally. Finally, I am aware of many other things in God which I can neither diminish nor change.

But no matter what proof or argument I employ, I always return to this, that I am fully convinced only by what I apprehend clearly and distinctly. Some of the things I thus apprehend are obvious to everyone, while others become apparent only after closer and more precise examination; yet the latter, once they have been discovered, are seen to be no less certain than the former. For example, the fact that the square of the hypotenuse of a right-angled triangle is equal to the sum of the squares of the other two sides is not at first so readily apparent as the fact that the hypotenuse subtends the largest angle, and yet when both these facts have been ascertained, they are accepted as equally certain. As for God, if my mind were not obscured by prejudices and overwhelmed by the images of sensible things, I would have known Him sooner and more easily than anything else. For what could be more manifest than the existence of a supreme being, that is, of God, to whose essence alone existence belongs?

It is true that I had to apply myself diligently in order to apprehend this; now, however, not only am I as certain of it as of everything else that seems to me most certain, but I also see that the certainty of all other things is so dependent on this knowledge that without it nothing could be known perfectly.

For although my nature is such that, as long as I apprehend something very clearly and distinctly, I cannot prevent myself from believing it to be true, nevertheless, because my nature is also such that I cannot keep my mind fixed always on one thing, I often remember having judged something to be true when I am no longer aware of the reasons for my judgment, and at those times other reasons may occur to me which, if I did not know that there is a God, could easily make me change my opinion, so that I would never have true and certain knowledge of anything, but only vague and shifting opinions. If, for example, I consider the nature of a triangle, it is quite evident to me, since I am acquainted with the principles of geometry, that its three angles are equal to two right angles, and it is impossible for me not to believe this as long as I am attentive to the demonstration. But as soon as I have turned my attention away from it, even though I recall having clearly understood it, I may easily come to doubt its truth if I am ignorant of God, for I may become convinced that I am so made by nature that I am sometimes mistaken in what I believe I understand with the greatest evidence, especially when I remember all the things which I once regarded as true and certain, but which other reasons later made me judge to be false.

But once I have recognized that there is a God, thereby recognizing at the same time that all things depend on Him and that He is not a deceiver, and further, that everything I apprehend clearly and distinctly is necessarily true, even though I am no longer aware of the reasons that made me judge it to be true, provided I remember that I have apprehended it clearly and distinctly, then I can never be confronted with any contrary reasons which will make me doubt it, and my knowledge of it is thus true and certain. And such knowledge also extends to all other things which I recall as having been demonstrated in the past, as is the case with the truths of geometry, and so on. For what objection can be raised that will make me doubt them? Will it be said that I am by nature prone to error? But I now know that I cannot be mistaken in whatever I understand clearly. Will it be said that I have regarded many things as true and certain which I later recognized as false? But I apprehended none of those things clearly and distinctly, and since I was still ignorant of this rule of truth, I was led to believe them by reasons which I later found to be less compelling than I had supposed. What else can be said? That perhaps I am asleep (an objection which I myself have already raised), or that all the thoughts I now have are no truer than those which come to me in sleep? But whether I am asleep or awake, anything that is clear and evident to my understanding is certainly true.

Thus I see clearly that the certainty and truth of all knowledge depends on knowledge of the true God, so that, before I knew him, I could have no perfect knowledge of anything else. And now that I know Him, it is possible for me to acquire perfect knowledge of countless things, not only concerning Him, but also concerning that corporeal nature which is the object of pure mathematics.*

MEDITATION VI

~§ Concerning the Existence of Material Things and the Real Distinction between Mind and Body.

It now remains for me to inquire as to whether material things exist. I already know that it is at least possible for them to exist insofar as they are objects of pure mathematics, since, as such, I apprehend them clearly and distinctly. For there is no doubt that God is capable of creating all things which I am capable of thus apprehending; and I have never judged it to be impossible for Him to do anything except something of which it would be contradictory to have a distinct apprehension. Furthermore, my faculty of imagination, which I use when I consider material things, is capable of convincing me of their existence; for when I carefully examine the question of what the imagination is, I find that it is nothing but a certain application of the cognitive faculty to a body which is intimately present to it, and which therefore exists.

To clarify this, I shall first consider the difference between the imagination and pure intellection. When I imagine a triangle, for example, not only do I understand it to be a figure bounded by three lines, but also, by an inner effort of my mind, I see these three lines as if they were present, and this is what I call imagining. If, however, I wish to think of a chiliagon, I understand it to be a figure composed of a thousand sides, as easily as I understand a triangle to be a figure composed of three sides, but I cannot imagine the thousand sides of a chiliagon as I do the three sides of a triangle, that is, I cannot see them as though they were present, so to speak, with the eyes of my mind. And although, in accordance with my habit of always imagining something when I think of corporeal things, I may confusedly represent some sort of figure to myself, this figure is obviously not a

---

* French version: "... countless things, not only of those which are in Him, but also of those which pertain to corporeal nature, insofar as it can serve as the object of the demonstrations of geometers, who are not concerned with its existence."

chiliagon, since it is in no way different from what I would represent to myself if I were thinking of a myriagon or any other many-sided figure, and it is of no use in determining the properties which distinguish the chiliagon from other polygons. In the case of a pentagon, I can understand what this figure is, just as I can understand what a chiliagon is, without the aid of the imagination; but I can also imagine it by applying my mental vision to each of its five sides and the area they enclose. Thus it is obvious to me that imagining requires a special effort of the mind which is not required in understanding, and this special effort of the mind clearly shows the difference between the imagination and pure intellection.

I note, further, that this power of imagining which is in me, insofar as it differs from the power of understanding, is not necessary to my essence, that is, to the essence of my mind: for if I did not have it, I would undoubtedly remain the same as I am now. From this it seems that I may conclude that my power of imagining depends on something other than my mind. And I can easily understand that if there exists some body to which my mind is so joined that it can contemplate it whenever it chooses, it may thus be able to imagine corporeal things, so that this way of thinking differs from pure intellection only in this, that in pure intellection the mind turns in upon itself, as it were, and considers one of the ideas that are in it, whereas in imagining it turns to the body and considers in it something in conformity with an idea which it has either formed by itself or received by way of the senses. I can easily understand that imagining may take place in this manner if it is true that bodies exist; and since I can find no other suitable way of explaining it, I conjecture that bodies probably exist. But it is only probable, and although I examine everything carefully, I find that, from the distinct idea of corporeal nature which is in my imagination, I can draw no conclusive argument for the existence of any body whatever.

Now I am accustomed to imagining many things besides that corporeal nature which is the object of pure mathematics, namely, colors, sounds, tastes, pain, and so on, although I imagine them less distinctly. Since I perceive these things better through the senses, by means of which, and of the memory, they seem to reach the imagination, I think that, in order to consider them more conveniently, I should also consider what sensing is, and try to determine whether, from the ideas which come into my mind through that way of thinking which I call sensing, I can obtain any certain proof of the existence of corporeal things.

First I shall recall those things, apprehended by means of the senses, which I believed to be true, along with the grounds on which my belief was based. Next I shall examine the reasons which later made me doubt them. Finally, I shall consider what I should now believe about them.

At first I sensed that I had a head, hands, feet, and all the other members composing the body which I considered to be part of myself, or perhaps all of myself. I also sensed that this body was only one among many others which were capable of affecting it in various agreeable or disagreeable ways, the agreeable effects being manifested by a sensation of pleasure, the disagreeable ones by a sensation of pain. Besides pleasure and pain, I also sensed in me hunger, thirst and other such appetites, as well as certain bodily inclinations toward joy, sorrow, anger and other such passions. And in the bodies outside of me, I sensed not only extension, shapes and movements, but also hardness, heat and other tactual qualities, and, further, light, colors, odors, tastes and sounds, the variety of which enabled me to distinguish the earth, the sky, the sea and all other bodies.

Since the ideas of all these qualities were constantly presenting themselves to my mind, and since they were all that I sensed properly and immediately, it was not unreasonable for me to believe that I was sensing things entirely different from my mind, namely, bodies from which those ideas proceeded. For experience showed me that they could present themselves to me without my consent, and that no matter how much I might wish to do so, I could not sense an object if it was not present to one of my sense organs, or prevent myself from sensing it if it was. And since the ideas that I received by way of the senses were much more vivid and precise, and even, in their way, more distinct, than any of the ideas which I could deliberately produce, or which I found imprinted in my memory, it seemed that they could not have proceeded from me, but must have come to me from things outside of myself. Having no knowledge of these things except what I derived from these same ideas, I could only assume that they resembled the ideas. Because I recalled that I had used my senses before my reason, and because I recognized that the ideas I formed by myself were less definite than those which I received by way of my senses, and were usually composed of parts of the latter, I readily believed that I had no idea in my mind which had not previously come from my senses.

As for the body which, by a certain special right, I called my own, it was not unreasonable for me to regard it as belonging to me more closely than any other, for I could never be separated from it as from other bodies, I experienced all my appetites in it and for it, and I was affected by sensations of pleasure and pain in its parts, but not in those of other bodies that were separate from it.

But when I sought to determine why a sensation of pain is followed by sadness, and a sensation of pleasure by joy, or why that twitching of the stomach which I call hunger makes me want to eat, while a feeling of dryness in the throat makes me want to drink, and so on, I could find no explanation except that I was so taught by nature; for there is no affinity (at least none that I can understand) between that twitching of the stomach and the desire to eat, or between the sensing of a thing that causes pain and the thought of sadness which follows this sensing. And it seemed to me that nature had taught me all the other judgments I made with regard to the objects of my senses, because I observed that these judgments were formed in me before I had time to weigh any reasons which might have obliged me to make them.

Later, however, many experiences destroyed all my faith in the senses. I often observed that towers which looked round from a distance appeared as square when seen at closer range, and that gigantic statues standing on top of these towers looked small when seen from the ground below; and so, in countless other instances, I found that judgments based on the external senses were erroneous. And not on the external senses only, but also on the internal senses. What could be more intimate, more internal, than pain? Yet I had been told by people who had had an arm or a leg amputated that it sometimes seemed to them that they felt pain in the amputated limb, and from this I concluded that I could not be completely certain that I had a pain in one of my limbs even when I seemed to feel it there. To these reasons for doubt I recently added two extremely general ones. The first one was that I had never believed myself to be sensing anything while awake which I could not also believe myself to be sensing while asleep; and since I did not believe that the things I seemed to sense in my dreams came to me from objects outside of myself, I did not see why I should hold that belief with regard to the things I seemed to sense when I was awake. The second reason was that, since I was still ignorant of the author of my being, or at least pretending to be so, I saw no reason why I should not have been so made by nature that I was mistaken even in those things which seemed truest to me. As for the reasons which had previously convinced me of the truth of sensible things, I had no difficulty in answering them. For since nature seemed to incline me toward many things which were contrary to reason, I did not think I should place much confidence in the teachings of nature. And although the ideas I received through my senses did not depend on my will, I did not think this justified the conclusion that they came from things outside of me, since there might be in me some faculty, hitherto unknown to me, which produced them.

However, now that I am beginning to know more about myself and the author of my being, I still do not think that I should rashly accept all the things which seem to come from the senses, but neither do I think that they should all be doubted.

In the first place, because I know that all the things which I apprehend clearly and distinctly can be created by God exactly as I apprehend them, my being able to apprehend one thing apart from another is enough to make me certain that one is different from the other, since they can be posited separately, at least by God; and it does not matter by what power this is done: I must still regard them as separate. Therefore, from the sole fact that I know I exist, and that I am not aware of anything which belongs to my nature or essence except that I am a thinking thing, I rightly conclude that my essence consists in this alone, that I am a thinking thing, that is, I am a substance whose whole essence or nature consists in thinking. And although perhaps (or, rather, certainly, as I shall soon say) I have a body with which I am closely conjoined, I have, on the one hand, a clear and distinct idea of myself as a thinking, non-extended thing, and, on the other hand, a distinct idea of my body as an extended, non-thinking thing; it is therefore certain that I am truly distinct from my body, and can exist without it.

Furthermore, I find in myself faculties or particular modes of thinking which are distinct from me, namely, the faculties of imagining and sensing. I can clearly and distinctly conceive of myself as complete without them, but I cannot conceive of them without me, that is, without an intelligent substance in which they reside. For in the notion we have of them, or (to use the terms of the School) in their formal concept, some sort of intellection is included, and from this I see that they are distinct from me, as shapes, movements and other modes or accidents of bodies are distinct from the bodies that sustain them.

I am also aware of other faculties, such as the powers of changing location, of assuming various postures, and so on, which, like those discussed above, cannot be conceived without a substance in which they reside, and therefore cannot exist without such a substance. But it is obvious that these faculties, if they exist, must reside in a corporeal or extended substance, not an intelligent substance, for the clear and distinct concept of them contains some sort of extension, but no intellection.

There is also in me a certain passive faculty of sensing, that is, of receiving and knowing ideas of sensible things, but it would be useless to me if there were not in me, or in some other being, an active faculty capable of producing these ideas. Now this active faculty cannot be in me, insofar as I am only a thinking thing, because it does not presuppose intellection, and because these ideas present themselves to me without my co-operation, and often against my will. This faculty must therefore be in some substance which contains, either formally or eminently, all the reality that is objectively in the ideas produced by the faculty (as I have previously observed). This substance is either a body, that is, a corporeal nature which contains formally and actually all that is in the ideas objectively and by representation, or else it is God or some creature of a higher order than body, in which all of it is eminently contained. But since God is not a deceiver, it is obvious that He does send these ideas to me immediately from Himself, or through some creature in which their reality is not contained formally, but only eminently. For since He has given me no faculty whereby I could know this, but has, on the contrary, given me a strong inclination to believe that these ideas come from corporeal things, I do not see how He could not be considered deceitful if they came from anything but corporeal things. Therefore, corporeal things exist.

However, they are perhaps not exactly as we perceive them by means of the senses, for such perception is often extremely obscure and confused; but at least everything I clearly and distinctly apprehend as being in them, that is, generally speaking, everything comprised in the object of pure mathematics, is truly in them.

As for those other things which are only particular, such as that the sun has this or that size or shape, etc., and those which are less clearly apprehended, such as light, sound, pain, etc., even though they are extremely dubious and uncertain, I may confidently conclude that it is possible for me to know them with certainty, for since God is not a deceiver, there can be no falsity in my opinions unless He has given me some faculty by which I can correct it. And there can be no doubt that there is some truth in whatever I am taught by nature, for by nature in general I now mean nothing other than God Himself, or the order of created things established by Him, and by my nature in particular I mean the aggregate of all the things that God has given me.

Now there is nothing that this nature teaches me more explicitly than that I have a body which is adversely affected when I feel pain, which needs food or drink when I feel hunger or thirst, and so on. I must therefore not doubt that there is some truth in all this.

Nature teaches me, further, that my body exists among other bodies, and that I ought to seek after some of them and avoid others. And certainly from the fact that I sense a great variety of colors, sounds, odors, tastes, heat, hardness, and so on, I rightly conclude that there are, in the bodies from which these various sensations proceed, variations which correspond to them, even though they may not resemble them; and since some of these sensations are agreeable to me while others are disagreeable, it is certain that my body, or rather I myself, insofar as I am composed of a body and a soul, can be affected beneficially or harmfully by the bodies around me.

However, there are many other things which seem to have been taught to me by nature, but which I have not actually learned in this way: they have entered my mind because of my habit of making ill-considered judgments which are often erroneous. Thus, for example, I may judge that all space in which there is nothing that affects my senses is a vacuum; that in a hot body there is something which resembles the idea of heat that is in me; that in a white or green body there is the same whiteness or greenness that I see; that a bitter or sweet body has the same bitterness or sweetness that I taste, and so on with the other senses; and that stars, towers and all other distant bodies have the same sizes and shapes that they present to my eyes, etc. But in order that there may be nothing in this which I do not apprehend with sufficient distinctness, I must define more precisely what I mean when

I say that something is taught by nature. I am here taking nature in a more restricted sense than when I refer to it as the aggregate of all things that God has given me, for that aggregate includes many things which belong to the mind alone, such as my awareness that once something has been done it can no longer not have been done, and all the other truths which I know by the natural light, about which I am not here speaking. It also includes many things which belong to body alone, such as the fact that it tends to move downward, and so on. I am not dealing with these things either, but only with those which God has given me insofar as I am composed of both mind and body. Taken in this sense, nature does teach me to avoid what makes me sense pain, and to pursue what causes me to sense pleasure. But I do not find that it also teaches me that I ought to draw any conclusions regarding things outside of me on the basis of these sensory perceptions before the mind has carefully examined them, for it would seem that it belongs to the mind alone, and not to the combination of mind and body, to know the truth of these things.

Thus, although a star makes no greater impression on my eye than the flame of a small torch, there is in me no real or positive propensity to believe that it is no larger than such a flame; I have simply assumed this since childhood, without reason. And, although when I come near a fire I feel heat, and even pain if I come too near it, there is no reason for me to believe that there is in the fire something which resembles that heat or pain; I am justified only in believing that there is something in the fire, whatever it may be, which produces those sensations of heat or pain in me. Similarly, although there are spaces in which I find nothing that affects my senses, it does not follow that there are no bodies in them. I see that in this case, as in many others, I have habitually perverted the order of nature. These sensory perceptions are given to me by nature only in order to signify to my mind which things are beneficial or harmful to the composite of which it is a part, and for this purpose they are sufficiently clear and distinct. But I have been using them as though they were infallible rules for discerning the nature of bodies outside of me, when actually the information they provide about them is extremely obscure and confused.

I have already sufficiently examined how it happens that, despite the supreme goodness of God, there may be falsity in judgments of this kind. At this point, however, a difficulty arises concerning those things which nature teaches me to pursue or avoid, and also concerning the internal sensations in which I seem to have sometimes detected error. Thus, for example, the pleasant taste of a poisoned food may induce me to eat it, and so deceive me. But in this case nature inclines me to eat only the pleasant-tasting food, not the poison, of which it knows nothing, so that I can conclude only that my nature is not omniscient. This is no cause for surprise, because man is a finite being and is therefore capable only of limited knowledge.

But it happens rather often that we are mistaken even in things to which nature inclines us directly, as when a sick man wishes to eat or drink something which would be harmful to him. It may be said that he is mistaken because his nature has been corrupted, but this does not remove the difficulty, for a sick man is no less truly God's creature than a man who is in good health, and it is therefore as inconsistent with God's goodness that a sick man should have a deceptive nature as that a healthy man should have one. A clock composed of wheels and counterweights observes all the laws of nature no less exactly when it is badly made and does not keep time correctly than when it completely fulfills its maker's wishes. Similarly, if I consider the human body as a machine which is so constructed and composed of bones, nerves, muscles, veins, blood and skin that even if there were no mind in it, it would still have all the movements it now has, except for those which proceed from the power of the will and therefore from the mind, I readily recognize that, while it is quite natural for a body to have a certain dryness in the throat which impels it to drink for its own good, it is no less natural for the same body, if it is suffering from dropsy, for example, to have the same dryness in the throat which usually communicates the sensation of thirst to the mind, and to be impelled by this dryness to move its muscles and other parts in the manner required for drinking, thereby worsening its malady. It is true that if I consider the purpose for which a clock was made, I can say that it deviates from its nature when it does not keep time correctly; and similarly, if I consider the machine of the human body as having been made to carry out those movements which usually occur in it, I have reason to think that it, too, deviates from its nature when it has a dryness in the throat even though drinking is detrimental to its preservation. But I recognize that I am here using the term "nature" in a sense which differs greatly from

the sense in which I was previously using it. It is merely an
appellation which depends on my mentally comparing a sick
man and a badly made clock with the idea of a healthy man
and a well-made clock, and which signifies nothing to be
found in the things to which it is applied. In my other use of
the term, however, it signifies something which is truly in the
things to which it is applied, and which is therefore not without some truth.

With regard to a body suffering from dropsy, it is indeed
only by means of an extrinsic appellation that we can speak
of its nature as having been corrupted when it has a dry throat
without having any need to drink. Nevertheless, with regard
to the composite whole, that is, the mind united with such a
body, it is not merely a manner of speaking, but a real error
of nature that it should be thirsty when drinking would be
harmful. Consequently, I must now seek to determine why
God's goodness does not prevent nature, taken in this sense,
from being deceptive.

My first step in this inquiry is to observe that there is a
great difference between mind and body, in that body is by
nature always divisible, while mind is completely indivisible.
For when I consider my mind, that is, myself insofar as I am
only a thinking thing, I can distinguish no parts in myself;
rather, I apprehend myself as a single whole. And although
my entire mind seems to be united to my entire body, I know
that nothing will be taken from my mind if a foot, an arm
or any other part of my body is cut off. The faculties of willing, sensing, understanding, etc., cannot be said to be parts of
my mind, for it is one and the same mind which wills, senses
and understands. The opposite is true of corporeal, or
extended, things: there is not one of them which I cannot
easily think of as being divided into parts, and which I do
not therefore know to be divisible. This alone would be
enough to convince me that the human mind, or soul, is
entirely different from the body, even if I had not already
learned it from other considerations.

Next I observe that the mind is not immediately affected
by all parts of the body, but only by one small part of it,
namely, that in which what is known as common sense is said
to be. Each time this part is disposed in a given way, it con-
veys the same thing to the mind, even though the other parts
of the body may be differently disposed, as is shown by countless experiences which there is no need to recall here.

I observe, further, that the nature of body is such that if

one of its parts can be moved by another and somewhat distant part, it can also be moved in the same way by any of the other parts between these two. Thus, for example, if the cord ABCD is held taut and its last part, D, is pulled, its first part, A, will be moved in exactly the same way as if one of the intermediate parts, B or C, were pulled while the last part, D, remained motionless. The case is similar when I feel a pain in my foot: physics teaches me that the sensation is communicated by means of nerves dispersed throughout the foot and extending, like cords, from it to the brain, and that when they are pulled in the foot, they pull the inner parts of the brain at which they end, causing in them a certain movement instituted by nature to make the mind sense pain as though it were in the foot. But because these nerves must pass through the calf, the thigh, the loins, the back and the neck in order to reach the brain, it may happen that, although their extremities in the foot are not moved, but only some of their intermediate parts, the movements caused in the brain are the same as those that would be caused by an injury to the foot, and the mind will then necessarily sense the same pain that it would sense if the foot had actually been injured.

Finally, I observe that since each of the movements that take place in the part of the brain by which the mind is immediately affected and always causes one particular sensation, nothing better can be conceived in this respect than that, of all the sensations it is capable of causing, each movement should cause the one which is most often of the greatest use in the preservation of a healthy body. Now experience shows that all the sensations aroused in us by nature are of this kind; consequently there is nothing in them which does not testify to the power and goodness of God. Thus, for example, when the nerves in the foot are moved more violently than usual, their movement passes through the spinal marrow to the brain, where it causes the mind to sense a pain as though it were in the foot, thereby inciting it to do everything possible to remove the cause of the injury to the foot. God could have constituted man's nature in such a way that this same movement in the brain would have made the mind aware of something else: of the movement itself, for example, as being in the brain, the foot, or some intermediate part of the body, or of something entirely different, whatever it might be; but nothing else would have been as useful in the preservation of the body. To take another example, when we need to drink, there is a certain dryness in the throat which moves its nerves and thereby moves the inner parts of the brain, and this movement makes the mind aware of a sensation of thirst, because in this particular situation there is nothing more useful to us than to know that we need to drink in order to preserve our health; and so on in other similar cases.

From all this it is manifest that, despite the infinite goodness of God, man's nature, insofar as he is a composite of mind and body, must occasionally be deceptive. For if some cause, not in the foot, but in some other part of the nerves that extend from the foot to the brain, or even in the brain itself, should give rise to the same movement that usually takes place when the foot is injured, pain will be sensed as though it were in the foot, and the sensation will be naturally deceptive; for since this particular movement in the brain must always cause the same sensation in the mind, and since it arises much more often from a cause which injures the foot than from one which acts elsewhere, it is reasonable that it should always convey to the mind a pain which is sensed as being in the foot, rather than in some other part of the body. And while dryness of the throat does not always arise, as it usually does, from a need to drink in order to preserve the health of the body, but sometimes from a contrary cause, as in the case of those afflicted with dropsy, it is far better that it should be deceptive in such cases than that it should always be so when the body is in good health; and the same is true in other similar instances.

And this consideration is extremely helpful to me, not only in making it possible for me to recognize all the errors to which my nature is subject, but also in making it easy for me to correct or avoid them. I now know that, with regard to things which concern the welfare of the body, the indications of my senses are much more often true than false. Furthermore, I can nearly always employ several of my senses in the examination of a single thing, and I can make use of my memory, which connects the present with the past, and of my understanding, which has already ascertained all the causes of my errors. For these reasons, I need no longer fear that the things represented to me every day by the senses may be false, and I must reject my recent doubts as hyperbolic and laughable. This is particularly true of my doubt concerning sleep, which I was unable to distinguish from the state of being awake. I now see a great difference between the two, in that memory can never connect my dreams with one another and with the entire course of my life, as it does in the case of things that occur while I am awake. If, while I am awake, someone should suddenly appear before me and then just as suddenly disappear, as happens in dreams, so that I could know neither where he had come from nor where he had gone, it would not be unreasonable for me to regard him as a specter or phantom formed in my own brain, rather than as a real man. But if, in perceiving something, I know whence, where and when it comes to me, and can uninterruptedly connect my perception of it with the rest of my life, I am fully certain that what I perceive is taking place while I am awake, and not in a dream. And I ought not to have the slightest doubt of its truth if, having called on all my senses, my memory and my understanding to examine it, I find that none of them tells me anything that is inconsistent with what I am told by the others. Since God is not a deceiver, it follows that I cannot be mistaken in such a case. But because the necessity for action does not always allow time for such careful examination, we must admit that human life is often subject to error with regard to particular things, and acknowledge the weakness of our nature.

End

THE PASSIONS OF THE SOUL

❧❦❧

PART ONE

OF THE PASSIONS IN GENERAL, AND INCIDENTALLY OF THE WHOLE NATURE OF MAN

ARTICLE 1

❧ *That what is passion with regard to a subject is always action in some other respect.* ❧

Nowhere does the defectiveness of the sciences handed down to us by the ancients appear more clearly than in what they wrote about the passions. This is a topic which has always been intensively studied, and which does not seem to be particularly difficult, since everyone feels the passions within himself and therefore has no need to borrow observations from elsewhere in order to discover their nature, and yet what the ancients have taught us about them is so slight, and for the most part so far from credible, that I cannot hope to approach the truth unless I depart from the paths they have followed. That is why I shall be obliged to write here as though I were dealing with a matter that had never been touched on before. To begin with, I observe that whatever takes place or happens anew is generally called by philosophers a passion with regard to the subject to which it happens, and an action with regard to what causes it to happen, so that although the agent and the recipient are often quite different, the action and the passion are always one and the same thing which has these two names because of the two separate subjects to which it can be referred.

ARTICLE 2

❧ *That in order to understand the passions of the soul we must distinguish its functions from those of the body.*

Next I note that we are not aware of any subject which acts more immediately on our soul than the body to which it is joined, and that we must therefore consider that what is a passion in the soul is usually an action in the body, so that there is no better way of gaining knowledge of the passions than by examining the differences between the soul and the body, in order to know to which of the two we must attribute each one of the functions that are in us.

ARTICLE 3

❧ *What rule we must follow in so doing.*

We shall not find great difficulty in this if we bear in mind that everything we experience as being within us, and which we observe to be capable of occurring in wholly inanimate bodies, must be attributed to our body alone, whereas everything that is in us, and which we cannot in any way consider as capable of appertaining to a body, must be attributed to our soul.

ARTICLE 4

❧ *That the heat and movement of the members proceed from the body, while thoughts proceed from the soul.*

Thus, because we cannot conceive of the body as thinking in any way, we are right in assuming that all of the various kinds of thoughts within us belong to our soul; and because we do not doubt that there are inanimate bodies which can move in at least as many various ways as our own body, and which have at least as much heat (as experience shows us in the case of a flame, which has much more heat and movement than any of our members), we must believe that all the heat and movement that are in us, insofar as they do not depend on thought, belong only to our body.

ARTICLE 5

◆§ *That it is an error to believe that the soul gives the body its heat and movement.*

Reasoning thus, we shall avoid a serious error into which many have fallen, and which I consider to be the primary cause of the fact that hitherto no one has been able to give a satisfactory explanation of the passions and other matters pertaining to the soul. The error has consisted in concluding, from the observation that dead bodies are devoid of heat and consequently of movement, that it was the absence of the soul which caused the heat and movement to cease. Thus it has been wrongly believed that our natural heat and all the movements of our body depend on the soul, whereas what we ought to believe is that, when we die, our soul departs only because this heat ceases and the organs which serve to move the body fall into decay.

ARTICLE 6

◆§ *The difference between a living body and a dead body.*

In order, then, that we may avoid this error, let us consider that death never comes through any fault of the soul, but because one of the principal parts of the body has deteriorated; and let us further consider that the body of a living man differs as much from that of a dead man as a watch or other automaton (i.e., a machine that moves of itself), when it is wound up and contains the corporeal principle of the movements for which it is designed, together with everything else required for its action, differs from the same watch, or other machine, when it is broken and the principle of its movement has ceased to act.

ARTICLE 7

◆§ *A brief explanation of the parts of the body and some of its functions.*

To make this more intelligible, I shall now explain in a few words the entire manner in which the machine of our body is composed. There is no one who does not know that we have in us a heart, a brain, a stomach, muscles, nerves, arteries, veins and other such things. We also know that the food we eat descends into the stomach and the intestines, from which its juice flows into the liver and all the veins, mingling with the blood they contain and thereby increasing its quantity. Those who have heard even a little about the science of medicine know, furthermore, how the heart is made, and how all the blood in the veins can easily flow from the vena cava into its right side, and from there pass into the lungs through the vessel known as the pulmonary artery, then return from the lungs into the left side of the heart through the vessel known as the pulmonary vein, and finally pass into the aorta, whose branches spread to all parts of the body. And all those who have not been blinded by the authority of the ancients, and who have been willing to open their eyes to examine Harvey's opinions concerning the circulation of the blood, do not doubt that all the veins and arteries of the body are like conduits through which the blood flows constantly and swiftly, taking its course from the right cavity of the heart through the pulmonary artery, whose branches spread over the entire lungs and are joined to those of the pulmonary vein, through which it passes from the lung into the left side of the heart; then from there it goes into the aorta, whose branches, spread throughout the rest of the body, are connected with the branches of the vein which carries the same blood back to the right cavity of the heart; so that these two cavities are like sluices through each of which all the blood passes in the course of each circuit it makes in the body. We know, further, that all the movements of the members depend on the muscles, and that these muscles are so related to one another that when one of them contracts it draws toward it the part of the body to which it is attached, which causes the muscle opposed to it to extend itself at the same time; and if, at another time, this second muscle contracts, it causes the first one to extend itself, and draws back toward itself the part of the body to which they are attached. Finally, we know that all these movements of the muscles, as well as all the senses, depend on the nerves, which are like little filaments, or little tubes which all come from the brain, and like it, contain a certain very subtle air or wind which is called animal spirits.

ARTICLE 8

❧ *The principle of all these functions.*

But it is not generally known in what way these animal
spirits and these nerves contribute to movements and the
senses, or what is the corporeal principle which causes them to
act. Therefore, although I have already touched on this matter
in some of my other writings, I shall say here succinctly that,
as long as we are alive, there is a continuous heat in our heart
which is a kind of fire maintained there by the blood of the
veins, and that this fire is the corporeal principle of the
movements of all our members.

ARTICLE 9

❧ *How the movement of the heart takes place.*

Its first effect is to dilate the blood with which the cavities
of the heart are filled. This causes the blood, which needs to
occupy a great space, to pass quickly from the right cavity into
the pulmonary artery, and from the left cavity into the aorta;
then, when this dilation ceases, new blood immediately enters
from the vena cava into the right cavity of the heart, and
from the pulmonary vein into the left cavity; for there are
little membranes at the entrances of these four vessels,
arranged in such a way that blood can enter the heart only
through the latter two, and flow out only through the two
others. The new blood that enters the heart is immediately
rarefied in the same manner as the blood that preceded it,
and this is what causes the pulse, or beating of the heart and
arteries: this beating is repeated each time new blood enters
the heart. And it is this alone which gives the blood its
movement and causes it to flow continuously and swiftly in
all the arteries and veins, whereby it carries the heat it acquires
in the heart to all the other parts of the body, and supplies
them with nourishment.

ARTICLE 10

❧ *How the animal spirits are produced in the brain.*

But what is here more notable is that all the most animated and subtle parts of the blood, which have been rarefied by heat in the heart, constantly enter the cavities of the brain in large quantities. And the reason why they go there rather than elsewhere is that all the blood which issues from the heart through the aorta takes its course toward there in a straight line, and that, since all of it cannot enter, for there are only very narrow passages, only its most agitated and subtle parts pass through, while the rest spreads into all the other portions of the body. Now these very subtle parts of the blood are composed of animal spirits, and as such they have no need to undergo any other change within the brain, except that they are separated there from the less subtle parts of the blood; for what I here name spirits are nothing but bodies, and their only peculiarity is that they are very small and move very quickly, like the parts of the flame that rises from a torch. They never stop anywhere, and as some of them enter the cavities of the brain, others go out through the pores that are in its substance. These pores lead them into the nerves, and from there into the muscles, by means of which they move the body in all the different ways in which it can be moved.

ARTICLE 11

❧ *How the movements of the muscles take place.*

For the sole cause of the movements of the members is that certain muscles contract while those opposed to them are extended, as has already been said; and the sole cause of one muscle's contracting rather than the one opposed to it is that it receives a slightly larger amount of animal spirits from the brain. Not that the spirits which come immediately from the brain are sufficient in themselves to move these muscles, but they cause the other spirits that are already in the two muscles to pass quickly from one of them entirely into the other. Thus the muscle from which they leave becomes longer and looser, and the one into which they pass, being quickly swollen by them, contracts and pulls the member to which it is attached. This is easy to understand, provided we know that there are very few animal spirits which constantly flow from the brain to each muscle, but that there are always many others enclosed in the same muscle which move very rapidly, sometimes only turning in the place where they are, when they find no passage open to them through which they can come out, and sometimes flowing into the opposite muscle. Since there are little openings in each of these muscles through which the spirits can flow from one into the other, and which are arranged in such a way that when the spirits coming from the brain to one of them have a little more force than those coming to the other, they open all the entrances through which the spirits in the second muscle can pass into the first, and at the same time they close all the entrances through which the spirits in the first muscle can pass into the second. Thus all the spirits formerly contained in both muscles quickly collect in one of them, swelling and shortening it while the other becomes longer and looser.

ARTICLE 12

ও§ *How external objects act on the organs of the senses.*

We still have to understand the reasons why the spirits do not always flow from the brain into the muscles in the same manner, and why more of them sometimes flow into some muscles than into others. For, aside from the action of the soul, which is truly one of these causes within us, as I shall explain later, there are two other causes which depend only on the body, and they must now be pointed out. The first consists in the diversity of the movements which are induced in the organs of the senses by their objects, as I have already explained rather fully in my *Dioptrics*; but in order that those who read the present work may not need to have read others, I shall repeat here that there are three things to consider in the nerves: their marrow, or innner substance, which extends in the form of little filaments from the brain, where it originates, to the extremities of the other members to which these filaments are attached; then there are the membranes which surround them and which, being conterminous with those that envelop the brain, form little tubes in which these filaments are enclosed; and finally there are the animal spirits which, being carried by these same tubes from the brain to the muscles, are the cause of the fact that the filaments remain entirely free and extended within the tubes, so that the least thing that moves the part of the body to which the end of any one of them is attached also moves the part of the brain from which it comes, just as when one pulls one end of a rope the other is also made to move.

ARTICLE 13

～§ *That this action of external objects may lead the animal spirits into the muscles in various ways.*

And I have explained in my *Dioptrics* how all the objects of sight communicate themselves to us only because they move locally, through the agency of the transparent bodies that are between them and us, the little filaments of the optic nerves which are at the backs of our eyes, and then the parts of the brain from which these nerves proceed; they move them, I explained, in as many different ways as the diversities they cause us to see in things, and it is not immediately the movements that take place in the eye, but those that take place in the brain which represent these objects to the soul. On the basis of this example, it is easy to understand that sounds, odors, tastes, heat, pain, hunger, thirst and, in general, all objects, whether from our outer senses or our inner appetites, also induce some movement in our nerves, which conduct it to the brain. In addition to the fact that these diverse movements of the brain cause our soul to have diverse sensations, they can also, without the soul, cause the spirits to flow to certain muscles rather than others, thus moving our members, as I shall prove here by one example only. If someone abruptly thrusts his hand toward our eyes as though to strike us, even though we know that he is our friend, that he is doing it only in fun, and that he will take care not to hurt us, we nevertheless have difficulty in preventing ourselves from closing them. This shows that it is not by the intervention of our soul that they close, since it is against our will, which is its only action, or at least its principal one, but that it is because the machine of our body is so made that the movement of the hand toward our eyes induces another movement in our brain which leads the animal spirits into the muscles which cause the eyelids to close.

ARTICLE 14

❧ *That the diversity which exists among the animal spirits may also diversify their course.*

The other cause which serves to conduct the animal spirits differently into the muscles is the unequal agitation of these spirits and the diversity of their parts. For when some of their parts are larger and more agitated than the others, they go further forward in a straight line into the cavities and pores of the brain, and are thus conducted into other muscles than those they would enter if they had less force.

ARTICLE 15

❧ *The causes of their diversity.*

And this inequality may arise from the diverse matters of which they are composed, as we see in those who have drunk much wine: the vapors of the wine, quickly entering the blood, rise from the heart to the brain, where they are converted into animal spirits which, being stronger and more abundant than those usually present there, are capable of moving the body in various strange ways. This inequality of spirits may also arise from the diverse dispositions of the heart, liver, stomach, spleen and all other parts which contribute to their production; for we must here notice principally certain little nerves at the base of the heart which serve to widen and narrow the entrances of its cavities, by means of which the blood, dilating there in various degrees, produces spirits disposed in various ways. We must also notice that, although the blood which enters the heart comes from all the other parts of the body, it nevertheless often happens that it is driven there more forcibly from some parts than from others, because the nerves and muscles which are connected to those parts press or agitate it with greater force, and that, according to the parts from which it comes most, it dilates diversely in the heart and then produces spirits which have different qualities. Thus, for example, the blood which comes from the lower part of the liver, where the bile is, dilates differently in the heart from that which comes from the spleen, and this differently from that which comes from the veins of the arms or legs, and this quite differently from the juice of food when, having just left the stomach and intestines, it rapidly passes through the liver to the heart.

ARTICLE 16

❧ *How all the members may be moved by the objects of the senses and by the animal spirits without the aid of the soul.*

Finally, we must consider that the machine of our body is so made that all the changes that occur in the movements of the animal spirits can make them open some of the pores of the brain more than others, and, reciprocally, that when one of these pores is opened even slightly more or less than usual by the action of the nerves which serve the senses, it makes a change in the movement of the spirits and causes them to be conducted into the muscles which serve to move the body in the way it is usually moved when such an action occurs, so that all the movements we make to which our will does not contribute (as often happens when we breathe, walk, eat or perform any of the other acts we have in common with the beasts) depend only on the conformation of our members and the course which the animal spirits, excited by the heat of the heart, follow naturally in the brain, nerves and muscles, just as the movements of a watch are produced solely by the force of its springs and the shape of its wheels.

ARTICLE 17

❧ *The functions of the soul.*

Having thus considered all the functions which pertain to the body alone, it is easy to understand that there remains nothing in us that we must attribute to our soul except our thoughts, which are of two kinds: those which are the actions of the soul, and those which are its passions. I name all our volitions its actions, because we experience them as coming directly from our soul and seeming to depend on it alone; on the other hand, we can generally give the name of passions to all the different forms of perception or awareness that are in us, because often it is not our soul which makes them what they are, and because it always receives them from the things they represent.

ARTICLE 18

❧ *The will.*

Our volitions are likewise of two kinds: some of them are actions of the soul which terminate in the soul itself, as when we will to love God or, in general, apply our thought to some non-material object; the others are actions which terminate in our body, as when from the sole fact that we will to walk, it follows that our legs move and we walk.

ARTICLE 19

❧ *Perception.*

Our perceptions are also of two kinds: some have the soul as their cause, the others the body. Those which have the soul as their cause are the perceptions of our volitions and all the imaginations or other thoughts which depend on them; for it is certain that we cannot will anything without perceiving by the same means that we will it; and although with respect to the soul it is an action to will something, we can say that it is also a passion in it to be aware that it wills. However, since this perception and this volition are actually the same thing, and since it is always named from what is the more noble, it is customary to call it an action rather than a passion.

ARTICLE 20

❧ *The imaginations and other thoughts that are formed by the soul.*

When our soul applies itself to imagining something that does not exist, such as an enchanted palace or a chimera, and also when it applies itself to considering something that is solely intelligible and not imaginable, as, for example, when it considers its own nature, the perceptions it has of these things depend chiefly on the volition which causes it to perceive them; therefore they are usually regarded as actions rather than passions.

ARTICLE 21

The imaginations that have the body alone as their cause.

Most of the perceptions which are caused by the body depend on the nerves, but there are some which do not. These are called imaginations, like the ones I discussed above, yet they differ from them in that our will is not used in forming them. Therefore they cannot be counted among the actions of the soul. They arise from the fact that the animal spirits, being agitated in various ways and encountering traces of diverse impressions which have preceded them in the brain, fortuitously take their course there through some pores rather than others. Such are the illusions of our dreams and daydreams, when our thought wanders aimlessly without deliberately applying itself to anything. Some of these imaginations are passions of the soul, taking the term in its most proper and exact meaning, and they may all be so named if we take it in a more general meaning; however, since they do not have so notable and determinate a cause as the perceptions which the soul receives by means of the nerves, and seem to be only their shadows and pictures, before we can distinguish them properly we must consider the differences that divide these other perceptions.

ARTICLE 22

The differences among the other perceptions.

All the other perceptions which I have not yet explained come to the soul by means of the nerves, and among them there are these differences: we refer some of them to the external objects that strike our senses, others to our body or some of its parts, and still others to our soul.

ARTICLE 23

The perceptions which we refer to external objects.

Those which we refer to things that are outside of us, namely, to the objects of our senses, are caused, at least when our opinion is not false, by those objects which, in inducing

certain movements in the organs of our outer senses, also
induce movements in the brain by means of the nerves, which
cause the soul to sense them. Thus when we see the light of
a torch and hear the sound of a bell, this sound and this
light are two distinct actions which, by the sole fact that they
induce movements in some of our nerves, and thereby in the
brain, give the soul two different sensations, which we so refer
to the subjects we assume to be their causes that we believe
we see the torch itself and hear the bell, and not that we are
merely sensing the movements that come from them.

ARTICLE 24

ᴇ§ *The perceptions which we refer to our body.*

The perceptions which we refer to our body or some of
its parts are those we have of hunger, thirst and our other
natural appetites, to which may be added pain, heat and
other sensations which we experience as being in our members, and not as being in external objects. Thus we can feel
at the same time, and by means of the same nerves, the cold
of our hand and the heat of the flame when it approaches;
or, conversely, the heat of our hand and the cold of the air to
which it is exposed, without there being any difference
between the actions that cause us to feel the heat or the cold
in our hand and those which cause us to feel what is external
to us, except that when one of these actions follows the other,
we judge that the first is already in us, and that the second
is not yet in us, but in the object which causes it.

ARTICLE 25

ᴇ§ *The perceptions which we refer to our soul.*

The perceptions which we refer to the soul alone are
those whose effects we experience as being in the soul itself,
and to which we are usually unable to assign any proximate
cause. Such are the feelings of joy, anger, etc., which are
sometimes aroused in us by the objects that move our nerves,
and sometimes also by other causes. Although all our perceptions, those we refer to external objects as well as those we
refer to the various sensations of our body, are truly passions

with regard to our soul when we take the word in its most general meaning, it is customary to restrict it to mean only those which are related to the soul itself, and it is these alone which I have undertaken to explain here under the name of passions of the soul.

ARTICLE 26

That the imaginations which depend only on the fortuitous movement of the animal spirits may be passions as truly as the perceptions which depend on the nerves.

It remains for us to note here that the same things which the soul perceives by means of the nerves may also be represented by the fortuitous course of the animal spirits without there being any difference other than that the impressions which come into the brain by way of the nerves are usually more vivid and distinct than those induced there by the spirits, which is what led me to say in Article 21 that the second are only, so to speak, the shadows and pictures of the first. We must also note that it sometimes happens that the picture is so similar to the thing it represents that we may be deceived with regard to perceptions which refer to external objects, or those which refer to certain parts of the body, but we cannot be deceived in the same way with regard to the passions, since they are so close and so interior to the soul that it is impossible for it to feel them other than they truly are. Thus often when we are asleep, and sometimes even when we are awake, we imagine certain things so vividly that we think we see them before us or feel them in our body, even though they are actually not there at all; but even though we are asleep and dreaming, we cannot feel sad or be moved by any other passion unless the soul truly has that passion within itself.

ARTICLE 27

Definition of the passions of the soul.

Having considered how the passions of the soul differ from all its other thoughts, it seems to me that we may generally define them as those perceptions, sensations or emotions of the soul which we refer specifically to it, and which are caused, maintained and fortified by some movement of the animal spirits.

ARTICLE 28

৯৪ *Explanation of the first part of this definition.*

We may call them perceptions when this word is used generally to signify all thoughts which are not actions of the soul or volitions, but not when it is used only to signify clear cognitions, for experience shows that those who are most agitated by their passions are not those who know them best, and that the passions are to be counted among the perceptions made confused and obscure by the close alliance between the soul and the body. They may also be called sensations, because they are received into the soul in the same fashion as the objects of the external senses, and are not otherwise known by it. But they may still better be called the emotions* of the soul, not only because this name can be given to all changes that take place in it, that is, to all the various thoughts that come to it, but particularly because, of all the different kinds of thoughts that the soul can have, there are no others which stir and shake it so powerfully as do these passions.

ARTICLE 29

৯৪ *Explanation of its other part.*

I add that they are specifically referred to the soul, in order to distinguish them from sensations such as odors, sounds and colors, which are referred to external objects, and others, such as hunger, thirst and pain, which are referred to the body. I also add that they are caused, maintained and fortified by some movement of the animal spirits, in order to distinguish them from our volitions, which may be called emotions of the soul which are referred to it, but which are caused by it, and also in order to explain their nearest and most immediate cause, which again distinguishes them from all other feelings.

* The French word *"émotion"* is stronger than the English "emotion": it has more definite connotations of excitement or agitation.—L.B.

ARTICLE 30

ॐ *That the soul is united to all parts of
the body conjointly.*

But in order to understand these things more thoroughly,
we must know that the soul is truly joined to the entire body,
and that we cannot properly say that it is in one of its parts
to the exclusion of the others, because the body is one and,
in a sense, indivisible, owing to the disposition of its organs,
which are so interrelated that when any one of them is
removed the whole body becomes defective, and because the
soul is of such a nature that it has no relation to extension,
dimensions, or other properties of the matter of which the
body is composed, but only to the whole assemblage of its
organs, as is obvious when we consider that we cannot conceive of half or a third of a soul, or imagine how much space
it might occupy, and that the soul does not become smaller
when part of the body is cut off, but that it departs from the
body entirely when the assemblage of the bodily organs dis-
integrates.

ARTICLE 31

ॐ *That there is a small gland in the brain in which the
soul exercises its functions more specifically than in the
other parts of the body.*

We must also know that, although the soul is joined to
the entire body, there is nevertheless one part of the body in
which it exercises its functions more specifically than in any
of the others. It is generally believed that this part is the
brain, or perhaps the heart: the brain because it is related to
the organs of the senses, the heart because we feel our passions as though they were within it. But in carefully examining the matter, it seems to me that I have clearly ascertained
that the part of the body in which the soul directly exercises
its functions is neither the heart nor the brain as a whole,
but is only the innermost part of the brain, which is a certain
very small gland, situated in the middle of its substance, and
so suspended over the passage through which the animal
spirits of the anterior cavities communicate with those of the

posterior that the slightest movement on its part can do a great deal to alter the course of these spirits, and, reciprocally, that the slightest change in the course of the spirits can do a great deal to alter the movements of this gland.

ARTICLE 32

❧ *How we know that this gland is the main seat of the soul.*

The reason which convinces me that this gland is the only part of the body in which the soul can exercise its functions directly is that I observe all the other parts of the brain to be double, just as we also have two eyes, two hands, two ears: in short, all the organs of our external senses are double; and that since we have only one single and simple thought of any one thing at any one time, there must necessarily be some place where the two images that come from the two eyes, and where the two impressions that come from a single object by way of the double organs of the other senses, can unite before they reach the soul, so that they will not present two objects to it instead of one. We can easily conceive of these images or other impressions uniting in this gland by means of the spirits which fill the cavities of the brain, and there is no other place in the body where they could unite before doing so in this gland.

ARTICLE 33

❧ *That the seat of the passions is not in the heart.*

As for the opinion of those who think that the soul receives its passions in the heart, it scarcely deserves consideration, for it is based only on the fact that the passions makes us feel certain changes there. It is easy to see that these changes are felt as taking place in the heart only through the mediation of a small nerve which descends to it from the brain, just as pain is felt as being in the foot through the mediation of the nerves of the foot, and the stars are seen as being in the sky through the mediation of their light and the optic nerves. Thus it is no more necessary for our soul to exercise its functions directly in the heart than it is necessary for it to be in the sky in order to see the stars there.

ARTICLE 34

❧ *How the soul and the body act on each other.*

Let us then consider here that the soul has its main seat in the small gland which is in the middle of the brain, from where it radiates throughout the rest of the body by means of the animal spirits, the nerves, and even the blood, which, participating in the impressions of the spirits, can carry them through the arteries to all the members. Let us recall what has been said above about the machine of our body, namely, that the little filaments of our nerves are so distributed in all its parts that, when various movements are induced in them by perceptible objects, they open the pores of the brain in various ways, thus enabling them to move the members in all the different ways in which they are capable of being moved, and also that all the other causes which can diversely move the spirits suffice to conduct them into diverse muscles. And let us add here that the little gland which is the main seat of the soul is so suspended between the cavities which contain these spirits that it can be moved by them in as many different ways as there are perceptible diversities in objects, but that it may also be moved in different ways by the soul, which is of such a nature that it receives as many diverse impressions within itself, that is, it has as many diverse perceptions, as there are diverse movements in this gland. And, reciprocally, the machine of the body is so made that, by the sole fact that this gland is diversely moved by the soul or by any other cause, it pushes the animal spirits which surround it into the pores of the brain, which conduct them through the nerves into the muscles, by means of which it causes them to move the members.

ARTICLE 35

❧ *An example of the way in which impressions from objects unite in the gland that is in the middle of the brain.*

Thus, for example, if we see an animal coming toward us, the light reflected from its body forms two images of it, one in each of our eyes, and, by means of the optic nerve, these two images form two others on the inner surface of the

brain which faces its cavities. Then, from there, by means of
the spirits with which its cavities are filled, these images
radiate in such a way toward the little gland which these
spirits surround that the movement which constitutes each
point of one of the images goes to the same point of the
gland as does the movement constituting that point of the
other image which represents the same part of the animal;
and so the two images in the brain form only one image on
the gland, which, acting immediately on the soul, causes it
to see the shape of the animal.

ARTICLE 36

&ഽ *An example of the way in which the passions are aroused
in the soul.*

Furthermore, if this shape is very appalling and fright-
ful, that is, if it is closely related to things which have previously been hurtful to the body, it arouses in the soul the
passion of apprehension, and then either courage or fear and
consternation, depending on the particular temperament of
the body, and according to whether it has been by self-defense
or by flight that one has previously protected oneself from the
hurtful things to which the present impression is related. For,
in some men, past reactions of flight have predisposed the
brain in such a way that the spirits reflected from the image
thus formed on the gland go partly to the nerves which serve
to turn the back and move the legs to take flight, and partly
to those which so widen or narrow the orifices of the heart,
or agitate the other parts from which blood is sent to it, that
the blood, being rarefied there in an unusual manner, sends
spirits to the brain which are capable of maintaining and
strengthening the passion of fear, that is, which are capable
of holding open or reopening the pores of the brain which
lead them to those same nerves. By the sole fact that these
spirits enter these pores, they arouse a particular movement
in this gland, a movement which is instituted by nature in
order to make the soul feel this passion; and since these pores
are primarily related to the little nerves which serve to widen
or narrow the orifices of the heart, the soul feels the passion
mainly in the heart.

ARTICLE 37

How it appears that the passions are all caused by some movement of the animal spirits.

The same is true of all the other passions, that is, they are principally caused by the animal spirits contained in the cavities of the brain, inasmuch as they flow toward the nerves which serve to widen or narrow the orifices of the heart, or to push toward it, in various ways, the blood that is in the other parts, or to maintain the same passion in some other manner. From this it can be clearly understood why, in my definition of the passions, I have stated that they are caused by some particular movement of the animal spirits.

ARTICLE 38

An example of the movements of the body which accompany the passions and do not depend on the soul.

Moreover, just as the course which these spirits take toward the nerves of the heart suffices to give the gland the movement through which fear is put into the soul, so, too, the simultaneous flowing of certain spirits to the nerves which serve to move the legs for flight causes in the same gland another movement by means of which the soul feels and perceives this flight, which may thus be aroused in the body solely by the disposition of the organs, with no contribution from the soul.

ARTICLE 39

How the same cause may arouse different passions in different men.

The same impression which the presence of a frightening object makes on the gland, and which causes fear in some men, may in other men arouse courage and resolution. The reason for this is that all brains are not disposed in the same way, and that the same movement of the gland, which in some men arouses fear, in others causes the animal spirits to enter the pores of the brain which lead them partly into the nerves which serve to move the hands for self-defense, and partly into those which agitate and drive the blood toward the heart in the manner required to produce the right spirits for continuing this self-defense and maintaining the will to do so.

ARTICLE 40

**๛ *The principal effect of the passions.* **

For we must note that the principal effect of all the passions in man is to incite and dispose the soul to will the things for which they are preparing the body. Thus the feeling of fear arouses a will to flee, that of boldness the will to fight, and so on with the others.

ARTICLE 41

**๛ *The power of the soul with regard to the body.* **

But the will is by nature so free that it can never be constrained; and of the two kinds of thoughts which I have distinguished in the soul—those which are its actions, i.e., its volitions, and those which are its passions, taking this word in its most general meaning, which includes all kinds of perceptions—the former are absolutely in its power and can be changed only indirectly by the body, while the latter are absolutely dependent on the actions that produce them, and can be changed only indirectly by the soul, except when it is itself their cause. And all the action of the soul consists in this, that merely by willing something it causes the little gland with which it is closely connected to move in the manner required to produce the effect appropriate to that volition.

ARTICLE 42

**๛ *How we find in our memory the things we wish to remember.* **

Thus when the soul wills to remember something, this volition causes the gland, leaning successively in various directions, to drive the animal spirits to various parts of the

brain, until they come to the part where the object we wish
to remember has left its traces. These traces consist in the
fact that the pores of the brain through which the animal
spirits have previously flowed because of the presence of that
object have thereby acquired a greater facility than the others
for being opened again in the same way by the spirits that
come to them. And so, when they reach these pores, the
spirits pass through them more easily than through the
others, and they then induce in the gland a particular movement which represents the same object to the soul and makes
it know that this is the object it has willed to remember.

ARTICLE 43

◄§ *How the soul can imagine, be attentive, and move the
body.*

When we wish to imagine something we have never
seen, this volition has the power to make the gland move in
the way required in order to drive the animal spirits to the
pores of the brain by means of whose openings the thing can
be represented. And when we wish to hold our attention on
one object for a certain time, this volition keeps the gland
leaning in the same direction during that time. And finally,
when we wish to walk or move our body in some other way,
this volition causes the gland to drive the animal spirits into
the muscles which serve that purpose.

ARTICLE 44

◄§ *That each volition is naturally connected with some
movement of the gland, but that by effort or habit it
can be connected with others.*

However, it is not always the will to induce some movement or other effect within us that enables us to induce it;
this varies with the way in which nature or habit has joined
each movement of the gland with each thought. Thus, for
example, if we wish to adjust our eyes to look at a very distant
object, this volition causes their pupils to dilate, and if we
wish to adjust them to look at a very near object, this volition
causes their pupils to contract; but if we think only of di-

lating our pupils, our volition fails to dilate them, for it is
not with the volition to dilate or contract that nature has
connected the movement of the gland which serves to dilate
or contract the pupils, but rather with the volition to look
at distant or near objects. And when, in speaking, we think
only of the meaning of what we wish to say, this makes us
move our tongue and lips much more quickly and much
better than if we thought of moving them in all the ways
required in order to say those same words, for the habits we
have acquired in learning to speak have caused us to connect
the action of the soul which, by means of the gland, can
move the tongue and lips, with the meaning of the words
that follow from these movements, rather than with the
movements themselves.

ARTICLE 45

❦ *The power of the soul with regard to its passions.*

Similarly, our passions cannot be aroused or suppressed
directly by the action of our will, but only indirectly through
the representation of the things that are usually connected
with the passions we wish to have, or are contrary to the
passions we wish to suppress. Thus, in order to arouse courage
and suppress fear within ourselves, it is not enough to have
a will to do so: we must deliberately consider reasons, objects
or examples which convince us that the danger is not great,
that there is always more safely in self-defense than in flight,
that we shall have the glory and joy of having conquered,
whereas we can expect nothing but regret and shame from
having run away, and so on.

ARTICLE 46

❦ *What prevents the soul from having complete control
of its passions.*

There is one particular reason why the soul cannot
readily change or arrest its passions, and it was this reason
which led me, in defining them, to state that they are not
only caused, but also maintained and strengthened by some
particular movement of the animal spirits. The reason to

which I am referring is that they are nearly all accompanied by a certain agitation that takes place in the heart, and therefore also in all the blood and animal spirits, so that, until this agitation has ceased, they remain present to our thought in the same way as sensible objects are present to it while they are acting on the organs of our senses. And just as the soul, in making itself very attentive to something else, can prevent itself from hearing a slight sound or feeling a small pain, but cannot in the same way prevent itself from hearing thunder or feeling fire burning the hand, so it can easily overcome the lesser passions, but not the stronger and more violent ones, except after the agitation of the blood and the animal spirits has subsided. The most the will can do while this agitation is in full force is not to consent to its effects, and to restrain some of the movements to which it disposes the body. For example, if anger makes us raise our hand to strike, our will can usually hold it back; if fear incites us to run away, our will can stop us, and so on with the other passions.

ARTICLE 47

In what consist the conflicts we are wont to imagine between the lower and higher parts of the soul.

All the conflicts we are wont to imagine between the lower part of the soul, which we call sensuous, and the higher part, which is rational, or between the natural appetites and the will, consist only in the repugnance there is between the movements which the body, by its animal spirits, and the soul, by its will, tend to induce in the gland at the same time. For there is in us but one soul, and that soul has no diversity of parts: it is both sensuous and rational, and all its appetites are volitions. The error that has been committed in making it play diverse roles which are usually contrary to one another lies in the failure to distinguish its functions from those of the body, to which alone we must attribute everything that can be observed in us as repugnant to our reason. There is, therefore, no conflict here except that which arises from the fact that, since the little gland in the middle of the brain can be pushed in one direction by the soul and in another direction by the animal spirits, which are only bodies, as I have said, it often happens that these two propulsions are opposed to each other, and that the stronges prevents the weaker from taking effect. Now we can distinguish two kinds of movements induced in the gland by the animal spirits: some of them represent to the soul the objects that move the senses, or the impressions that are encountered in the brain and exert no force on the will, while others do exert force on the will, namely, those which cause the passions or the movements of the body that accompany them. Although the former often hinder the actions of the soul or are hindered by them, they are not directly opposed to them, and we notice no conflicts between them. We notice conflicts only between the latter kind of movements and the volitions that are repugnant to them: for example, between the force which the spirits exert on the gland to arouse a desire for something in the soul and the force which the soul exerts on the gland in the opposite direction by its will to shun that same thing. And what makes this conflict apparent is, chiefly, that the will, not having the power to arouse the passions directly, as has already been said, is forced to use ingenuity and successively consider various things, one of which may have the power to change the course of the animal spirits for a moment, while the one that follows may not have that power, so that the spirits immediately resume their original course, since the previous disposition in the nerves, heart and blood has not changed. The soul therefore feels impelled to desire and not to desire the same thing at almost the same time, and this is what has given rise to the idea that it has two conflicting powers within itself. However, we may still recognize a certain conflict, in that often the same cause which arouses a passion in the soul also arouses certain movements in the body to which the soul does not contribute, and which it stops or tries to stop as soon as it becomes aware of them, as we experience when what arouses fear also causes the spirits to enter the muscles that serve to move the legs for flight, while at the same time the legs are held in check by the will to be brave.

ARTICLE 48

How we can recognize the strength or weakness of souls, and what is the evil in those that are weakest.

It is by the outcome of these conflicts that everyone can ascertain the strength or weakness of his soul. Those whose will is by nature most easily able to overcome the passions

nd arrest the movements of the body that accompany them
ave, no doubt, the strongest souls. But there are some who
nnot test their strength, because they never make their
ul fight with its own weapons, but only with those supplied
it by some passions in order to resist others. What I call
its own weapons are firm, definite judgments concerning good
and evil, in accordance with which it has resolved to conduct
the actions of its life; and the weakest souls are those whose
will does not thus determine itself to follow certain judgments, but constantly lets itself be carried away by present
passions which, often being contrary to one another, draw it
first in one direction, then in another, and, making it fight
against itself, reduce the soul to the most deplorable state
possible. Thus, when fear represents death as an extreme
evil which can be avoided only by flight, ambition may at
the same time represent this flight as an evil worse than
death. These two passions agitate the will in different ways;
obeying each in turn, it is constantly opposed to itself, and
so makes the soul enslaved and unhappy.

ARTICLE 49

*That the strength of the soul is insufficient without
knowledge of the truth.*

It is true that there are very few men so weak and
irresolute that they want only what their passions dictate to
them. Most men have definite judgments in accordance with
which they regulate part of their actions. These judgments
are often false, or even based on passions by which the will
has previously let itself be overcome or seduced, and yet,
because the will continues to follow them when the passion
that caused them is absent, they can be regarded as its own
weapons, and we may consider that souls are stronger or
weaker according to their ability to follow these judgments
and resist present passions which are contrary to them. There
is, however, a great difference between resolutions which
proceed from some false opinion and those which rest only
on knowledge of the truth, so much so that if we follow the
latter we are assured that we shall never have to regret it or
repent of it, whereas we always have to do so if we follow
the former, when we discover our error.

ARTICLE 50

That there is no soul so weak that it cannot, if well directed, acquire absolute power over its passions.

And it is useful to know here that, as has already been said above, although each movement of the gland seems to have been connected by nature with each one of our thoughts since the beginning of our life, we can nevertheless connect them with others through habit, as experience shows in the case of words: they induce movements in the gland which, as instituted by nature, represents to the soul only their sound when they are spoken, or the shape of their letters when they are written, and yet, through the habit we have acquired in thinking of their meaning when we hear their sound or see their letters, they usually make us aware of that meaning rather than of the shape of their letters or the sound of their syllables. It is also useful to know that although the movements, whether of the gland, the animal spirits or the brain, which represent certain objects to the soul, are naturally connected with those which arouse certain passions in it, they can nonetheless, by habit, be separated from them and be connected with other and very different ones, and that this habit can be acquired by a single action, without long usage. Thus, when we unexpectedly find something very dirty in food which we are eating with relish, the shock of finding it may so change the disposition of our brain that we can never again see such food without abhorrence, whereas we previously ate it with pleasure. And the same thing can be observed in animals, for although they have no reason, and perhaps no thought of any kind, all the movements of the spirits and the gland which arouse the passions in us are also in them, and serve to maintain and strengthen, not the passions, as in us, but the movements of the nerves and muscles which usually accompany them. Thus, when a dog sees a partridge, he is naturally disposed to run toward it; and when he hears a gun fired, the sound naturally incites him to flee. Nevertheless, setters are usually so trained that the sight of a partridge makes them stop, and that the sound they hear later, when the partridge is shot, makes them run toward it. Now these things are useful to know in order to give us the determination to practice controlling our passions, for since it is possible, with a little skill, to change the movements of the brain in animals devoid of reason, it is obvious that it can be done even better in men, and that even those who have the weakest souls can acquire absolute sway over all their passions if they use enough skill in training and guiding them.

PART TWO

OF THE NUMBER AND ORDER OF THE PASSIONS, AND AN EXPLANATION OF THE SIX PRIMARY PASSIONS

ARTICLE 51

The first causes of the passions.

We know from what has been said above that the nearest and most immediate cause of the passions of the soul is none other than the agitation with which the animal spirits move the little gland in the middle of the brain. But that is not enough to enable us to distinguish them from one another; we need to investigate their sources and examine their first causes. Although they can sometimes be caused by the action of the soul when it resolves to conceive this or that object, and also solely by the temperament of the body, or by the impressions that are fortuitously encountered in the brain, as happens when we feel sad or happy without being able to say why, it nevertheless appears from what has been said that all these same passions can also be aroused by the objects that move the senses, and that these objects are their principal and most common cause; hence it follows that in order to find them all, it is sufficient to consider all the effects of these objects.

ARTICLE 52

Their function, and how they can be enumerated.

I note, furthermore, that the objects which move the senses do not arouse diverse passions in us because of the diversities that are in them, but only because of the diverse ways in which they can harm or benefit us, or, in general, be important, and that the function of all the passions consists solely in the fact that they dispose the soul to will the things which nature tells us are useful to us, and to persist in so willing. Also, the same agitation of the animal spirits which usually causes them disposes the body to the movements useful in carrying out these things. Therefore, to enumerate them it is necessary only to make an orderly examination of the various important (to us) ways in which our senses can be moved by their objects; and I shall here make an enumeration of all the principal passions according to the order in which they may thus be found.

THE ORDER AND ENUMERATION OF THE PASSIONS

ARTICLE 53

Wonder.

When our first encounter with an object surprises us and we judge it to be new, or very different from what we have previously known or from what we supposed it ought to be, this causes us to wonder and be astonished. Since this can happen before we have any idea of whether the object is beneficial to us or not, it seems to me that wonder is the first of all the passions. And it has no opposite, for if the object that presents itself has nothing in it which surprises us, we are not moved by it at all, and we consider it without passion.

ARTICLE 54

Esteem or contempt, magnanimity or pride, and humility or baseness.

To wonder is joined esteem or contempt, according to whether it is the greatness or the smallness of an object that arouses our wonder. And we may thus esteem or despise ourselves, hence the passions, and then the habits, of magnanimity or pride, and of humility or baseness.

ARTICLE 55

❧ *Veneration and scorn.*

But when we esteem or despise other objects which we consider as free causes capable of doing good or evil, from esteem comes veneration, and, from ordinary contempt, scorn.

ARTICLE 56

❧ *Love and hatred.*

All the preceding passions can be aroused in us without our perceiving whether the object that causes them is good or bad. But when something is presented to us as being good with regard to us, that is, as being beneficial to us, this makes us have love for it; and when it is represented as bad or harmful, this arouses hatred in us.

ARTICLE 57

❧ *Desire.*

All the other passions arise from the same consideration of good or evil; but in order to place them in order I make distinctions with regard to time, and, considering that the passions incline us to look to the future much more than to the present or the past, I begin with desire. For not only when we desire to acquire a good which we do not yet have, or to avoid an evil which we judge to be capable of occurring, but also when we merely wish to preserve a good or the absence of an evil, which is as far as this passion can extend, it is obvious that it always looks to the future.

ARTICLE 58

❧ *Hope, apprehension, jealousy, confidence, and despair.*

It is sufficient to think that the acquisition of a good or the avoidance of an evil is possible in order to be incited to desire it. But when we go on to consider whether it is likely or unlikely that we shall obtain what we desire, that which indicates to us that it is likely arouses hope in us, and that which indicates that it is unlikely arouses apprehension, of which jealousy is a species. When hope is extreme, it changes its nature and is called confidence or assurance, just as, on the other hand, extreme apprehension becomes despair.

ARTICLE 59

❧ *Irresolution, courage, daring, emulation, cowardice, and terror.*

And we can be hopeful and apprehensive even though the outcome of what we are awaiting does not depend on us in any way; but when it is represented to us as depending on us, there may be difficulty in the choice of means, or in carrying them into action. From the first comes irresolution, which disposes us to deliberate and take counsel. To the latter is opposed courage or daring, of which emulation is a species. And cowardice is contrary to courage, as fear or terror is contrary to daring.

ARTICLE 60

❧ *Remorse.*

And if we are moved to take action before irresolution has been dispelled, this gives rise to remorse, which, unlike the preceding passions, does not look to the future, but to the present or the past.

ARTICLE 61

❧ *Joy and sadness.*

And the consideration of a present good arouses joy in us, that of an evil, sadness, when it is a good or an evil which is represented to us as pertaining to us.

ARTICLE 62

❧ *Mockery, envy, pity.*

But when it is represented to us as pertaining to other men, we may regard them as worthy or unworthy of it; and when we regard them as worthy of it, this arouses in us no other passion than joy, inasmuch as it gives us some satisfaction to see things happening as they should. There is only this difference, that joy which comes from a good is serious, while that which comes from an evil is accompanied by laughter and mockery. But if we regard them as unworthy, the good arouses envy and the evil arouses pity, which are two species of sadness. And it should be noted that the same passions which are related to present goods or evils may often also be related to those which are yet to come, insofar as the opinion that they will come represents them as already present.

ARTICLE 63

❧ *Self-satisfaction and repentance.*

We may also consider the cause of the good or the evil, whether past or present. Good which has been done by ourselves gives us an inner satisfaction which is the sweetest of all the passions, while evil arouses repentance, which is the bitterest.

ARTICLE 64

❧ *Favor and gratitude.*

But good which has been done by others causes us to regard them with favor, even though it is not to us that it has been done; and if it is to us, we join gratitude to favor.

ARTICLE 65

❧ *Indignation and anger.*

Similarly, evil which is done by others, but which does not affect us, causes us to feel only indignation; and when it does affect us, it also arouses anger.

ARTICLE 66

◄§ *Vainglory and shame.*

Furthermore, good which is or has been in us, being referred to the opinion that others may have of it, arouses vainglory in us, and evil arouses shame.

ARTICLE 67

◄§ *Disgust, nostalgia, and gladness.*

And sometimes the duration of a good causes boredom or disgust, while the duration of an evil diminishes the sadness that goes with it. Finally, from a good that has passed comes nostalgia, which is a species of sadness, and from an evil that has passed comes gladness, which is a species of joy.

ARTICLE 68

◄§ *Why this enumeration of the passions is different from that which is commonly accepted.*

Such is the order that seems to me the best one in which to enumerate the passions. In this I know well that I am departing from the opinion of all those who have previously written on the subject, but it is not without serious reason that I do so. For they derive their enumeration from the fact that they distinguish in the sensuous part of the soul two appetites which they name *concupiscent* and *irascible*. And because I recognize no distinction of parts in the soul, as I have said above, this seems to me to mean nothing but that it has two faculties, one of desire and one of anger; and since it has in the same way the faculties of wondering, loving, hoping and fearing, and thus of receiving all the other passions within itself, or of bringing about the actions to which these passions drive it, I do not see why they have all been referred to concupiscence or anger. Furthermore, such an enumeration does not comprehend all the principal passions, as I believe this one does. I am speaking only of the principal ones, for it is possible to distinguish other more particular ones, and their number is indefinite.

ARTICLE 69

⮂ *That there are only six primary passions.*

But the number of those which are simple and primary is not very great. For, in looking over all those which I have enumerated, we can easily see that there are only six which are such, namely, wonder, love, hatred, desire, joy, and sadness, and that all the others are either composed of some of these six, or are species of them. Therefore, in order that their multiplicity may not perplex the reader, I shall here treat each of the six primary passions separately, and later I shall show how all the others originate from them.

ARTICLE 70

⮂ *Wonder: its definition and cause.*

Wonder is a sudden surprise of the soul which inclines it to consider attentively those objects which seem to it rare and extraordinary. Thus it is caused first by an impression in the brain which represents the object as unusual and therefore worthy of attentive consideration, then by the movement of the animal spirits, which are made by this impression to flow with great force to the part of the brain where it is located, in order to strengthen and maintain it there; and it also makes them pass from there into the muscles which serve to hold the organs of the senses in the same situation, so that it will still be maintained by them, if it is by them that it has been formed.

ARTICLE 71

⮂ *That in this passion no change occurs in the heart or the blood.*

One particular characteristic of this passion is that, unlike the other passions, it is not observed to be accompanied by any change in the heart or the blood. The reason for this is that, not having good or evil as its object, but only knowledge of the thing that arouses wonder, it has no connection with the heart and the blood, on which all the good of the body depends, but only with the brain, which contains the organs of the senses which serve in acquiring this knowledge.

ARTICLE 72

In what the strength of wonder consists.

This does not prevent its having great strength because of surprise, that is, the sudden and unexpected occurrence of the impression which changes the movement of the animal spirits. Surprise is proper and peculiar to this passion, so that when it is found in other passions—and it is found in nearly all of them as an element which augments them—it means that wonder is joined to them. And its strength depends on two things: novelty, and the fact that the movement it causes has its full strength from the beginning. For it is certain that such a movement has more effect than those which, being weak at first and growing only little by little, can easily be turned aside. It is certain also that objects of the senses which are new touch the brain in parts not accustomed to being touched, and that since these parts are more tender or less firm than those which have been hardened by frequent agitation, the effect of the movements they induce is thereby increased. We shall not find this difficult to believe if we consider that, similarly, the soles of our feet are accustomed to a rather harsh contact by the weight of the body they support, so that we feel it very little when we walk, whereas if someone tickles them, we find this much softer and gentler contact almost unbearable, because it is unusual to us.

ARTICLE 73

What astonishment is.

And this surprise has so much power to cause the animal spirits which are in the cavities of the brain to flow to the place where the impression of the object of our wonder is located, that sometimes it drives them all there and causes them to be so thoroughly occupied in maintaining this impression that there are none which pass from there into the muscles or even depart in any way from the paths they have been following in the brain. This causes the whole body to remain as motionless as a statue, limits us to perceiving only the first facet of the object that has presented itself to us, and consequently prevents us from acquiring more particular knowledge of it. This is what is commonly called being astonished, and astonishment is an excess of wonder which can never be anything but bad.

ARTICLE 74

❦ How the passions can be useful or harmful.

From what has been said above, it is easy to understand that the usefulness of all the passions consists in their strengthening and prolonging in the soul thoughts which are good for it to conserve, and which might otherwise be effaced from it. And all the harm they can do consists in their strengthening and conserving these thoughts more than is necessary, or in strengthening and conserving others on which it is not good to dwell.

ARTICLE 75

❦ The particular usefulness of wonder.

And we may particularly say of wonder that it is useful in that it causes us to apprehend and remember things of which we were previously ignorant, for we wonder only at what appears rare and extraordinary to us, and nothing can appear to us as such unless we have previously not known it, or unless it is also different from the things we have already known, for it is this difference which makes us call it extraordinary. Now even though something which was unknown to us presents itself to our understanding or our senses, we cannot retain it in our memory unless our idea of it is strengthened in our brain by some passion, or by an effort of our understanding when our will has disposed it to special attention and reflection. The other passions may serve to make us take note of things which appear to be good or bad, but we have only wonder to make us take note of things which appear only to be rare. Hence we see that those who have no natural inclination to this passion are usually very ignorant.

ARTICLE 76

&ﬁ *How it can be harmful, and how we can make up for
its deficiency and correct its excess.*

But it happens much more frequently that we wonder
too much, and that we are astonished on perceiving things
which deserve little or no attention, than that we wonder too
little. And this may entirely prevent or pervert the use of
reason. Therefore, even though it is good to have been born
with some inclination to this passion, since it is what disposes
us to the acquisition of the sciences, we must nevertheless
try afterward to free ourselves from it as much as possible.
For it is easy to make up for a deficiency of it by special
reflection and attention, to which our will can always con-
strain our understanding when we judge that the object
which presents itself to be worth the effort; but the only
remedy for excessive wonder is to acquire knowledge of many
things and train ourselves to consider those which seem to
be the rarest and strangest.

ARTICLE 77

&ﬁ *That it is neither the most stupid nor the most intelligent
who are most strongly inclined to wonder.*

Moreover, although only those who are dull and stupid
are by their nature not disposed to wonder, this does not
mean that those who are most intelligent are always those
who are most strongly inclined to it, for it is chiefly those
who, though well endowed with common sense, do not have
too high an opinion of their own abilities.

ARTICLE 78

&ﬁ *That excessive wonder may become a habit if we fail
to correct it.*

This passion seems to diminish with use, since the more
unusual things we find to wonder at, the more we become
accustomed to ceasing to wonder at them and thinking that

all those which we later encounter are commonplace; and yet, when it is excessive and causes us to fix our attention only on the first image of the objects that present themselves to us, without acquiring any further knowledge of them, it gives rise to a habit which disposes the soul to dwell in the same way on all the other objects that present themselves, as long as they appear to be even slightly new. And this is what sustains the malady of those who are blindly curious, that is, those who seek out rarities only to wonder at them, and not in order to acquire knowledge of them; for they gradually become so susceptible to wonder that things of no importance are no less capable of arresting their attention than those which it would be more useful to examine.

ARTICLE 79

∞§ Definition of love and hatred.

Love is an emotion of the soul, caused by the movement of the animal spirits, which incites it to will to join itself to objects which appear to be beneficial to it. And hatred is an emotion caused by the spirits which incites the soul to will to be separated from objects which are presented to it as harmful. I say that these emotions are caused by the spirits in order to distinguish love and hatred, which are passions and depend on the body, both from the judgments which also incline the soul to will to join itself to things it regards as good and to separate itself from those it regards as bad, and from the emotions aroused in the soul by these judgments alone.

ARTICLE 80

∞§ What it means to will to join oneself or separate oneself.

By the word "will," I do not here intend to speak of desire, which is a passion apart and relates to the future, but of the consent by which we consider ourselves as henceforth joined to what we love, so that we imagine a whole with ourselves as one part and what we love as another. In hatred, on the other hand, we consider ourselves as alone, and as entirely separated from that for which we feel aversion.

ARTICLE 81

⋙ *The distinction that is usually made between concupiscent and benevolent love.*

Two kinds of love are usually distinguished: one is called
benevolent love, i.e., that which incites us to wish well to the
object of our love, and the other is called concupiscent love,
i.e., that which makes us desire the object of our love. But it
seems to me that this distinction concerns only the effects of
love, and not its essence, for as soon as we have willed to
join ourselves to some object, no matter what its nature, we
have for it a feeling of benevolence, i.e., we also will to join
to it the things we believe to be beneficial to it, which is one
of the principal effects of love. And if we judge that it is
good to possess it or to be associated with it in some way
other than through the will, we desire it, which is also one
of the commonest effects of love.

ARTICLE 82

⋙ *How extremely different passions are in accord with one
another, insofar as they share some of the characteristics
of love.*

There is also no need to distinguish as many kinds of
love as there are diverse objects which we may love, because,
for example, although the passions of an ambitious man for
glory, of a miser for money, of a drunkard for wine, of a
brutal man for a woman he wants to rape, of a man of honor
for his friend or his mistress, and of a good father for his
children, are very different from one another, they are all
similar in that they share some of the characteristics of love.
But the first four have love only for the possession of the
objects to which their passion is related, and have none for the
objects themselves, for which they have only desire mingled
with other particular passions, whereas the love of a good
father for his children is so pure that he does not desire to
obtain anything from them and does not wish to possess them
otherwise than he does, or to be joined with them more
closely than he is already; regarding them as an extension of
himself, he seeks their good as his own, or with even greater

care, for, considering that he and they form a whole of which he is not the best part, he often places their interests before his and is not afraid of losing himself in order to save them. The affection which men of honor have for their friends is of this nature, although it is seldom so perfect, and that which they have for their mistresses is of a closely similar nature, although it also has some characteristics in common with the other kind.

ARTICLE 83

◁§ *The differences among simple affection, friendship, and devotion.*

We can, it seems to me, more rightly make distinctions in love according to the esteem we feel for what we love as compared to ourselves: when we esteem the object of our love less than ourselves, we have only simple affection for it; when we esteem it as much as ourselves, we feel what is known as friendship; and when we esteem it more than ourselves, the passion we have may be called devotion. Thus we may have affection for a flower, a bird or a horse, but unless we have a seriously deranged mind, we can have friendship only for men. And they are so truly the object of this passion that there is no man so imperfect that we cannot feel very perfect friendship for him if we think he loves us and if we have a truly noble and magnanimous soul, as will be explained later in Articles 154 and 156. As for devotion, its principal object is no doubt the sovereign Divinity, to whom we cannot fail to be devoted when we know Him as we should. But we may also be devoted to our ruler, our country, our city, and even to a private individual, when we esteem him much more than ourselves. Now the differences among these three kinds of love appear to lie chiefly in their effects; for inasmuch as in all three of them we regard ourselves as being joined to and united with the object of our love, we are always ready to abandon the lesser part of the whole which we compose with it in order to preserve the other part, which means that in simple affection we always prefer ourselves to what we love, and that, on the contrary, in devotion we so prefer the object of our love to ourselves that we are not afraid to die in order to preserve it. Examples of this have often been seen in those who have exposed themselves to certain death for the defense

of their ruler or their city, or sometimes even for private individuals to whom they were devoted.

ARTICLE 84

❧ *That there are not as many kinds of hatred as of love.*

Although hatred is directly opposed to love, we do not
divide it into as many different kinds, because we do not to
the same extent notice differences among the evils from which
we will to be separated as we do among the goods to which
we will to be joined.

ARTICLE 85

❧ *Delight and abhorrence.*

And I find only one noteworthy distinction that is common to both. It consists in the fact that the objects of both
love and hatred can be represented to the soul by the external
senses, or by the inner senses and its own reason. For we
usually call good or evil what our inner senses or our reason
make us judge to be agreeable or contrary to our nature, but
we call beautiful or ugly what is thus represented to us by
our external senses, chiefly by the sense of sight, which is
more highly considered than any of the others. Hence arise
two kinds of love: that which we have for good things, and
that which we have for beautiful things. The latter may be
called delight, in order not to confuse it with the former, or
with desire, which is often given the name of love. And
hence, in the same way, arise two kinds of hatred, one of
which is directed against bad things, the other against ugly
things; and the latter may be called abhorrence or aversion,
in order to distinguish it from the former. But what is most
remarkable here is that these passions of delight and abhorrence are usually more violent than the other kinds of love or
hatred, because what comes to the soul by means of the senses
affects it more strongly than what is represented to it by its
reason, even though these two passions generally have less
truth. And so, of all the passions, these are the ones which
deceive the most, and against which we should guard ourselves
most carefully.

ARTICLE 86

✑ *Definition of desire.*

The passion of desire is an agitation of the soul caused by the animal spirits which dispose it to wish for the future those things which it represents to itself as agreeable. Thus we desire not only the presence of an absent good, but also the preservation of a present good, and, further, the absence of evil, whether it be that which we have already, or that which we believe may come to us in the future.

ARTICLE 87

✑ *That it is a passion which has no opposite.*

I am well aware that in the Schools the passion which incites us to seek good, and which alone is called desire, is commonly set in opposition to that which incites us to shun evil, and which is known as aversion. But since there is no good whose privation is not an evil, nor any evil, considered in a positive sense, whose privation is not a good, and since in seeking wealth, for example, we necessarily shun poverty, and in shunning illness we seek health, and so on with other things, it seems to me that it is always the same movement which incites us both to seek a good and to shun the evil that is contrary to it. I note only this difference, that the desire we have when we seek a good is accompanied by love, and then by hope and joy, whereas the same desire, when we seek to shun the evil which is contrary to this good, is accompanied by hatred, apprehension and sadness, which is why we judge it to be contrary to ourselves. But if we wish to consider it when at the same time it relates to a good in order to seek it, and to the opposed evil in order to shun it, we can see quite clearly that it is only one passion which causes one as well as the other.

ARTICLE 88

✑ *Its different species.*

There would be more reason to distinguish desire into as many different species as there are different objects which we seek, because curiosity, for example, which is nothing but a desire for knowledge, differs greatly from the desire for glory, which differs greatly from the desire for vengeance, and so on. But it is sufficient here to know that there as many species of desire as of love or hatred, and that the strongest and most noteworthy are those which arise from delight and abhorrence.

ARTICLE 89

The desire which arises from abhorrence.

Now although it is but a single desire which incites us to seek a good and shun the evil that is contrary to it, as has already been said, the desire which arises from delight is nevertheless very different from that which arises from abhorrence, for delight and abhorrence, which are truly opposites, are not the good and the evil which serve as objects for these desires, but only two emotions of the soul which dispose it to seek two very different things. Abhorrence is instituted by nature to represent sudden and unexpected death to the soul, so that although it is sometimes only the touch of an earthworm, or the sound of a quivering leaf, or our own shadow which arouses abhorrence in us, we feel at first as much emotion as though an obvious danger of death had presented itself to our senses, and this suddenly gives rise to the agitation which disposes the soul to employ all its forces to avoid such a present evil. It is this kind of desire which is commonly called avoidance or aversion.

ARTICLE 90

The desire which arises from delight.

Delight, on the other hand, is specially instituted by nature to represent the enjoyment of that which pleases us as the greatest of all the goods that belong to man, and we therefore ardently desire this enjoyment. It is true that there are various sorts of delight, and that the desires which arise from them are not all equally powerful. The beauty of flowers, for example, incites us only to look at them, and that of fruits to eat them. But the principal one is that which comes from the perfections we imagine in a person who we think can become another self to us; for with the difference of sex which nature has placed in men as well as in animals without reason, it has also placed certain impressions in the brain which, at a certain age and at a certain time, cause us to regard ourselves as incomplete and as though we were only half of a whole of which a person of the opposite sex ought to be the other half. The acquisition of this other half is confusedly represented by nature as the greatest of all goods imaginable. And although we see many persons of the opposite sex, we do not wish to have many of them at the same time, since nature does not make us imagine that we need more than one half. But when we observe something in one person which is more pleasing than what we observe in others at the same time, it determines the soul to feel for that one alone all the inclination which nature gives it to seek the good that is represented to it as the greatest which can be possessed; and the inclination or desire that thus arises from delight is more commonly given the name of love than the passion of love which has been described above. It also has more extraordinary effects, and it is what serves as the principal material for novelists and poets.

ARTICLE 91

◁§ *Definition of joy.*

Joy is an agreeable emotion of the soul in which consists the enjoyment it has of the good which the impressions of the brain represent to it as being its own. I say that it is in this emotion that the enjoyment of the good consists, for the soul receives no other fruit from all the goods it possesses; and while it has no joy from them, it can be said that it enjoys them no more than if it did not possess them. I add also that it is of the good which the impressions of the brain represent to it as being its own, in order not to confuse this joy, which is a passion, with the purely intellectual joy that comes into the soul through the action of the soul alone, and which can be said to be an agreeable emotion aroused in itself and in which consists the enjoyment it has of the good which its understanding represents to it as being its own. It is true that while the soul is joined to the body this intellectual joy can scarcely fail to be accompanied by that which is a passion, for as soon as our understanding perceives that we possess a good, even though this good may be so different from everything which pertains to the body that it is not at all imaginable, imagination is sure to make some impression on the brain, and from this impression follows the movement of the animal spirits which arouses the passion of joy.

ARTICLE 92

Definition of sadness.

Sadness is a disagreeable languor in which consists the discomfort which the soul receives from evil, or from the deficiency which the impressions of the brain represent to it as belonging to it. And there is an intellectual sadness which is not the passion, but which scarcely ever fails to be accompanied by it.

ARTICLE 93

The causes of these two passions.

Now when intellectual joy or sadness thus arouses that which is a passion, their cause is rather obvious; and we see from their definitions that joy comes from our opinion that we possess some good, and sadness from our opinion that we have some evil or deficiency. But we often feel sad or joyful without being able to observe distinctly the good or the evil which causes our feeling. This happens when the good or the evil makes its impression in the brain without the intervention of the soul, sometimes because it belongs only to the body, and sometimes also, even though it belongs to the soul, because the soul does not consider it as good or evil, but under some other form whose impression is joined to that of good or evil in the brain.

ARTICLE 94

How these passions are aroused by goods and evils which concern only the body, and in what titillation and pain consist.

Thus when we are in full health and the weather is better than usual, we feel within us a gaiety which does not come from any function of the understanding, but solely from the impressions which the movement of the animal spirits causes in the brain; and we feel sad in the same way only when the body is indisposed, even though we are unaware of it. Thus the titillation of the senses is followed so closely by joy, and pain by sadness, that most men do not distinguish them. And yet they differ so greatly that we may sometimes undergo pain with joy, and experience titillations that are unpleasant. But the cause which makes it happen that joy usually follows titillation is that everything we call titillation or agreeable sensation consists in the fact that the objects of the senses arouse some movement in the nerves which would be capable of harming them if they did not have enough strength to resist it, or if the body were not well disposed; and this produces in the brain an impression which, being instituted by nature to evince this good disposition and strength, represents it to the soul as a good which belongs to it, inasmuch as the soul is united with the body, and thus arouses joy in it. It is almost the same reason which makes us naturally take pleasure in being moved to all sorts of passions, even sadness and hatred, when these passions are caused only by the strange adventures we see represented on the stage, or by other similar means, which, being unable to harm us in any way, seem to touch our soul in such a manner as to give it pleasurable stimulation. And the cause which makes it happen that pain usually produces sadness is that the sensation known as pain always comes from some action so violent that it injures the nerves, so that, being instituted by nature to signify to the soul the injury which the body receives from this action, and its weakness in not being able to resist it, it represents both of them to the soul as evils which are always disagreeable to it, except when they bring about goods which it regards as more important.

ARTICLE 95

❧ *How they may also be aroused by goods and evils which the soul does not notice, even though they belong to it, such as the pleasure that is taken in running a risk, or in recalling a past evil.*

Thus the pleasure which young people often derive from undertaking difficult tasks and exposing themselves to great danger, even when they expect no profit or glory from doing so, comes to them from the fact that the thought that what they are undertaking is difficult makes an impression in their brains which, being joined to that which they might form if they were to think that it is good to feel courageous, fortunate, skillful or strong enough to run such a risk, causes them to take pleasure in it. And the satisfaction which old people feel when they recall the evils they have suffered comes from the fact that they consider it good to have been able to go on living in spite of them.

ARTICLE 96

❧ *The movements of the blood and the animal spirits which cause the five preceding passions.*

The five passions which I have here begun to explain are so joined or opposed to one another that it is easier to consider them all together than to treat each of them separately, as I have treated wonder. And, unlike wonder, their cause is not in the brain alone, but also in the heart, the spleen, the liver and all the other parts of the body, inasmuch as they serve to produce the blood and subsequently the animal spirits; for although all the veins conduct the blood they contain to the heart, it sometimes happens that the blood in some of them is driven there with greater force than the blood in others, and it may also happen that the openings through which it enters the heart, or those through which it flows out, are more widened or narrowed at one time than at another.

ARTICLE 97

❧ *The principal experiences which give us knowledge of these movements in love.*

Now in considering the various alterations which experience shows us in our body while our soul is agitated by various passions, I note that in love, when it is alone, that is, when it is accompanied by no strong joy, or desire, or sadness, the pulse is steady and much greater and stronger than usual, we feel a pleasant warmth in the chest, and the digestion of food takes place very quickly in the stomach, so that this passion is useful to health.

ARTICLE 98

❧ *In hatred.*

In hatred, however, I note that the pulse is unsteady, weaker, and often quicker, that we have sensations of cold in the chest mingled with a harsh, biting heat which is difficult to describe, and that the stomach ceases to perform its functions and is inclined to vomit and reject the food we have eaten, or at least to corrupt it and convert it into evil humors.

ARTICLE 99

❧ *In joy.*

In joy, I note that the pulse is steady and quicker than usual, but that it is not so great or strong as in love, that we feel a pleasant warmth which is not only in the chest but spreads into all the outer parts of the body with the blood which we observe to flow to them in abundance, and that nevertheless we sometimes lose our appetites, because digestion takes place less actively than usual.

ARTICLE 100

❧ *In sadness.*

In sadness, I note that the pulse is weak and slow, that we feel as though our heart were being constricted by tight bands around it and frozen by ice which communicates its cold to the rest of the body, and that nevertheless we sometimes have a good appetite and feel that the stomach is not failing to do its duty, provided there is no hatred mingled with our sadness.

ARTICLE 101

❧ *In desire.*

Finally, I note this particularity in desire, that it agitates the heart more violently than any of the other passions, and supplies the brain with more animal spirits which, passing

from there into the muscles, make all the senses more acute
and all the parts of the body more mobile.

ARTICLE 102

❧ *The movement of the blood and the animal spirits in
love.*

These observations, and many others which would take
too long to write, have led me to judge that when the understanding represents some object to itself in love, the impression which this thought makes in the brain conducts the
animal spirits, by way of the nerves of the sixth pair, to the
muscles around the intestines and the stomach in the manner
required to cause the juice of the food, which is converted
into new blood, to pass quickly to the heart without stopping
in the liver; and that, being driven there with greater force
than the blood in the other parts of the body, it enters in
greater abundance and arouses stronger heat in the heart,
because it is coarser than the blood which has already been
rarefied several times in passing and repassing through the
heart. This causes it to send to the brain animal spirits whose
parts are larger and more agitated than usual, and these spirits,
strengthening the impression which the first thought of the
lovable object has made in the brain, oblige the soul to linger
over this thought; and it is in this that the passion of love
consists.

ARTICLE 103

❧ *In hatred.*

In hatred, however, the first thought of the object which
arouses aversion so conducts the animal spirits that are in the
brain to the muscles of the stomach and the intestines that
they prevent the juice of the food from mingling with the
blood by constricting all the openings through which it usually flows; and it also conducts them in such a way to the
little nerves of the spleen and of the lower part of the liver,
where the gall bladder is located, that the parts of the blood
which are usually thrown back to those places issue from them
and flow toward the heart with the blood that is in the

branches of the vena cava. This causes many inequalities in its heat, since the blood that comes from the spleen is scarcely heated and rarefied at all, whereas that which comes from the lower part of the liver, where the gall is always present, is quickly inflamed and dilated. Consequently the animal spirits which go to the brain also have very unequal parts and very extraordinary movements; from this it results that they strengthen the ideas of hatred that are already imprinted in the brain, and dispose the soul to thoughts that are full of harshness and bitterness.

ARTICLE 104

◄§ *In joy.*

In joy it is not so much the nerves of the spleen, liver, stomach or intestines which act, as those which are in all the rest of the body, particularly the one that is around the orifices of the heart, which, opening and widening these orifices, provides a means whereby the blood which the other nerves drive toward the heart through the veins may enter the heart and flow out of it in greater quantity than usual. And because the blood which then enters the heart has already passed through it several times, having come from the arteries into the veins, it dilates very easily and produces animal spirits whose parts, being extremely equal and subtle, are capable of forming and strengthening the impressions of the brain which give gay and tranquil thoughts to the soul.

ARTICLE 105

◄§ *In sadness.*

In sadness, however, the openings of the heart are greatly contracted by the little nerve that surrounds them, and the blood in the veins is not agitated at all, so that very little of it goes to the heart. And yet the passages through which the juice of the food flows from the stomach and intestines to the liver remain open, so that the appetite is not diminished, except when they are closed by hatred, which is often joined to sadness.

ARTICLE 106

◦§ *In desire.*

Finally, the passion of desire has this peculiarity, that our volition to obtain some good or to avoid some evil quickly sends the animal spirits from the brain to all parts of the body which may be of service in the actions required for that purpose, particularly to the heart and the parts which supply it with the most blood, so that in receiving a greater abundance than usual, it sends a greater quantity of animal spirits to the brain, in order that they may maintain and fortify the idea of this volition there, and also in order that they may pass from there into all the organs of the senses and all the muscles which may be employed in obtaining what we desire.

ARTICLE 107

◦§ *The cause of these movements in love.*

And I deduce the reasons for all this from what has been said above: that there is a connection between our soul and our body such that when we have joined some bodily action with some thought, one of the two never presents itself to us afterward without the other presenting itself to us also, as we see in the case of those who, having taken some potion with great aversion during an illness, can never again eat or drink anything that has a similar taste without again feeling the same aversion; and we also note that they cannot think of their aversion to the medicine without the same taste coming back to them in thought. For it seems to me that the first passions which our soul had when it began to be joined to the body must have arisen from the fact that sometimes the blood, or other juice, which entered the heart was a more suitable nutriment than usual for the maintenance there of heat, which is the principle of life, and this caused the soul to will to join itself to that nutriment, i.e., to love it, while at the same time the animal spirits flowing from the brain to the muscles which could press or agitate the parts from which it had come to the heart, thus causing them to send still more of it; and these parts were the stomach and the intestines, whose agitation increases the appetite, and also perhaps the liver and the lungs, which can be pressed by the muscles of the diaphragm. That is why this same movement of the animal spirits has always accompanied the passion of love ever since.

ARTICLE 108

◦§ *In hatred.*

Sometimes, however, there came to the heart some strange juice which was not capable of maintaining heat, or which was even capable of extinguishing it. This caused the animal spirits rising from the heart to the brain to arouse the passion of hatred in the soul, and at the same time also these spirits went from the brain to the nerves which were able to drive blood from the spleen and the little veins of the liver toward the heart, in order to prevent the harmful juice from entering it; and, further, they went to those nerves which were able to drive back this same juice to the intestines and the stomach, or were also able sometimes to make the stomach vomit it. From this it results that these movements usually accompany the passion of hatred. And it can be shown to the eye that there are in the liver a number of rather broad veins or ducts through which the juice of the food can pass from the portal vein into the vena cava, and from there to the heart, without stopping in the liver at all; but there are also a number of smaller ones in which it can stop, and which, like the spleen, always contain blood in reserve. This blood, being coarser than that which is in the other parts of the body, is better able to nourish the fire that is in the heart when the stomach and the intestines fail to supply it with nourishment.

ARTICLE 109

◦§ *In joy.*

It also happened in the beginning of our life that the blood contained in the veins was a nutriment sufficiently well suited to the maintenance of the heat of the heart, and that they contained so much of it that the heart had no need to draw nourishment from elsewhere. This aroused in the soul the passion of joy, and at the same time made the orifices of the heart open more widely than usual and caused the animal spirits flowing abundantly from the brain, not only into the nerves which serve to open these orifices but also generally into all the others which drive the blood through the veins toward the heart, to prevent any more blood from coming from the liver, spleen, intestines and stomach. That is why these same movements accompany joy.

ARTICLE 110

⋙ *In sadness.*

Sometimes, however, it happened that the body lacked nourishment, and that must have been what made the soul feel its first sadness, or at least its first sadness that was not joined to hatred. And it was also the cause of the fact that the orifices of the heart contracted, since they received only a little blood, and that a considerable part of this blood came from the spleen, since it is like the last reservoir which serves to supply the heart with blood when it does not receive enough from elsewhere. That is why the movements of the spirits and nerves which serve thus to contract the orifices of the heart, and to conduct blood to it from the spleen, always accompany sadness.

ARTICLE 111

⋙ *In desire.*

Finally, all the first desires which the soul can have had when it was newly joined to the body were to receive the things that were agreeable to it and to reject those that were harmful to it; and it was in order to bring about these same effects that the animal spirits began from then on to move all the muscles and all the organs of the senses in all the ways in which they can move them. That is why now, when the soul desires something, the whole body becomes more agile and more strongly disposed to move than it usually is otherwise. And when it happens for other reasons that the body is thus disposed, the desires of the soul are thereby made stronger and more ardent.

ARTICLE 112

❧ *The external signs of these passions.*

What I have set down here is enough to give an understanding of the cause of the differences in the pulse and of all the other characteristics I have attributed to these passions, without there being any need for me to stop to explain them further. But since I have noted in each one of them only that which can be observed in it when it is alone, and which serves to give us knowledge of the movements of the blood and animal spirits which produce them, it still remains for me to deal with a number of external signs which usually accompany them, and which are much better observed when several of them are mingled, as they usually are, than when they are separate. The most important of these signs are the actions of the eyes and the face, changes of color, tremors, languor, fainting, laughter, tears, moans, and sighs.

ARTICLE 113

❧ *The actions of the eyes and the face.*

There is no passion which is not manifested by some particular action of the eyes, and this is so obvious in some of them that even the most stupid servants can tell from their master's eyes whether or not he is angry with them. But although we easily perceive these actions of the eyes and know what they mean, it is not easy to describe them, because each one of them is composed of several changes that occur in the movement and conformation of the eyes, and these changes are so special and so slight that each of them cannot be perceived separately, even though what results from their conjunction is very easy to observe. Almost the same can be said of the actions of the face which also accompany the passions, for although they are greater than those of the eyes, it is nevertheless difficult to distinguish them, and they differ so slightly that there are men who have almost the same expression when they weep as other men have when they laugh. It is true that some of these actions are rather outstanding, such as the wrinkling of the forehead in anger, and certain movements of the nose and lips in indignation and mockery, but they seem to be less natural than voluntary. And, in general, all the actions of both the face and the eyes can be changed by the soul when, wishing to hide its passion, it strongly imagines a contrary one, so that we can use them to dissimulate our passions as well as to manifest them.

ARTICLE 114

✑ *Changes of color.*

We cannot so easily prevent ourselves from blushing or turning pale when some passion disposes us to do so, because, unlike those discussed above, these changes do not depend on the muscles and nerves, and they come more immediately from the heart, which can be called the source of the passions, inasmuch as it prepares the blood and the animal spirits to produce them. Now it is certain that the color of the face comes solely from the blood, which, constantly flowing from the heart through the arteries into the veins, and through all the veins into the heart, colors the face in varying degrees, according to how fully it fills the little veins that go toward its surface.

ARTICLE 115

✑ *How joy makes us blush.*

Thus joy makes the color brighter and redder, because in opening the sluices of the heart it makes the blood flow more swiftly into all the veins, and because, becoming warmer and more subtle, the blood swells all parts of the face to a certain extent, which gives it a gayer and livelier appearance.

ARTICLE 116

✑ *How sadness makes us turn pale.*

Sadness, however, by contracting the orifices of the heart, makes the blood flow more slowly through the veins and become colder and thicker. Thus, needing to occupy less space in the veins, the blood withdraws into the broadest ones, which are those nearest to the heart, and leaves the more distant ones, the most apparent of which are those of the face. This makes the face appear pale and gaunt, particularly when the sadness is great or when it comes quickly, as we see in the case of sudden terror, whose surprise augments the action which constricts the heart.

ARTICLE 117

❧ *How we often blush when we are sad.*

But it often happens that we do not turn pale when we are sad, and that on the contrary we turn red. This must be attributed to the other passions which are joined to sadness, namely, love or desire, and sometimes also hatred. For these passions heat or agitate the blood which comes from the liver, intestines and other inner parts of the body, drive it to the heart, and then from there, by way of the aorta, to the veins of the face; and this cannot be prevented by the sadness which contracts the orifices of the heart here and there, except when it is extremely intense. But even if it is only moderate it can easily prevent the blood which has thus come into the veins of the face from descending to the heart while love, desire or hatred drive other blood to it from the inner parts. That is why this blood, being arrested around the face, makes it red, and even redder than during joy, because the color of the blood appears more vividly due to the fact that it is flowing less swiftly, and also because more of it can collect in the veins of the face than when the orifices of the heart are more open. This appears chiefly in shame, which is composed of self-love and a pressing desire to avoid a present disgrace, which makes the blood flow from the inner parts to the heart, then from there through the arteries to the face, and with this there is also a moderate sadness which prevents this blood from returning to the heart. The same thing usually appears when we weep, for, as I shall say later, it is love joined to sadness which causes most tears; and the same thing also appears in anger, in which a sudden desire for vengeance is often mingled with love, hatred and sadness.

ARTICLE 118

◆§ *Tremors.*

Tremors have two different causes: one is that sometimes
too little of the animal spirits in the brain comes into the
nerves, and the other is that sometimes there comes too much
to allow the precise closing of the little passages in the muscles which, in accordance with what has been said in Article
11, must be closed in order to determine the movements of
the members. The first cause appears in sadness and in fear,
as also when we shiver with cold, for these passions, as well
as the coldness of the air, can so thicken the blood that it
does not supply enough animal spirits to the brain to enable
it to send some of them into the nerves. The other cause
often appears in those who ardently desire something, in
those who are strongly moved by anger, and in those who are
drunk, for these two passions, as well as wine, sometimes make
so many spirits go to the brain that they cannot be properly
conducted from there into the muscles.

ARTICLE 119

◆§ *Languor.*

Languor is an inclination to relax and be motionless which
is felt in all the members. Like tremors, it comes from the fact
that not enough spirits go into the nerves, but in a different
manner, for the cause of tremors is that there are not enough
spirits in the brain to obey the impulsions of the gland when
it drives them toward some muscle, whereas languor comes
from the fact that the gland does not impel them to go
toward some muscles rather than others.

ARTICLE 120

◆§ *How it is caused by love and by desire.*

And the passion which most commonly brings about
this effect is love, joined to a desire for something whose
acquisition is not imagined as possible at the present time; for

love so occupies the soul in considering the loved object that it employs all the spirits which are in the brain in representing its image to it, and stops all movements of the gland which do not serve that purpose. And with regard to desire it must be noted that the property I have attributed to it of making the body more mobile belongs to it only when we imagine the desired object as being such that we can immediately do something that will serve in acquiring it; for if, on the contrary, we imagine that it is impossible for the time being to do anything that will be useful to that end, all the agitation of our desire remains in the brain, without passing into the nerves in any way, and, being wholly employed in strengthening the idea of the desired object in the brain, it leaves the rest of the body in a state of languor.

ARTICLE 121

&§ *That it may also be caused by other passions.*

It is true that hatred, sadness and even joy may thus cause some languor when they are extremely violent, because they occupy the soul entirely in considering their object, particularly when a desire for something to whose acquisition we can contribute nothing at the present time is joined to it. But because we spend much more time in considering objects to which we will to join ourselves than those from which we will to separate ourselves, or any others, and because languor does not depend on surprise, but requires a certain time in which to be formed, it is encountered much more in love than in all the other passions.

ARTICLE 122

&§ *Fainting.*

Fainting is not far removed from death, for we die when the fire in the heart is extinguished altogether, and we only faint when it is smothered in such a way that there remain some traces of heat which can later rekindle it. Now there are several indispositions of the body which can cause us thus to fall into a faint, but among the passions it is only extreme joy which we observe to have this power. I believe that it brings about this effect in the following manner: by opening the orifices of the heart to an extraordinary extent, it causes the blood from the veins to flow into the heart so suddenly and in such great quantities that it cannot be rarefied there quickly enough to raise the little membranes which close the entrances of these veins, and thus it smothers the fire which it usually maintains when it enters the heart only in moderate amounts.

ARTICLE 123

◦§ *Why we do not faint from sadness.*

It would seem that a great sadness which befalls us unexpectedly should so close the orifices of the heart that it could also extinguish the fire of the heart, but we do not observe this to happen, or, if it does happen, it is only very rarely. I believe the reason for this to be that there can scarcely be so little blood in the heart as to be insufficient to maintain its heat when its orifices are nearly closed.

ARTICLE 124

◦§ *Laughter.*

Laughter consists in the fact that the blood which comes into the right cavity of the heart through the pulmonary artery swells the lungs suddenly and repeatedly, thus forcing the air they contain to go out precipitously through the windpipe, where it forms an inarticulate and explosive utterance; and the lungs in expanding, as well as this air in rushing out, push all the muscles of the diaphragm, the chest and the throat, by means of which they cause motion in the facial muscles which have some connection with them. And it is only this action of the face, along with the inarticulate and explosive utterance, that we call laughter.

ARTICLE 125

◦§ *Why it does not accompany the greatest joys.*

Although it would seem that laughter were one of the principal signs of joy, nevertheless joy cannot cause it except when it is only moderate and when it is mingled with some admiration or hatred; for we learn from experience that when we are extraordinarily joyful the subject of our joy never makes us burst into laughter, and it is even more difficult for us to be moved to laughter by some other cause than when we are sad. The reason for this is that in great joy the lungs are always so full of blood that they cannot be repeatedly inflated further.

ARTICLE 126

❧ *Its principal causes.*

And I can observe only two causes which make the lungs thus inflate suddenly. The first is the surprise of wonder, which, being joined to joy, can open the orifices of the heart so quickly that a great abundance of blood suddenly enters its right side through the vena cava, is rarefied there, and then, passing through the pulmonary artery, inflates the lungs. The other is the admixture of some liquid which increases the rarefaction of the blood; and I can find nothing suitable for that purpose except the most free-flowing part of the blood which comes from the spleen. This part of the blood, being driven to the heart by some slight emotion of hatred, aided by the surprise of wonder, and mingling there with the blood that comes from the other parts of the body, which joy causes to enter there abundantly, can make this blood dilate there much more than usual, just as we see many other liquids suddenly expand when they are over a fire and we throw a little vinegar into the vessel that contains them, for the most free-flowing part of the blood which comes from the spleen is of a nature similar to that of vinegar. Experience also shows us that, in all the occurrences which can produce the explosive laughter which comes from the lungs, there is always some small element of hatred, or at least of wonder. And those whose spleen is not in a very healthy condition are subject to being not only sadder, but also, intermittently, more strongly disposed to laughter than others; for the spleen sends two kinds of blood to the heart, one very thick and coarse, which causes sadness, the other very fluid and subtle, which causes joy. And often, after having laughed a great deal, we feel naturally inclined to sadness, because when the most fluid part of the blood from the spleen has been exhausted, the coarser part follows it to the heart.

ARTICLE 127

❧ *Its cause in indignation.*

As for the laughter which sometimes accompanies indignation, it is usually artificial and feigned; but when it is natural it seems to come from our joy in seeing that we cannot be harmed by the evil over which we are indignant, and also from the fact that we are surprised by the novelty or unexpected occurrence of this evil, so that joy, hatred and wonder all contribute to our laughter. I am inclined to believe, however, that it can also be produced without any joy, solely by a movement of aversion which sends blood from the spleen to the heart, where it is rarefied and driven into the lungs, which it easily inflates when it finds them almost empty. And, in general, anything that can suddenly inflate the lungs in this way causes the external action of laughter, except when sadness changes it into that of the moans and cries which accompany tears. In this connection, Vives writes of himself that after he had gone a long time without eating, the first pieces of food he put into his mouth made him laugh, which may have happened because his lungs, empty of blood from lack of nourishment, were quickly inflated by the first juice which passed from his stomach toward his heart, and which the mere imagination of eating could conduct there, even before the arrival of the juice of the food he was eating.

ARTICLE 128

❧ *The origin of tears.*

As laughter is never caused by the greatest joys, so tears never come from extreme sadness, but only from a moderate sadness which is accompanied or followed by some feeling of love, or also of joy. And in order to understand their origin properly, we must note that, although vapors are constantly and abundantly issuing from all parts of the body, there is no other part from which they issue so abundantly as from the eyes, because of the size of the optic nerves and the multitude of little arteries through which the vapors reach them; and just as perspiration is composed only of the vapors that issue from the other parts of the body and are converted into water on their surface, so tears are made of the vapors that issue from the eyes.

ARTICLE 129

❧ *The way in which vapors change into water.*

As I have written in my *Meteors*, in explaining the way in which the vapors of the air are converted into rain, namely, that it is owing to the fact that they are less agitated or more abundant than usual, so I believe that when those which issue from the body are much less agitated than usual, even though they are not so abundant, they are converted into water, which causes the cold sweats that sometimes come from weakness when we are ill. And I believe that when they are much more abundant, provided that they are not at the same time more agitated, they are also converted into water, which is the cause of the sweat that comes when we exercise. But then the eyes do not perspire, because while the body is exercising, most of the animal spirits go into the muscles that serve to move it, and a smaller quantity of them goes to the eyes by way of the optic nerve. And it is one and the same matter which composes the blood when it is in the veins or arteries, the animal spirits when it is in the brain, the nerves or the muscles, the vapors when it issues forth in the form of air, and sweat or tears when it thickens into water on the surface of the body or of the eyes.

ARTICLE 130

❧ *How that which causes pain in the eye incites it to weep.*

And I can observe only two causes which make the vapors that issue from the eyes change into tears. The first is when the shape of the pores through which they pass is altered by some sort of accident, for, by retarding the movement of the vapors, such an alteration may cause them to be converted into water. Thus a wisp of straw falling into the eye is enough to draw tears from it, for by arousing pain in the eye it alters the disposition of its pores; when some of them become narrower, the smaller parts of the vapors pass through them less rapidly, and, whereas previously they passed through equally distant from the one another, thereby remaining separate, they now come into contact with one another because the order of the pores has been disturbed, and are therefore joined and converted into tears.

ARTICLE 131

⋙ *How we weep from sadness.*

The other cause is sadness followed by love or joy, or, in general, some cause which makes the heart drive much blood through the arteries. Sadness is required in weeping because, by cooling all the blood, it narrows the pores of the eyes; but since in proportion as it narrows them it also diminishes the quantity of vapors which they ought to allow to pass, it is not sufficient to produce tears if the quantity of these vapors is not at the same time increased by some other cause; and there is nothing which increases it more than the blood that is sent to the heart in the passion of love. Thus we see that those who are sad do not shed tears constantly, but only intermittently, when they make some new reflection on the objects of their affection.

ARTICLE 132

⋙ *The moans which accompany tears.*

And then the lungs are also sometimes suddenly inflated by the abundance of the blood which enters them and drives out the air they contained, which, issuing from the windpipe, gives rise to the moans and cries which usually accompany tears. And these cries are, as a rule, shriller than those which accompany laughter, even though they are produced in almost the same way. The reason for this is that the nerves which serve to expand or contract the organs of the voice in order to make it lower or shriller, being joined to those which open the orifices of the heart during joy and contract them during sadness, make these organs expand or contract at the same time.

ARTICLE 133

⮞ *Why children and old people weep easily.*

Children and old people are more inclined to weep than those of intermediate age, but for different reasons. Old people often weep from affection and joy, for these two passions joined together send much blood to their heart, and from there a great quantity of vapors to their eyes; and the agitation of these vapors is so retarded by the coldness of their constitution that they are easily converted into tears, even though no sadness has gone before. And if some old people also weep very easily from vexation, it is not so much the temperament of their body as that of their soul which disposes them to do so; and it happens only to those who are so weak that they let themselves be entirely overcome by small causes of sorrow, fear or pity. The same occurs with children, who hardly ever weep from joy, but much more often from sadness, even when it is not accompanied by love; for they always have enough blood to produce a great deal of vapors, which, when their movement is retarded by sadness, are converted into tears.

ARTICLE 134

⮞ *Why some children turn pale instead of weeping.*

There are, however, some children who turn pale instead of weeping when they are angry. This may be evidence of extraordinary judgment and courage on their part, in cases when it comes from the fact that they are considering the magnitude of the evil and preparing themselves for firm resistance, in the same way as older people; but it is more commonly a sign of a bad temperament, when it comes from an inclination to hatred or fear, for these are passions which diminish the material of tears, and we see that, on the other hand, those who weep very easily are inclined to love and pity.

ARTICLE 135

❦ *Sighs.*

The cause of sighs is very different from that of tears,
even though, like tears, they presuppose sadness; for whereas
we are moved to weep when the lungs are full of blood, we
are moved to sigh when they are nearly empty, and when
some imagination of hope or joy opens the orifice of the
pulmonary vein, which sadness has contracted, because then,
when the little blood remaining in the lungs has abruptly
entered the left side of the heart through the pulmonary vein,
having been driven there by the desire to achieve the imagined
joy, which at the same time agitates all the muscles of the
diaphragm and the chest, air is quickly driven through the
mouth and into the lungs to fill the space left vacant by
the blood; and this is what we call sighing.

ARTICLE 136

❦ *Whence come the effects of the passions that are peculiar to certain men.*

For the rest, in order to cover in a few words everything
else that might be added concerning the various effects and
causes of the passions, I shall content myself with repeating
the principle that underlies everything I have written about
them, namely, that our soul and our body are so connected
that once we have joined a certain bodily action to a certain
thought, one of them never presents itself to us later without
the other presenting itself also, and that the same actions are
not always joined to the same thoughts. This will suffice to
give a reason for anything we can observe as peculiar to ourselves or to others in this matter, and which has not been
here explained. For example, it is easy to conceive that the
strange aversions of some people which make them unable to
endure the smell of roses, the presence of a cat, or similar
things, come only from the fact that at the beginning of their
life they were made to suffer by such objects, or that they
sympathized with their mother's feelings when she was made
to suffer by them while she was pregnant; for it is certain that
there is a relation between all the movements of the mother

and those of the child in her womb, so that what is adverse to one is harmful to the other. And the smell of roses may have given a child a severe headache while he was still in the cradle, or a cat may have frightened him greatly, without anyone's having been aware of it and without his retaining any memory of it later, although the idea of aversion which he then felt for the roses or the cat remains imprinted in his brain until the end of his life.

ARTICLE 137

≈§ *The function of the five passions here explained, insofar as they relate to the body.*

Having given the definitions of love, hatred, desire, joy and sadness, and having treated of all the bodily movements which cause or accompany them, it now remains for us here only to consider their function. Concerning this it must be noted that, as they have been instituted by nature, they all relate to the body, and are given to the soul only insofar as it is joined to the body; so that their natural function is to incite the soul to consent and contribute to actions which may serve to preserve the body or make it more perfect in some way. And in this regard, sadness and joy are the two foremost that are employed, for the soul is immediately made aware of things useful to the body only by its feeling of pain, which first produces in it the passion of sadness, then hatred of what causes the pain, and finally a desire to free itself of it; just as, also, the soul is immediately made aware of things useful to the body only by some sort of titillation which arouses joy in it, then gives rise to love of what it believes to be its cause, and finally to a desire for what can bring about a continuation of that joy or a later enjoyment of a similar one. This shows that all five of these passions are very useful with regard to the body, and even that sadness is, in a sense, primary and more necessary than joy, and hatred more necessary than love, because it is more important to repel things which harm us, and may destroy us, than to acquire those which add some perfection without which we can still go on living.

ARTICLE 138

✍ *Their defects, and the means of correcting them.*

But although this function of the passions is the most
natural one that they can have, and though all the animals
without reason lead their lives entirely by bodily movements
similar to those which usually follow the passions in us, it is
nevertheless not always good, since there are many things
harmful to the body which at first cause no sadness, or even
give joy, and others which are useful to it even though they
are at first disagreeable. Furthermore, the passions nearly
always cause the goods and evils they represent to appear
much greater and more important than they are, thus inciting
us to seek the former and flee the latter with more ardor and
care than is proper, as we see also that animals are often
deceived by bait, and that to avoid small evils they rush into
greater ones. That is why we ought to make use of experience
and reason to distinguish good from evil and recognize their
just value, in order not to mistake one for the other, and not
to give ourselves over to anything in excess.

ARTICLE 139

✍ *The function of these same passions, insofar as they pertain to the soul; and, firstly, some remarks concerning
love.*

This would be sufficient if we were composed only of a
body, or if it were the better part of us; but since it is only
the lesser part, we must consider the passions chiefly as they
pertain to the soul, with regard to which love and hatred
come from knowledge and precede joy and sadness, except
when these latter two take the place of knowledge, of which
they are species. And when this knowledge is true, that is,
when the things it incites us to love are truly good, and those
it incites us to hate are truly evil, love is incomparably better
than hatred; it cannot be too great, and it never fails to
produce joy. I say that this love is extremely good because,
joining true goods to us, it perfects us accordingly. I say also
that it cannot be too great, for all that the most extreme love
can do is to join us so perfectly to those goods that the love

we have in particular for ourselves makes no distinction
between them and us, and this, I believe, can never be bad.
And it is necessarily followed by joy because it represents what
we love as a good which belongs to us.

ARTICLE 140

◄§ *Hatred.*

Hatred, on the other hand, can never be so small that it
is not harmful; and it is never without sadness. I say that it
cannot be too small because we are not incited to any action
by the hatred of evil to which we cannot be still better
incited by the love of good which is opposed to it, at least
when the good and the evil are sufficiently known. For I
confess that the hatred of evil which is manifested only by
pain is necessary with regard to the body, but I am not here
speaking of that which comes from clearer knowledge, and
I relate it only to the soul. I say also that it is never without
sadness, because since evil is only a privation, it cannot be
conceived without some real object in which it resides, and
there is nothing real which does not have some goodness in
it, so that the hatred which moves us away from an evil
also moves us away from the good to which it is joined, and
the privation of this good, being represented to our soul as
a defect that belongs to it, arouses sadness in us. For example,
the hatred which makes us shun someone's evil behavior also
makes us shun converse with him in which we might otherwise find some good which we regret being deprived of. And
thus in all other hatreds we may note some cause of sadness.

ARTICLE 141

◄§ *Desire, joy, and sadness.*

As for desire, it is obvious that when it proceeds from
true knowledge it cannot be bad, provided that it is not
excessive, and that this knowledge controls it. It is obvious
also that joy cannot fail to be good, or sadness to be bad, with
regard to the soul, because all the discomfort which the soul
receives from evil consists in the latter, and all the enjoyment
of the good that belongs to it consists in the former, so that

if we did not have a body, I would go so far as to say that we could not too greatly abandon ourselves to love and joy, or too greatly shun hatred and sadness. But the bodily movements which accompany them may all be harmful to our health when they are too violent, and, on the other hand, they may be useful to it when they are moderate.

ARTICLE 142

◄§ *Joy and love, compared with sadness and hatred.*

Moreover, since hatred and sadness ought to be rejected by the soul, even when they proceed from true knowledge, this should with still greater reason be the case when they come from some false opinion. But we may doubt whether love and joy are good when they are thus badly founded, and it seems to me that if we consider them precisely only as what they are in themselves with regard to the soul, we may say that, even though joy is less solid and love less advantageous than when they have a better foundation, they are nevertheless preferable to hatred and sadness when the foundation of the latter is equally bad; so that in the vicissitudes of life in which we cannot avoid the risk of being deceived, we always do much better to incline toward passions which make for good, rather than toward those that are related to evil, even if it be only to avoid it; and often even a false joy is worth more than a sadness whose cause is true. But I dare not say the same of love with respect to hatred, for when hatred is justified it removes us only from what contains the evil from which it is good to be separated, whereas love that is unjustified joins us to things which may be harmful, or at least which do not deserve to be considered by us as much as they are, which demeans and degrades us.

ARTICLE 143

◄§ *The same passions insofar as they relate to desire.*

And it must be carefully noted that what I have just said about these four passions takes place only when they are considered precisely in themselves and do not incite us to any action, for inasmuch as they arouse desire in us, by means of which we regulate our conduct, it is certain that all those whose cause is false can be harmful, and that, on the other hand, all those whose cause is true can be useful, and even that when their foundations are equally bad, joy is usually more harmful than sadness, because the latter, by giving us restraint and fear, disposes us in a certain degree to prudence, whereas those who abandon themselves to the former are made thoughtless and rash.

ARTICLE 144

◄§ Desires whose outcome depends only on us.

But since these passions can incite us to action only by means of the desire they arouse, it is particularly this desire which we ought to be careful to control, and it is in this that the principal use of morality consists. As I have said that it is always good when it follows true knowledge, so it cannot fail to be bad when it is founded on some error. And it seems to me that the error we most commonly commit with regard to desire is that we do not sufficiently distinguish things which depend entirely on us from those which do not. For as to those which depend only on us, that is, on our free will, knowing that they are good is enough to prevent us from desiring them too ardently, for it is following virtue to do good things which depend on us, and it is certain that we cannot have too ardent a desire for virtue, and furthermore, since what we desire in this way cannot fail to be favorable to us, because it depends on us alone, we always receive all the satisfaction we have expected of it. But the mistake which is commonly made in this is never that we desire too much, but only that we desire too little. The sovereign remedy against this is to free our mind as much as possible of all sorts of other less useful desires, then to try to know clearly and consider attentively the goodness of what is to be desired.

ARTICLE 145

◄§ Those which depend only on other causes; and the meaning of chance.

As for things which do not depend on us in any way, no matter how good they may be, we ought never to desire them with passion, not only because they may fail to occur, thereby making us suffer all the more as we have wished for them more intensely, but chiefly because by occupying our thoughts they turn us away from applying our affection to other things whose acquisition depends on us. And there are two general remedies against these vain desires: the first is magnanimity, of which I shall speak later, and the second is that we ought frequently to reflect on divine Providence and tell ourselves that it is impossible for anything to occur unless it has been determined by that Providence from all eternity, so that Providence is like a fatality or an immutable necessity which must be opposed to chance in order to destroy it as an illusion which comes to us only through an error of our understanding. For we cannot desire anything which we regard as in some way impossible, and we can regard things which do not depend on us as possible only insofar as they depend on chance, that is, insofar as we judge that they may occur, and that other similar things have occurred before. Now this opinion is founded only on our ignorance of all the causes which contribute to each effect, for when something we have regarded as depending on chance does not occur, this indicates that one of the causes which were necessary to produce it has failed, and consequently that it was absolutely impossible, and that a similar thing—that is, one in whose production a similar cause was lacking—has never occurred, so that if we had not been ignorant of this beforehand, we would never have regarded it as possible, and would therefore not have desired it.

ARTICLE 146

❧ *Those which depend on us and on others.*

We must, then, entirely reject the common opinion that there is outside of us a Fortune which makes things occur or not occur, according to its own pleasure, and we must recognize that everything is directed by divine Providence, whose eternal decree is so infallible and immutable that, except for things which that same decree has willed to depend on our free will, we ought to consider that nothing happens to us which is not necessary and, so to speak, ordained by fate, so that we cannot without error desire it to happen otherwise. But because most of our desires extend to things which depend neither wholly on us nor wholly on others, we ought to distinguish exactly in them what depends only on us, so that we can extend our desire to that alone; and as for what remains, even though we ought to regard its outcome as entirely fated and immutable, in order that our desire may not concern itself with it, we ought nevertheless to consider the reasons which make us more or less expect it, so that they may serve to direct our actions. Thus, for example, if we have some matter which requires our presence in a place to which we may go by two different roads, one of which is usually much safer than the other, even though the decree of Providence may be such that if we go by the road which is considered to be safer we are sure to be robbed, and that on the other hand we can take the other one without any danger, we should not therefore be indifferent as to which one we choose, or rest on the immutable fatality of that decree, for reason requires that we choose the road which is usually the safer, and our desire ought to be fulfilled in that respect when we have taken it, whatever evil may thereby befall us, for that evil was inevitable as far as we were concerned, and we therefore had no reason to wish to be exempt from it, but only to do our best in accordance with what our understanding could discern, as I assume to have been the case. And it is certain that when we thus apply ourselves to distinguishing fatality from chance, we easily accustom ourselves to regulating our desires in such a way that, since their fulfillment will depend only on us, they may always give us complete satisfaction.

ARTICLE 147

ᴥᣥ *The inner emotions of the soul.*

I shall here add only a consideration which seems very useful to me in preventing us from being adversely affected by the passions: it is that our good and our evil depend chiefly on the inner emotions which are aroused in the soul only by the soul itself. In this they differ from passions which always depend on some movement of the animal spirits; and although these emotions of the soul are often joined to passions that are similar to them, they may often also be found with others, and may even arise from those which are contrary to them. For example, when a husband laments the death of his wife, whom (as sometimes happens) he would be sorry to see brought back to life, it may be that his heart is oppressed by the sadness aroused in him by the appurtenances of the funeral and the absence of someone to whose company he had become accustomed, and it may also be that genuine tears are drawn from his eyes by a few remnants of love or pity, even though he simultaneously feels a secret joy in the innermost part of his soul, the emotion of which is so powerful that the sadness and tears which accompany it can do nothing to diminish its strength. And when we read of extraordinary adventures in a book, or see them represented on the stage, it arouses in us sometimes sadness, sometimes joy, or love, or hatred, and generally all the passions, according to the diversity of the objects which are offered to our imagination. But at the same time we have pleasure in feeling them aroused in us, and this pleasure is an intellectual joy which can arise from sadness as well as from any of the other passions.

ARTICLE 148

⋐ *That the practice of virtue is a sovereign remedy against the passions.*

Now inasmuch as these inner emotions affect us more closely and therefore have much more power over us than the passions that differ from them and are found in conjunction with them, it is certain that, provided our soul always has something with which to content itself inwardly, none of the disturbances that come from elsewhere ever have any power to harm it, but rather serve to increase its joy, since it is made aware of its perfection by seeing that they can do it no harm. And in order that our soul may thus have something with which to be content, it needs only to follow virtue exactly. For whoever has lived in such a way that his conscience cannot reproach him with having ever failed to do all the things he has judged to be best (which is what I here call following virtue) receives from this a satisfaction so powerful in making him happy that the most violent efforts of the passions never have enough power to trouble the tranquillity of his soul.

PART THREE

OF THE PARTICULAR PASSIONS

ARTICLE 149

&§ *Esteem and contempt.*

Having explained the six primary passions, which are, so
to speak, genera of which all the others are species, I shall
here note succinctly the particular characteristics of each of
these others, and I shall keep the same order in which I have
enumerated them above. The first two are esteem and contempt; for although these names usually signify only passion-
less opinions concerning the value of things, nevertheless,
because these opinions often give rise to passions which have
been given to particular names, it seems to me that such
names can be attributed to them. And esteem, insofar as it
is a passion, is an inclination of the soul to represent to itself
the value of the thing esteemed. This inclination is caused
by a particular movement of the animal spirits when they
are conducted into the brain in such a way that they
strengthen the impressions that serve to produce that effect.
The passion of contempt, on the other hand, is an inclination
of the soul to consider the baseness or smallness of what it
despises, and is caused by the movement of the spirits which
strengthen the idea of that smallness.

ARTICLE 150

&§ *That these two passions are only species of wonder.*

Thus these two passions are only species of wonder, for
when we are not moved to wonder by the greatness or smallness of an object, we attach no more or no less importance to
it than reason tells us we should, so that we then esteem or
despise it without passion. And although esteem is often

aroused in us by love, and contempt by hatred, this is not invariably so, and comes only from the fact that we are more or less inclined to consider the greatness or smallness of an object according to whether we have more or less affection for it.

ARTICLE 151

◦§ *That we may esteem or despise ourselves.*

Now these two passions may generally relate to all sorts of objects, but they are chiefly remarkable when we relate them to ourselves, that is, when it is our own merit that we esteem or despise; and the movement of the animal spirits which causes them is then so manifest that it even changes the expression, gestures, bearing, and, in general, all the actions of those who conceive a better or worse opinion of themselves than usual.

ARTICLE 152

◦§ *For what cause we may esteem ourselves.*

And because one of the principal parts of wisdom is to know in what way and for what cause each of us ought to esteem or despise himself, I shall here try to state my opinion on the matter. I see in us only one cause which can give us good reason to esteem ourselves, namely, the use of our free will and the control we have over our volitions, because it is only for the actions which depend on our free will that we can rightly be praised or blamed, and, in making us masters of ourselves, it makes us like God to some extent, provided we do not through laxity lose the rights it gives us.

ARTICLE 153

◦§ *In what magnanimity consists.*

Thus I believe that true magnanimity, which makes a man esteem himself as highly as he legitimately can, consists only partly in the fact that he knows there is nothing which truly belongs to him except this free control of his volitions and that there is no reason why he should be praised or blamed except that he uses it well or badly, and partly in the fact that he feels in himself a firm and constant resolution to use it well, that is, never to lack the will to undertake and carry out all the things he judges to be the best, which is following virtue perfectly.

ARTICLE 154

That it prevents us from despising others.

Those who have this knowledge and feeling about themselves readily convince themselves that every other man also has it about himself, for there is nothing in it which depends on others. That is why they never despise anyone; and although they see that others commit transgressions which show their weakness, they are more inclined to excuse them than to blame them, and to believe that it is rather through lack of knowledge than through lack of good will that they commit them. And since they do not think themselves greatly inferior to those who have more wealth or honors, or even more intelligence, or, generally speaking, who surpass them in other perfections, they do not consider themselves much above those whom they surpass, because all those things seem to them to be of very little worth compared to the good will for which alone they esteem themselves, and which they assume to exist, or at least to be capable of existing, in all other men.

ARTICLE 155

In what virtuous humility consists.

Thus the most magnanimous are usually the most humble; and virtuous humility consists only in the fact that our reflections on the infirmity of our nature and on the transgressions we may have committed in the past or are still capable of committing, which are not less serious than those which may be committed by others, causes us not to prefer ourselves to anyone, and to think that others, having free will the same as ourselves, are equally capable of using it.

ARTICLE 156

❧ *The properties of magnanimity, and how it serves as a remedy against the disorders of the passions.*

Those who are magnanimous in this way are naturally inclined to do great things, yet not to undertake anything which they do not feel capable of carrying out; and because they regard nothing as greater than to do good to other men and to despise their own interests, they are always perfectly courteous, kind and obliging to everyone. And at the same time they are entirely in control of their passions, particularly of desire, jealousy and envy, because there is nothing whose acquisition does not depend on them which they regard as being of sufficient value to deserve being greatly desired; they are also entirely in control of hatred for other men, because they esteem them all; and of fear, because their confidence in their virtue makes them secure; and finally of anger, because, esteeming very little all things which depend on others, they never give their enemies the advantage of acknowledging that they have been offended by them.

ARTICLE 157

❧ *Pride.*

All those who form a good opinion of themselves for some other reason, whatever it may be, do not have true magnanimity, but only a kind of pride which is always extremely vicious, although it is all the more so as the cause for which we esteem ourselves is more unjust; and the most unjust cause of all occurs when we are proud without any reason, that is, when we do not think we have any merit for which we ought to be appreciated, not only because, attaching no importance to merit and regarding glory as nothing but usurpation, we believe that those who attribute the most of it to themselves actually have the most. This vice is so unreasonable and absurd that it would be difficult for me to believe that there are men who sink into it if no one had ever been unjustly praised; but flattery is so common everywhere that there is no man so defective that he does not often see himself esteemed for things which deserve no praise, or which even deserve blame; and this gives occasion to the most ignorant and stupid to fall into this kind of pride.

ARTICLE 158

֍ *That its effects are contrary to those of magnanimity.*

But whatever may be the reason for which we esteem ourselves, if it is other than a resolution always to make good use of our free will, from which resolution I have stated that magnanimity proceeds, it always produces a very reprehensible pride which is so different from true magnanimity that it has completely opposite effects. For since all other goods, such as intelligence, beauty, wealth, honors, etc., are usually esteemed more highly as they are found in fewer persons, and since most of them are even of such a nature that they cannot be communicated to many, this causes the proud to try to lower all other man, and because they are the slaves of their desires, their souls are constantly agitated by hatred, envy, jealousy or anger.

ARTICLE 159

֍ *Vicious humility.*

As for baseness or vicious humility, it consists chiefly in the fact that a man feels weak or irresolute, and that, as though he did not have the entire use of his free will, he cannot prevent himself from doing things of which he will later repent; and it also consists in his believing that he cannot subsist by himself or do without many things whose acquisition depends on others. Thus it is directly opposed to magnanimity, and it often happens that those who have the basest minds are the most arrogant and haughty, just as the most magnanimous are the most modest and humble. But, whereas those who have strong and magnanimous minds do not change their humor in relation to the prosperity or adversity that comes to them, those who have weak and abject minds are led only by fortune, and prosperity puffs them up no less than adversity makes them humble. Often we even see that they ignominiously lower themselves before those from whom they expect some benefits or fear some evil, and that at the same time they insolently raise themselves above those from whom they neither expect nor fear anything.

ARTICLE 160

✑ The movement of the animal spirits in these passions.

Moreover, it is easy to recognize that pride and baseness are not only vices but also passions, because their emotions appear clearly in those who are suddenly puffed up or cast down by some new turn of events. But we may doubt whether magnanimity and humility, which are virtues, can also be passions, because their movements are less apparent, and it seems that virtue is less closely related to passion than is vice. However, I see no reason why the same movement of the animal spirits which strengthens a thought when it has a bad foundation cannot also strengthen it when its foundation is legitimate. And because pride and magnanimity consist only in the good opinion that a man has of himself, and differ only in that this opinion is unjustified in one case and justified in the other, it seems to me that they can be related to a single passion which is aroused by a movement composed of the movements of wonder, joy and love, both of ourselves and of that which makes us esteem ourselves. On the other hand, the movement which arouses humility, whether virtuous or vicious, is composed of those of wonder, sadness and love of ourselves, mingled with hatred of our faults, which make us despise ourselves. And the only difference I see in these movements is that the movement of wonder has two properties: the first, that surprise makes it strong from the beginning; the second, that it is equal in its continuance, i.e., that the spirits continue to move in the same way in the brain. Of these properties, the first is encountered much more in pride and baseness than in magnanimity and virtuous humility, whereas the second is better seen in the latter two than in the former two. The reason for this is that vice usually comes from ignorance, and that it is those who know themselves the least who are most likely to become proud or humiliate themselves more than they should, because everything new that happens to them surprises them, and because, attributing it to themselves, they wonder at themselves, so that they esteem or despise themselves according to whether what happens to them is to their advantage or not. But because something which has made them proud is often followed by something which humiliates them, the movement of their passions is variable. In magnanimity, however, there is nothing that is not compatible with virtuous humility, or anything elsewhere which might change them, which makes their movements firm, constant and always very similar to what they have been before. But they do not come so much from surprise, because those who esteem themselves in this manner are sufficiently well aware of the causes that make them esteem themselves; and yet we may say that these causes (namely, the power of using our free will, which makes us value ourselves, and the infirmities of the subject in whom this power resides, which prevent us from esteeming ourselves too highly) are so wonderful that each time we consider them they give us a new feeling of wonder.

ARTICLE 161

✑ *How magnanimity may be acquired.*

And it must be noted that what are commonly called virtues are habits in the soul which dispose it to certain thoughts in such a way that they are different from these thoughts, but can produce them and, reciprocally, be produced by them. It must be noted also that these thoughts can be produced by the soul alone, but that it often happens that they are strengthened by some movement of the animal spirits, and that they are then both actions of virtue and passions of the soul. Thus, although there is no virtue to which good birth seems to contribute so much as to that which makes a man esteem himself at his just value, and although it is easy to believe that all the souls which God places in the bodies of men are not equally noble and strong (which is why I have called this virtue *générosité*,* in accordance with the usage of our language, rather than *magnanimité*, in accordance with the usage of the School, where it is not very well known), it is nevertheless certain that good education and upbringing are of great service in correcting the faults of birth, and that if we frequently occupy ourselves in considering what free will is, and how great are the advantages

---

* In the preceding pages I have translated *"générosité"* as "magnanimity" rather than "generosity," because the latter usually has a more restricted meaning in English.—L.B.

which come from a firm resolution to make good use of it, as well as, on the other hand, how vain and useless are all the concerns which torment those who are consumed with ambition, we may arouse in ourselves the passion, and then acquire the virtue, of magnanimity; and since this virtue is, so to speak, the key to all the others and a general remedy against all the disorders of the passions, it seems to me that this consideration is quite worthy of notice.

ARTICLE 162

❧ *Veneration.*

Veneration, or respect, is an inclination of the soul not only to esteem the object it reveres, but also to submit itself to it with a certain fear, in order to try to make the object more favorable to it. We therefore have veneration only for free causes which we judge to be capable of doing us good or evil, without knowing which of the two they will do; for we have love and devotion, rather than simple veneration, for those from which we expect only good, and we have hatred for those from which we expect only evil; and if we do not judge that the cause of this good or evil is free, we do not submit ourselves to it in order to try to make it favorable to us. Thus when the pagans had veneration for forests, springs or mountains, it was not, properly speaking, dead things that they revered, but the divinities they believed to preside over them. And the movement of the animal spirits which arouses this passion is composed of that which arouses fear, of which I shall speak later.

ARTICLE 163

❧ *Disdain.*

Similarly, what I call disdain is an inclination of the soul to despise a free cause in judging that, although it is by nature capable of doing good and evil, it is nevertheless so far beneath us that it can do neither to us. And the movement of the animal spirits which arouses it is composed of those which arouse wonder and confidence or boldness.

ARTICLE 164

❧ *The function of these two passions.*

And it is magnanimity and weakness of mind or baseness which determine the good or bad use of these two passions, for the nobler and more magnanimous our soul is, the more we are inclined to give everyone his due, so that not only do we have a very profound humility with regard to God, but we also render without reluctance all the honor and respect that is due to each man according to his rank and authority in the world, and we despise nothing but vices. Those who have base and weak minds, however, are likely to sin by excess, sometimes in revering and fearing things which deserve only contempt, and sometimes in insolently disdaining those which most deserve to be revered; and they often pass quickly from extreme impiety to superstition, then from superstition back to impiety, so that there is no vice or disorder of the mind of which they are not capable.

ARTICLE 165

❧ *Hope and apprehension.*

Hope is a disposition of the soul to persuade itself that what it desires will come about, and it is caused by a particular movement of the animal spirits, namely, by that of joy and desire mingled together. And apprehension is another disposition of the soul which persuades it that what it desires will not come about. It must be noted that, although these two passions are contrary, we may nevertheless have them both together when we represent to ourselves different reasons at the same time, some of which make us judge that the fulfillment of our desire is easy, while others make it appear difficult.

ARTICLE 166

❧ *Confidence and despair.*

And one of these passions never accompanies desire without leaving some room for the other, for when hope is so strong that it completely drives away apprehension, it changes its nature and is called confidence or assurance, and when we are confident that what we desire will come about, even though we continue to will its occurrence, we nevertheless cease to be agitated by the passion of desire, which makes us seek its fulfillment with anxiety. Similarly, when apprehension is so extreme that it removes all reason for hope, it is converted into despair, and this despair, representing the thing as impossible, completely extinguishes desire, which extends only to things that are possible.

ARTICLE 167

꿎§ *Jealousy.*

Jealousy is a species of apprehension which relates to a desire on our part to preserve our possession of some good; and it comes not so much from the strength of the reasons which make us judge that we may lose it as from the high esteem in which we hold it, which makes us examine even the slightest subjects of suspicion and regard them as worthy of serious attention.

ARTICLE 168

꿎§ *How this passion may be right.*

And because we ought to be more careful in preserving goods which are very great than in preserving those which are smaller, this passion may be just and right in some circumstances. Thus, for example, a military leader who is defending a position of great importance is justified in being jealous of it, that is, in being wary of every means by which it might be taken by surprise; and an honorable woman is not blamed for being jealous of her honor, that is, not only guarding herself against doing wrong, but also avoiding even the slightest reasons for gossip.

ARTICLE 169

꿎§ *How it is reprehensible.*

But a miser is derided when he is jealous of his treasure, that is, when he gloats over it and never wants to go away from it for fear it may be stolen from him; for money is not worth being guarded with such great care. And we despise a man who is jealous of his wife, because it shows that he does not love her in the right way and that he has a bad opinion either of himself or of her. I say that he does not love her in the right way, for if he had real love for her he would have no inclination to mistrust her. It is not she who is actually the object of his love, but only the good he imagines to consist in having sole possession of her, and he would not be afraid of losing that good if he did not judge himself to be unworthy of it, or his wife to be unfaithful. Moreover, this passion relates only to suspicion and mistrust, for it is not, properly speaking, being jealous to try to avoid an evil when we have good reason to fear it.

ARTICLE 170

ᛈᴥᵍ *Irresolution.*

Irresolution is also a species of apprehension which, holding the soul as though suspended among several actions which it can perform, prevents it from carrying out any of them, thus giving it time to choose before deciding, and in this it truly has a certain function which is good; but when it lasts longer than it should, and causes the time required for action to be spent in deliberation, it is very bad. Now I say that it is a species of apprehension, even though it may happen, when we have a choice among several things which all seem equally good, that we remain uncertain and irresolute without having any apprehension, for this kind of irresolution comes only from the subject which presents itself, and not from any agitation of the animal spirits; that is why it is not a passion, except insofar as our apprehension of making a wrong choice increases our uncertainty. But this apprehension is so common and so strong in some men that often, even when they have no choice to make and see only one thing which they may take or leave, it holds them back and makes them stop uselessly in order to seek other things. It is then an excess of irresolution which comes from too great a desire to do right, and a weakness of the understanding, which, having no clear and distinct conceptions, has only a great many confused ones. That is why the only remedy against this excess is to accustom ourselves to forming certain and definite judgments concerning all things that present themselves to us, and to believe that we have always done our duty when we have done what we judge to be best, even though we may have judged very badly.

ARTICLE 171

◂§ *Courage and daring.*

Courage, when it is not a habit or a natural inclination, is a certain heat or agitation which disposes the soul to apply itself powerfully to the execution of the things it wants to do, no matter what their nature; and daring is a species of courage which disposes the soul to the execution of those things which are most dangerous.

ARTICLE 172

◂§ *Emulation.*

And emulation is also a species of courage, but in another sense; for we may regard courage as a genus divided into as many species as there are different objects, and into as many others as there are causes. In the first case, daring is one species of it; in the other, emulation. And the latter is nothing but a heat which disposes the soul to undertake things in which it hopes to be able to succeed, because it sees others succeed in them; and thus it is a species of courage whose external cause is example. I say the external cause because there must also be an internal one, which consists in the fact that the body is so disposed that the power of desire and hope to make a large amount of blood flow to the heart is greater than the power of apprehension or despair to prevent it.

ARTICLE 173

◂§ *How daring depends on hope.*

For it must be noted that although the object of daring is difficulty, from which usually follows apprehension or even despair, so that it is in the most dangerous and desperate matters that we employ the most daring and courage, we nevertheless need to hope, or even be confident, that we can achieve the end we have proposed to ourselves, in order that we may vigorously oppose the difficulties we encounter. But this end is different from this object, for we cannot be confident and hopeless with regard to the same thing at the same time. Thus when the Decii threw themselves against their enemies and rushed to certain death, the object of their daring was the difficulty of preserving their lives during that action, for which difficulty they had only despair, because they were certain of dying; but their end was to stir their soldiers by example, and to make them win the victory, for which they had hope; or their end may also have been to achieve glory after their death, of which they were confident.

ARTICLE 174

৶ৡ *Cowardice and fear.*

Cowardice is directly opposed to courage, and it is a languor or coldness which prevents the soul from proceeding to the execution of the things it would do if it were free of this passion; and fear or terror, which is contrary to daring, is not only a coldness, but also a perturbation and astonishment of the soul which deprives it of the power to resist evils which it believes to be close at hand.

ARTICLE 175

৶ৡ *The function of cowardice.*

Although I cannot convince myself that nature has given men any passion which is always vicious and has no good and praiseworthy function, it is difficult for me to guess what end these two may serve. It seems to me only that cowardice is of some use when it dispenses us from the efforts we might be incited to make by plausible reasons if other more certain reasons, which have made us judge them to be futile, had not aroused this passion; for besides dispensing the soul from these effects, it is then often useful to the body, in that by retarding the movement of the animal spirits it prevents us from dissipating our forces. But it is usually very harmful, because it turns the will away from useful actions; and since it comes only from the fact that we do not have enough hope or desire, we need only increase these two passions within ourselves in order to correct it.

ARTICLE 176

✑§ The function of fear.

As for fear or terror, I do not see that it can ever be praiseworthy or useful. It is therefore not a particular passion, but only an excess of cowardice, astonishment and apprehension which is always vicious, just as daring is an excess of courage which is always good, provided that the end in view is good. And because the principal cause of fear is surprise, there is no better way to rid ourselves of it than to practice forethought and prepare ourselves for all eventualities which may give rise to it through the apprehension they arouse.

ARTICLE 177

✑§ Remorse.

Remorse is a species of sadness which comes from a doubt as to whether a thing we are doing or have done is good, and it necessarily presupposes doubt, for if we were entirely convinced that what we were doing was bad, we would refrain from doing it, since the will applies itself only to things which have some appearance of goodness; and if we were convinced that what we had already done was bad, we would feel repentance, and not only remorse. Now the function of this passion is to make us seek to determine whether the thing we doubt is good or not, or to prevent us from doing it again while we are still not convinced that it is good. But because it presupposes evil, it would be best for us never to have any reason to feel it, and we forestall it by the same means whereby we can free ourselves of irresolution.

ARTICLE 178

~§ *Mockery.*

Derision or mockery is a species of joy mingled with hatred, and it comes from our perception of some small evil in a person we consider to deserve it: we have hatred for the evil, and joy in seeing it in someone who deserves it. And when this happens unexpectedly, surprise and wonder cause us to burst into laughter, in accordance with what has previously been said about the nature of laughter. But this evil must be small, for if it is great we cannot believe that the person who has it deserves it, unless we are of a very evil nature or feel great hatred for him.

ARTICLE 179

~§ *Why those who are least perfect are usually most strongly inclined to mockery.*

And we see that those who have some very obvious defects, such as those who are lame, one-eyed, or hunchbacked, or those who have received some affront in public, are particularly inclined to mockery; for, wishing to see everyone else as ill-favored as themselves, they are glad of the evils which befall others, and feel that they deserve them.

ARTICLE 180

~§ *The function of banter.*

As for good-natured banter in which we reprove vices by making them appear ridiculous, yet without laughing at them ourselves or bearing any hatred toward the persons concerned, it is not a passion, but a quality of the true gentleman which shows the gaiety of his humor and the tranquillity of his soul, which are marks of virtue, and often also the adroitness of his mind, in that he is able to give a pleasant appearance to the things he ridicules.

ARTICLE 181

✑ *The function of laughter in banter.*

And it is not improper to laugh when we hear banter from someone else; it may, in fact, be such that it would be rude not to laugh at it. But when we ourselves jest, it is more seemly to refrain from laughter, in order not to appear to be surprised by the things we are saying, and not to seem to admire our own cleverness in inventing them; and this makes those who hear them all the more surprised.

ARTICLE 182

✑ *Envy.*

What is commonly called envy is a vice which consists in a perverseness of nature which makes some people resent any good that they see coming to others; but I am here using the word to signify a passion which is not always vicious. Envy, then, insofar as it is a passion, is a species of sadness mingled with hatred which arises from our seeing good things come to those whom we consider to be unworthy of them. And we can rightly think this only with regard to the goods of fortune, for as to those of the soul or even of the body, insofar as they are inborn, having received them from God before one was capable of doing any evil makes one sufficiently worthy of them.

ARTICLE 183

✑ *How it can be just or unjust.*

But when fortune gives goods to someone who is truly unworthy of them, and when envy is aroused in us only because, naturally loving justice, we resent that it has not been observed in the distribution of those goods, it is a zeal which may be excusable, particularly when the good we envy in others is of such a nature that it may be converted into evil in their hands, as when it is some charge or office in the exercise of which they may behave badly. When we desire the same good for ourselves and are prevented from having it because it is possessed by others who are less worthy of it, the passion is made more violent, but it is still excusable, provided that the hatred it contains is directed against the bad distribution of the good we envy, and not against the persons who possess it or distribute it. But there are few who are so just and magnanimous that they have no hatred for those who prevent them from acquiring a good which is not communicable to many, and which they had desired for themselves, even though those who have acquired it are equally worthy of it, or more so. And what is usually most envied is glory, for although the glory of others does not prevent us from being able to aspire to it, it does makes access to it more difficult, and increases the price that must be paid for it.

ARTICLE 184

🙚 *Why the envious tend to have a leaden complexion.*

Moreover, there is no vice so harmful to the felicity of men as that of envy, for besides the fact that those who are tainted with it make themselves suffer, they also do everything in their power to disturb the pleasure of others, and they usually have a leaden complexion, that is, one of mingled yellow and black, as though bruised, whence it comes that envy is called *livor* in Latin, which accords very well with what has been said above about the movement of the blood in sadness and hatred; for hatred causes yellow bile which comes from the lower part of the liver, and black bile which comes from the spleen, to spread from the heart through the arteries and into all the veins, and sadness causes the blood in the veins to have less heat and flow more slowly than usual, which is enough to make the complexion livid. But because bile, yellow as well as black, can be sent into the veins by many other causes, and because envy does not send it into them in quantities large enough to change the complexion unless it is very great and of long duration, we must not think that all those in whom we observe this color are inclined to envy.

ARTICLE 185

❧ *Pity.*

Pity is a species of sadness mingled with love or good will toward those whom we see suffering from some evil which we think they do not deserve. Thus it is contrary to envy because of its object, and to mockery because it considers them in a different way.

ARTICLE 186

❧ *Those who are most strongly inclined to pity.*

Those who feel very weak and subject to the adversities of fortune seem to be more strongly inclined to this passion than are others, because they regard the evil of others as capable of happening to themselves, and they are thus moved to pity more by their love for themselves than by their love for others.

ARTICLE 187

❧ *How the most magnanimous are touched by this passion.*

Nevertheless, those who are most magnanimous and strongest in mind, so that they fear no evil for themselves and hold themselves beyond the power of fortune, are not exempt from compassion when they see the infirmity of other men and hear their complaints, for it is part of magnanimity to have good will toward everyone. But the sadness of this pity is no longer bitter, and, like that aroused by the tragic actions we see represented on the stage, it is more in the exterior and in the senses than in the interior of the soul, although the soul does have the satisfaction of knowing that it is doing its duty in sympathizing with the afflicted. And there is here this difference, that whereas the ordinary man has compassion for those who complain, because he thinks that the evils from which they are suffering are extremely trying, the principal object of the pity of the greatest men is the weakness of those whom they hear complaining, because they consider that no possible accident could be so great an evil as the cowardice of those who cannot endure it with constancy; and although they hate vices, they do not hate those whom they see subject to them, but only pity them.

ARTICLE 188

☙ *Those who are not touched by it.*

But it is only the malicious and envious who naturally hate all men, or those who are so brutal and so blinded by good fortune or made so hopeless by bad fortune that they think no further evil can befall them, who are insensitive to pity.

ARTICLE 189

☙ *Why this passion moves us to tears.*

Moreover, we weep very easily in this passion, because love, sending much blood to the heart, causes many vapors to issue from the eyes, and because the cold of sadness, retarding the agitation of those vapors, causes them to change into tears, in accordance with what has been said above.

ARTICLE 190

☙ *Self-satisfaction.*

The satisfaction which is always experienced by those who follow virtue constantly is a habit in their soul which is called tranquillity and peace of conscience; but that which is newly acquired when we have just done some action which we think to be good is a passion, namely, a species of joy, which I believe to be the sweetest of all, since its cause depends only on ourselves. However, when this cause is not just, that is, when the actions from which we draw much satisfaction are not of great importance, or are even vicious, it is ridiculous and serves only to produce pride and impertinent arrogance. We can see this particularly in those who, believing themselves to be devout, are only bigoted and superstitious: that is, on the pretext that they go to church often, recite many prayers, wear their hair short, observe fasts and give alms, they think they are absolutely perfect, and imagine that they are such great friends of God that they could do nothing that would displease Him, and that everything dictated to them by their passion is virtuous zeal, even though it sometimes dictates to them the greatest crimes that can be committed by men, such as betraying cities, killing princes and exterminating whole peoples for the sole reason that they do not follow their opinions.

ARTICLE 191

✍ *Repentance.*

Repentance is directly opposed to self-satisfaction, and is a species of sadness which comes from our believing that we have committed some evil action; and it is very bitter, since its cause comes only from us. This does not, however, prevent it from being very useful when it is true that the action of which we repent is evil, and when we have certain knowledge of it, because it incites us to do better in the future. But it often happens that weak minds repent of things they have done without knowing surely that they are evil: they convince themselves of it only because they are afraid of it, and if they had done the opposite they would repent of it in the same way. This is an imperfection in them which deserves pity, and the remedies against this defect are the same as those which serve to remove irresolution.

ARTICLE 192

✍ *Favor.*

Favor is, properly speaking, a desire to see good come to someone for whom we have good will, but I am here using the word to signify that will insofar as it is aroused in us by some good action on the part of the person for whom we have it; for we are naturally inclined to love those who do things we judge to be good, even though no benefit comes to us from them. In this sense, favor is a species of love, not of desire, even though it is always accompanied by a desire to see good come to the person we favor; and it is usually joined to pity, because when we see adversity befalling the unfortunate it makes us reflect more on their merits.

ARTICLE 193

ᴇᴈ *Gratitude.*

Gratitude is also a species of love aroused in us by some action on the part of the person for whom we feel it, and by which we believe that he has done us some good, or at least that he intended to do so. Thus it has the same content as favor, and all the more so because it is based on an action which affects us, and for which we desire to make a return. That is why it has much greater strength, particularly in souls that are to any extent noble and magnanimous.

ARTICLE 194

ᴇᴈ *Ingratitude.*

As for ingratitude, it is not a passion, for nature has not placed in us any movement of the animal spirits which arouses it; it is only a vice directly opposed to gratitude, in that the latter is always virtuous and one of the principal bonds of human society. That is why this vice is found only in brutal and foolishly arrogant men who think that all things are their due, or in stupid men who do not reflect on the benefits they receive, or in weak and abject men who, feeling their infirmity and their need, basely seek the help of others, then, after they have received it, hate them because, having no will to return the favor, or no hope of being able to do so, and imagining that everyone is as mercenary as themselves and that no one does good without the hope of being rewarded for it, they think they have deceived them.

ARTICLE 195

ᴇᴈ *Indignation.*

Indignation is a species of hatred or aversion which we naturally feel for those who do some evil, no matter what its nature; and it is often mingled with envy or pity, but it nevertheless has a very different object, for we are indignant only with those who do good or evil to people who do not deserve it, but we are envious of those who receive the good, and we pity those who receive the evil. It is true that it is, in a sense, doing evil to possess a good which we do not deserve, which may be the reason why Aristotle and his followers, assuming that envy is always a vice, have given the name of indignation to that envy which is not vicious.

ARTICLE 196

✑ *Why it is sometimes joined to pity, and sometimes to mockery.*

It is also, in a sense, receiving evil to do evil; therefore some men join pity to their indignation, and others mockery, according to whether they bear good or ill will toward those whom they see committing transgressions, and it is thus that the laughter of Democritus and the tears of Heraclitus may have proceeded from the same cause.

ARTICLE 197

✑ *That it is often accompanied by wonder, and is not incompatible with joy.*

Indignation is often also accompanied by wonder, for we usually assume that all things will be done in the way in which we feel they ought to be done. That is why, when they are done otherwise, we are surprised and moved to wonder. Indignation is also not incompatible with joy, even though it is more commonly joined to sadness, for when the evil over which we are indignant cannot harm us, and when we consider that we would not wish to do the same, it gives us a certain pleasure; and this may be one of the causes of the laughter which sometimes accompanies this passion.

ARTICLE 198

✑ *Its function.*

Moreover, indignation is seen much more in those who wish to appear virtuous than in those who really are so; for although those who love virtue cannot see the vices of others without some aversion, they become impassioned only against the greatest and most extraordinary ones. It is being irritable and querulous to have great indignation over things of little importance; it is being unjust to have it over things which are not reprehensible at all; and it is being impertinent and absurd not to restrict this passion to the actions of men, but to extend it to the works of God or of nature, as is done by those who, never content with their condition or fortune, dare to criticize the management of the world and the secrets of Providence.

ARTICLE 199

&§ *Anger.*

Anger is also a species of hatred or aversion which we feel for those who have done some evil, or who have tried to harm not anyone in general, but ourselves in particular. Thus it has the same content as indignation, and all the more so because it is based on an action which affects us, and for which we desire to take vengeance, for it is nearly always accompanied by this desire; and it is directly opposed to gratitude, as indignation is to favor, but it is incomparably more violent than these three other passions, because the desire to repel harmful things and take vengeance is the most pressing of all. It is desire joined to self-love which gives anger all the agitation of the blood which courage and daring can cause; and hatred brings it to pass that it is chiefly the bilious blood which comes from the spleen and the small veins of the liver that undergoes this agitation and enters the heart, where, because of its abundance and the nature of the bile with which it is mingled, it arouses a heat which is keener and more ardent than that which can be aroused there by love or joy.

ARTICLE 200

&§ *Why those whom it causes to turn red are less to be feared than those whom it causes to turn pale.*

And the external signs of this passion vary according to personal temperaments and the diversity of the other passions which compose it or are joined to it. Thus we see some men

who turn pale or tremble when they become angry, and we
see others who turn red or even weep; and it is generally
believed that the anger of those who turn pale is more to be
feared than the anger of those who turn red. The reason for
this is that when a man will not or cannot take vengeance
other than by his expression and his words, he uses all his
heat and strength as soon as he is moved to anger, which
causes him to turn red; and furthermore, sometimes his regret
and self-pity, arising from the fact that he cannot take vengeance in any other way, cause him to weep. On the other
hand, those who hold themselves back and resolve to take
greater vengeance become sad when they think themselves
obliged to do so by the action which has made them angry,
and sometimes they also fear the evils which may follow from
their resolution, which makes them at first pale, cold and
trembling; but when they later come to carry out their vengeance they become all the warmer in proportion as they were
cold at the beginning, just as we observe that fevers which
begin with a chill are usually the most severe.

ARTICLE 201

*That there are two kinds of anger, and that those who
have the most goodness are the most strongly inclined
to the first.*

This shows us that we can distinguish two kinds of
anger: the first is very quick and manifests itself very much
on the surface, but it has little effect and can easily be quelled;
the second is not so apparent at the beginning, but it gnaws
the heart more powerfully and has more dangerous effects.
Those who have much goodness and love are inclined to the
first, for it does not come from deep hatred, but from a quick
aversion which surprises them because, being inclined to
imagine that all things should go in the way they judge to be
the best, as soon as it happens otherwise they wonder and feel
offended, often even when the matter does not affect them
personally, because, having much affection, they are as inter-
ested in those they love as in themselves. Thus what would
be only a cause for indignation to someone else is to them
a cause for anger. And because their inclination to love makes
them have much heat and much blood in their heart, the
aversion which surprises them cannot send so little bile there

that it does not at first cause great agitation in the blood; but this agitation does not last long, because the strength of the surprise does not continue, and because as soon as they perceive that the matter which has angered them should not have stirred them so violently, they repent of it.

ARTICLE 202

✑ *That it is weak and base minds that let themselves be carried away by the second kind.*

The second kind of anger, in which hatred and sadness predominate, is not so apparent at first, except perhaps in that it makes the face turn pale; but its strength is gradually augmented by the agitation of an ardent desire for vengeance aroused in the blood, which, being mingled with the bile that is driven to the heart from the spleen and the lower part of the liver, arouses there a very keen and stinging heat. And as it is the most magnanimous souls that have the most heat, so it is those which are basest and weakest that allow themselves to be most carried away by this kind of anger; for offenses seem greater in proportion as pride makes us esteem ourselves more, and also as we esteem more highly the goods they take away, and these goods are esteemed more as the soul is weak and base, because they depend on others.

ARTICLE 203

✑ *That magnanimity serves as a remedy against its excesses.*

Moreover, although this passion is useful in giving us vigor with which to repeal offenses, there is no other passion whose excesses ought to be more carefully avoided, because, disturbing our judgment, they often make us commit transgressions which we later regret, and because sometimes they even prevent us from repelling those offenses as well as we could if we had less emotion. But as there is nothing which makes it more excessive than pride, so I think that magnanimity is the best remedy we can find against this excess, for by causing us to have little esteem for all goods which may be taken away, and on the other hand to have great esteem for the freedom and absolute dominion over ourselves which we cease to have when we can be offended by someone, it makes us have only contempt, or at most indignation, for the offenses which others usually resent.

ARTICLE 204

⋐ *Vainglory.*

What I here call vainglory is a species of joy which is based on self-love, and which comes from a belief or hope of being praised by certain other people. It is thus different from the inner satisfaction that comes from our belief that we have performed some good action, for we are sometimes praised for things we do not believe to be good, and blamed for things we believe to be better. But they are both species of self-esteem, as well as of joy, for seeing that we are esteemed by others is a reason for esteeming ourselves.

ARTICLE 205

⋐ *Shame.*

Shame, on the other hand, is a species of sadness which is also based on self-love, and which comes from our belief or fear of being blamed; it is, furthermore, a species of modesty or humility and self-mistrust, for if we esteem ourselves so highly that we cannot imagine ourselves to be despised by anyone, we cannot easily be ashamed.

ARTICLE 206

⋐ *The function of these two passions.*

Vainglory and shame have the same function in that they incite us to virtue, one by hope, the other by fear. We need only to train our judgment concerning what is truly deserving of blame or praise, in order not to be ashamed of doing good, and not to draw vanity from our vices, as many people do. But it is not good to rid ourselves entirely of these passions, as the Cynics used to do, for although common people judge very badly, nevertheless, because we cannot live without them, and because it is important to us to be esteemed by them, we should often follow their opinions rather than our own, concerning the external aspects of our actions.

ARTICLE 207

Impudence.

Impudence or effrontery, which is a contempt of shame, and often also of vainglory, is not a passion, because there is in us no particular movement of the animal spirits which arouses it; but it is a vice which is opposed to shame, and also to vainglory, insofar as they are both good, just as ingratitude is opposed to gratitude, and cruelty to pity. And the principal cause of effrontery comes from a man's having frequently received great affronts; for there is no one who, when he is young, does not imagine that praise is a good and disgrace an evil which is much more important to life than it is found to be by experience, when, having received some flagrant affronts, he sees himself entirely deprived of honor and despised by everyone. That is why those men become impudent who, measuring good and evil only by the well-being of the body, see that they enjoy it just as well after these affronts as before, or sometimes even much better, because they are relieved of many constraints which honor had imposed on them, and because, if the loss of their goods is joined to their disgrace, there are always charitable persons who will give to them.

ARTICLE 208

Disgust.

Disgust is a species of sadness which comes from the same cause as that from which joy has previously come; for we are so made that most of the things we enjoy are good with regard to us only for a certain time, and eventually become tiresome. This is particularly apparent in the case of eating and drinking, which are useful only while we have an appetite and become harmful when we no longer have it; and because they then cease to be pleasing to the taste [*goût*], this passion has been named disgust [*dégoût*].

ARTICLE 209

⇜ *Nostalgia.*

Nostalgia is a species of sadness which has a particular bitterness, in that it is always joined to a certain despair and to the memory of the pleasure which a certain enjoyment once gave us, for we feel nostalgia only over goods which we have enjoyed, and which are lost in such a way that we have no hope of recovering them in the time and form in which we look back on them with nostalgia.

ARTICLE 210

⇜ *Gladness.*

Finally, what I call gladness is a species of joy in which there is this particularity, that its sweetness is augmented by the recollection of the evils we have suffered, and of which we feel relieved in the same way as if we felt ourselves freed of a heavy burden that we had been carrying on our shoulders for a long time. And I see nothing very remarkable in these three passions; I have therefore placed them here only to follow the order of the enumeration I have previously made; but it seems to me that this enumeration has been useful in showing that we have omitted no passion worthy of particular consideration.

ARTICLE 211

⇜ *A general remedy against the passions.*

And now that we are acquainted with them all, we have much less reason to fear them than we had before, for we see that they are all good in their nature, and that we have nothing to avoid except their evil uses or their excesses, against which the remedies I have explained might be sufficient if everyone were careful to practice them. But because I have placed among these remedies the forethought and ingenuity by which we may correct our natural defects by applying ourselves to separating within us the movements of the blood and animal spirits from the thoughts to which they are usually joined, I confess that there are few people who are sufficiently prepared in this way to meet any contingency, and that these movements aroused in the blood by the objects of the passions follow so promptly from the single impressions made in the brain and from the disposition of the organs, although the soul in no way contributes to them, that there is no human wisdom capable of withstanding them when one is not sufficiently prepared for them. Thus many people cannot prevent themselves from laughing when they are tickled, even though it gives them no pleasure, for the impression of joy and surprise which has previously made them laugh for the same reason, being reawakened in the imagination, causes their lungs to be suddenly inflated against their will by the blood sent there from the heart. And thus those who are naturally inclined to the emotions of joy and pity, or fear, or anger, cannot prevent themselves from fainting, or weeping, or trembling, or having their blood agitated as though they had a fever, when their imagination is strongly affected by the object of one of these passions. But what we can always do on such occasions, and what I believe I can set down here as being the easiest and most general remedy against all the excesses of the passions, is that, when we feel our blood thus agitated, we ought to take warning and remember that everything which presents itself to the imagination tends to deceive the soul and to make the reasons in favor of the object of its passion appear to be much stronger than they are, and those opposed to it much weaker. And when the passion urges us to do only things which need not be done immediately, we should refrain from passing judgment on them for the present, and divert ourselves with other thoughts until time and rest have entirely calmed the agitation in the blood. And finally, when it incites us to actions with regard to which it is necessary to make a decision without delay, our will should apply itself chiefly to considering and following the reasons contrary to those presented by the passion, even though they appear to be less strong; as when we are unexpectedly attacked by an enemy, the situation does not permit us to spend any time in deliberation. But it seems to me that there is something which can always be done by those who are accustomed to reflecting on their actions, namely, when they feel themselves seized by fear, they can try to divert their thoughts from the danger by representing to themselves the reasons for which there is much more safety and honor in resistance than in flight; and when, on the other hand, they feel that anger and a desire for vengeance are inciting them to throw themselves heedlessly against those who are attacking them, they can remind themselves that it is foolhardy to lose one's life when one can save oneself without dishonor, and that, if the match is very unequal, it is better to retreat honorably, or ask quarter, than to expose oneself doggedly to certain death.

ARTICLE 212

That it is on them alone that all the good and evil of this life depends.

Moreover, the soul may have pleasures of its own, but those which are common to it and the body depend entirely on the passions, so that those men who can most be moved by the passions are most capable of savoring the enjoyments of this life. It is true that such men may also find the most bitterness when they do not know how to employ them well, and when fortune is contrary to them. But wisdom is here useful chiefly in that it teaches us to acquire such control over our passions, and to govern them with such skill, that all the evils they cause are quite bearable, and even bring us joy.

End

THE IMPORTANT LETTERS

❦

To ——————
November, 1640

I am obliged to you for telling me about the passage in Saint Augustine to which my *"I think, therefore I am"* has some relation. I went to read it today in the library of this city [Leyden], and I find that actually he uses it to prove the certainty of our being, and then to show that there is in us some image of the Trinity, in that we are, we know that we are, and we love this being and this knowledge that are in us. I, however, use it to show that this "I" that thinks is an *immaterial substance* which has nothing corporeal about it. These are two different things. And to infer that we exist from the fact that we doubt is something so simple and natural that it might have come from anyone's pen; nevertheless, I am glad to be in accord with Saint Augustine on this principle, if only to silence those small minds who have tried to quibble about it. The little I have written on metaphysics is already on its way to Paris, where I think it will be printed, and I have here only a first draft in which so many words are crossed out that I myself would have difficulty in reading it. I therefore cannot offer it to you, but as soon as it is printed I will send you one of the first copies of it, since you do me the honor of wishing to read it, and I shall be very happy to hear your judgment of it.

❦

To Marin Mersenne
July, 1641

If I am not mistaken, the author of the Latin letter, written to you, which you have sent me is not a man who is still trying to determine how we ought to judge things. He expresses himself so well when he explains his own thoughts that I cannot believe he has not understood those of others; I am convinced, rather, that, being biased in favor of his own opinions, it is difficult for him to appreciate anything that opposes his judgments. Thus I foresee that this will not be the last disagreement between us; on the contrary, I view this first letter as a challenge he has issued to me to see how I shall take it, and whether, after I myself have opened the battlefield to all comers, I shall hesitate to pit my weapons and strength against his. I admit to you that it would give me great pleasure to enter into a discussion with a man of his intelligence if, from what he has shown me of his thoughts, he did not seem to be too strongly committed already; I am afraid that all my efforts will be wasted on him, and that no matter how hard I try to satisfy him and withdraw him from the unfortunate commitment in which he appears to be, he will plunge still deeper into it of his own accord by seeking means of contradicting me.

Is it credible that, as he says, he was unable to understand what I meant by the idea of God, the idea of the soul, and the ideas of insensible things, since I mean by them nothing other than what he himself must necessarily have meant by them when he wrote to you that he did not understand them? For he does not say that he understood nothing by the name of God, the name of the soul and the name of insensible things; he says only that he does not know what is to be understood by the ideas of them. But if he understood something by these names, as he surely did, he knew at the same time what is to be understood by these ideas, since it is exactly what he understood by the names. For I do not simply give the name of "ideas" to those images which are depicted in the imagination. On the contrary, I do not call them by this name insofar as they are in the corporeal imagination; in general, I apply the word "idea" to anything that is in our mind when we conceive something, no matter how we conceive it.

But I am afraid he may be one of those who believe themselves unable to conceive something when they cannot imagine it, as though there were in us only that one way of thinking and conceiving. He has seen clearly that I do not hold that opinion, and he has also shown that he does not hold it either, in that he himself says that God cannot be conceived by the imagination. But if it is not by the imagination that we conceive God, then either we conceive nothing when we speak of Him (which would indicate a terrible blindness), or else we conceive Him in some other way; but no matter how we conceive Him, we have the idea of Him, for we can express nothing by our words, when we understand what we are saying, unless it is certain that we have in us the idea of the thing that is signified by our words.

If, therefore, he will take the word "idea" in the manner in which I expressly said I took it, without dwelling on the ambiguity of those who restrict it to the images of material things that are formed in the imagination, it will be easy for him to see that by the idea of God I mean nothing other than what all men usually mean when they speak of Him, and what he himself must necessarily have meant, for otherwise how could he have said that God is infinite and incomprehensible, and that He cannot be represented by our imagination? And if he did not have the idea of God, how could he say that these attributes, and countless others which express His greatness to us, are applicable to Him? It must therefore be agreed that we have the idea of God, and that we cannot fail to know what it is, or what is to be understood by it; for otherwise it would be impossible for us to know anything at all about God, and if someone said, for example, that he believed that God existed and that a certain attribute or perfection belonged to Him, these would be only empty words, because they would convey no meaning to our mind; and that would be the most impious and impertinent thing in the world.

As for the soul, it is something even clearer. Since, as I have demonstrated, it is only a thinking thing, it is impossible for us ever to think of anything without at the same time having the idea of our soul as a thing that is capable of thinking of everything we think. It is true that a thing of this nature cannot be imagined, that is, cannot be represented by a corporeal image. But this is not surprising, because our imagination is able to represent only things which affect the senses; therefore, since our soul has no color, odor, taste or anything else that belongs to body, it is not possible to imagine it, or form an image of it. But this does not mean that it is inconceivable; on the contrary, since it is by means of the soul that we conceive everything, it alone is more conceivable than all other things together.

After this, I am obliged to tell you that your friend utterly fails to grasp my meaning when, in order to point up the distinction between ideas that are in the imagination and those that are in the mind, he says that the former are expressed by names, while the latter are expressed by propositions. For the fact that they are expressed by names or propositions has nothing to do with whether they belong to the mind or to the imagination; both kinds of ideas may be expressed in either way, but it is the way of conceiving them that makes the difference. Anything that we conceive without an image is an idea of the pure mind, and anything we conceive with an image is an idea of the imagination. And since the limits of our imagination are extremely short and narrow, while our mind has almost no limits at all, there are few things, even corporeal things, which we can imagine, even though we are capable of conceiving them. Indeed, that whole science which might be regarded as the one that is most thoroughly dependent on the imagination, since it deals only with sizes, shapes and movements, is not founded on the phantoms of the imagination, but only on the clear and distinct notions of the mind, as is well known by those who have studied it with any thoroughness.

But by what induction has he been able to draw from my writings that the idea of God must be expressed by the proposition "God exists," and then to conclude, as he does, that my chief argument in proof of His existence is a begging of the question? He must be extremely clear-sighted to see something in my writings which I never intended to place in them, and which had never even occurred to me before I saw his letter. I have drawn the proof of the existence of God from the idea I find in myself of a supremely perfect being, which is the usual notion that one has of Him. And it is true that the mere consideration of such a being leads us so easily to the knowledge of His existence that conceiving God is almost the same thing as realizing that He exists. Nevertheless, the idea we have of God, or of a supremely perfect being, is quite different from the proposition "God exists," and one cannot be used as a means or antecedent for proving the other.

And it is certain that, after reaching knowledge of the nature of our soul by means of the steps I employed, and after thereby recognizing that it is a spiritual substance, since I see that all the attributes which belong to spiritual substances belong to it, I did not have to be a great philosopher to conclude, as I did, that it is therefore not corporeal. But it is no doubt necessary to have an extremely open mind, and think quite differently from most men, in order to see that one does not follow from the other, and find flaws in this argument. That is what I beg him to make clear to me, and what I hope to learn from him if he will take the trouble to teach me. As for myself, I will not refuse my little enlightenments to him if he needs them, and if he will act in good faith with me. I am, etc.

❧§§❧

To Princess Elizabeth of Bohemia
May 21, 1643

The favor with which you have honored me, Your Highness, in sending me your commands in writing, is greater than I would ever have dared to hope, and it relieves my defects better than the favor I had passionately desired, which was to receive your commands from you in person, if I had been granted the honor of paying my respects to you and offering you my very humble services when I was recently in The Hague. For I would have had too many wonders to admire at the same time; and, on hearing superhuman discourse issuing from a body so similar to those which painters give to angels, I would have been entranced, I believe, in the same way as those who have just left earth and entered heaven, and that would have made me less capable of answering you. You doubtlessly noticed that defect in me when I previously had the honor of speaking to you, and, in your clemency, you have decided to relieve me of it by leaving me the traces of your thoughts on paper. After rereading them several times, and accustoming myself to considering them, I am less dazzled by them, but I have all the more admiration for them, because I see that not only do they appear ingenious at first sight, but also that they appear to be more judicious and sound the more one examines them.

And I can truthfully say that the question Your Highness has raised [how the soul can move the body] seems to me to be the one that can most reasonably be asked of me on the basis of the writings I have published. For there are two things in the human soul on which all the knowledge we can have of its nature depends: one of them is that it thinks, the other is that, being united to the body, it can act and suffer with it. I have said almost nothing about the latter, and have taken pains only to make the former understood, because my chief purpose was to prove the distinction between the soul and the body, and only the former could be useful in this, while the latter would have been harmful. But since Your Highness sees so clearly that nothing can be concealed from her, I shall now try to explain the way in which I conceive the union of the soul with the body, and how the soul has the power to move the body.

First, I consider that there are in us certain primary notions that are, so to speak, originals on the pattern of which we form all our other knowledge. And there are only very few such notions, for after the most general ones, those of being, number, duration, etc., which apply to everything we can conceive, we have, for body in particular, only the notion of extension, from which follow those of shape and movement; and for the soul by itself, we have only the notion of thought, in which are comprised the perceptions of the understanding and the inclinations of the will; finally, for the soul and the body together, we have only the notion of their union, on which depends that of the power of the soul to move the body, and of the body to act on the soul by causing its sensations and passions.

I consider also that all human science consists solely in rightly distinguishing these notions, and in attributing each one of them only to those things to which it pertains. For if we try to explain some difficulty by means of a notion that does not pertain to it, we cannot fail to be mistaken, and we shall also be mistaken if we try to explain one of these notions by another, for, since they are primary, each of them can be understood only by itself. And because the use of the senses has made the notions of extension, shape and movement much more familiar to us than the others, the chief cause of our errors is that we commonly try to use these notions to explain things to which they do not pertain, as when we try to use the imagination in conceiving the nature of the soul, or when we try to understand the way in which the soul moves the body by thinking of the way in which one body moves another.

Therefore, since in my *Meditations*, which Your Highness has deigned to read, I have tried to clarify the notions which pertain to the soul alone by distinguishing them from those which pertain to the body alone, the first thing I must next explain is the way to understand those which pertain to the union of the soul with the body, without those which pertain to the body alone, or to the soul alone. In this it seems to me that what I have written in my replies to the sixth objections may be useful, for we may seek these simple notions nowhere except in our soul, which contains them all by its nature, but which does not always distinguish them well enough from one another, or attribute them to the objects to which they ought to be attributed.

Thus I believe that we have hitherto confused the notion of the power whereby the soul moves the body with that whereby one body acts in another, and that we have attributed them both, not to the soul, for we do not yet know it, but to the various qualities of bodies, such as weight, heat, and so on, which we have imagined to be real, that is, to have an existence distinct from that of body, and therefore to be substances, even though we have named them qualities. And in order to apprehend them we have made use sometimes of notions that are in us for knowing the body, and sometimes of those that are in us for knowing the soul, according to whether what we have attributed to them has been material or immaterial. For example, if we assume that weight is a real quality about which we know only that it has the power to move the body in which it is toward the center of the earth, we have no difficulty in apprehending how it moves this body, or how it is joined to it; and we do not think that it takes place by an actual contact of one surface against another, for we experience in ourselves that we have a particular notion for apprehending this; and I believe that we misuse this notion when we apply it to weight, which is nothing really distinct from body, as I hope to show in my *Physics*, because I believe that it has been given to us for apprehending the way in which the soul moves the body.

I would be showing lack of acquaintance with your incomparable mind, Your Highness, if I were to use any more words in explaining myself, and I would be too presumptuous if I dared to think that my reply could entirely satisfy you; but I will try to avoid both by adding only that if I am capable of writing or saying anything which may please you, I shall always be honored to take up my pen or go to The Hague for that purpose, and that there is nothing in the world so dear to me as to be able to obey your commands. But I can find here no place for the observance of the Hippocratic oath you enjoin upon me, since you have communicated to me nothing which does not deserve to be seen and admired by all men. I can only say on this subject that, having infinite esteem for the letter I have received from you, I shall treat it as misers treat their treasures: they hide them all the more as they esteem them, and, jealous of everyone else's sight, they take their supreme satisfaction in looking at them. Thus I shall be happy to be alone in enjoying the good of seeing your letter, and my greatest ambition is to be able to say that I am, and truly to be, etc.

❦

To Princess Elizabeth of Bohemia
June 28, 1643

I am greatly obliged to you, Your Highness, for still deigning to have the patience to listen to me on the same subject, after finding that I explained myself badly in my previous letter concerning the question it pleased you to propose to me, and for giving me the opportunity of pointing out the things I have omitted. The principal ones seem to me to be that, after distinguishing three kinds of primary ideas or notions which are known each in a particular manner and not by comparison with any other, namely, the notions we have of the soul, the body, and the union of the soul with the body, I ought to have explained the differences among these three kinds of notions, and among the operations of the soul by which we have them, and to have stated the means by which we may make each one of them familiar and easy; then, having said why I used the comparison of weight, I ought to have shown that, although we may try to apprehend the soul as material (which is actually apprehending its union with the body), we know afterward that it is inseparable from the body. This, I believe, is the whole task that Your Highness has set for me.

First, then, I note these great differences among the three kinds of notions: the soul can be apprehended only by the pure understanding; body, i.e., extension, shapes and movements, can also be known by the understanding alone, but it is known much better by the understanding aided by the imagination; and finally, the things which pertain to the union of the soul and the body can be known only obscurely by the understanding alone, and even by the understanding aided by the imagination, but they are known very clearly by means of the senses. Hence those who never philosophize, and who make use only of their senses, do not doubt that the soul moves the body and that the body acts on the soul; they consider them both as a single thing, that is, they apprehend their union, for apprehending the union between two things is apprehending them as a single thing. And metaphysical thoughts, which exercise the pure understanding, serve to make the notion of the soul familiar to us; and the study of mathematics, which exercises chiefly the imagination in the consideration of shapes and movements, accustoms us to forming distinct notions of body; and finally, it is in dealing only with life and everyday affairs, and in refraining from studying and meditating on things which exercise the imagination, th·it we learn to apprehend the union of the soul and the body.

I am almost afraid, Your Highness, that you may think I am not speaking seriously here; but that would be contrary to the respect I owe to you, and which I shall never fail to render to you. I may truthfully say that the rule I have always observed in my studies, and the one which I believe to have been of greatest service to me in acquiring knowledge, has been that I have never spent more than a few hours a day on thoughts which occupy the imagination, or more than a few hours a year on those which occupy the understanding alone, and that I have devoted all the rest of my time to the relaxation of the senses and the repose of the mind; and among the exercises of the imagination, I even count all serious conversation and anything that requires attention. That is what has made me retire to the country; for even though, in the busiest city in the world, I might still have as many hours to myself as I now devote to study, I could not employ them so usefully if my mind were wearied by the worries and bothers of life. I take the liberty of writing this to you, Your Highness, in order to express my wonder when I consider that, amid the affairs and concerns which never fail to beset those who are of both great intelligence and high birth, you have been able to occupy yourself with the meditations that are required for rightly understanding the distinction between the soul and the body.

But I have judged that it was these meditations, rather than thoughts that require less attention, which made you find obscurity in the notion we have of their union. It does not seem to me that the human mind is capable of apprehending distinctly, at the same time, the union of the soul and the body and the distinction between them, because in order to do so we would have to apprehend them as a single thing while at the same time apprehending them as two things, and these two apprehensions are incompatible. In this connection (assuming that you still had the reasons that prove the distinctness of the soul from the body strongly present to your mind, and not wishing to ask you to set them aside in order to represent to yourself the notion of the union which everyone always experiences in himself without philosophizing, namely, that he is a single person who has both a body and a mind which are of such a nature that the mind can move the body and sense the accidents which befall it), I previously made use of the comparison of weight and the other qualities we commonly imagine to be united to certain bodies, as thought is united to our own body; and I was not concerned by the fact that this comparison was amiss in that these qualities are not real, as we imagine them, because I believed that you were already entirely convinced that the soul is a substance distinct from the body.

But since you observe that it is easier to attribute matter and extension to the soul than to attribute to it the ability to move a body and be moved by it without having any matter, I beg you freely to attribute this matter and extension to the soul, for that is nothing other than conceiving it as united to the body. And after you have thoroughly conceived this, and have experienced it for yourself, it will be easy for you to consider that the matter you have attributed to thought is not thought itself, and that the extension of this matter is of a different nature from the extension of thought, in that the former is determined in a certain location from which it excludes all other corporeal extension, which is not true of the latter. And thus, Your Highness, you will easily return to knowledge of the distinctness of the soul from the body, even though you have conceived their union.

Finally, while I believe that it is very necessary to have thoroughly understood, once in one's life, the principles of metaphysics, since it is they which give us knowledge of God and of our soul, I also believe that it would be very harmful to occupy one's understanding often in meditating on them, since it would not be able to concern itself so well with the functions of the imagination and the senses, and that it is best to content ourselves with retaining in our memory and belief the conclusions we have already drawn, then spend the rest of the time we have for study in thoughts in which the understanding acts with the imagination and the senses.

The extreme devotion which I have to your service, Your Highness, makes me hope that my frankness will not be disagreeable to you, and it would have committed me to a longer discourse here, in which I would have tried to clear up all the difficulties of the question you have proposed to me, were it not for the fact that some unfortunate news which I have just received from Utrecht—where the Magistrate has summoned me in order to verify what I have written about one of their ministers, even though he is a man who has infamously slandered me, and what I have written about him is only too well known to everyone—forces me to end this letter here so that I may go and seek to determine how I can extricate myself from these chicaneries as soon as possible. I am, etc.

❧

To Father Mesland
May 2, 1644 (?)

I know that it is very difficult to enter into another man's thoughts, and experience has shown me how difficult my own thoughts seem to others; I am therefore greatly obliged to you for having taken pains to examine them, and I can only have a very high opinion of you on seeing that you have such a firm grasp of them that they are now more yours than mine. And the difficulties it has pleased you to propose to me are in the matter itself, and in the insufficiency of my expression, rather than in any insufficiency of your comprehension, for you have added the solutions of the principal ones. But I will nevertheless tell you my feelings here about all of them.

I admit that in physical and moral causes which are particular and limited, we often find that those which produce a certain effect are not always capable of producing many others which seem lesser to us. Thus a man, who can produce another man, cannot produce an ant; and a king who makes an entire people obey him sometimes cannot make a horse obey him. But when it is a question of a universal and undetermined cause, it seems to me that it is an extremely common notion that "he who can do the most can also do the least," and that "the whole is greater than any of its parts." And this common-sense notion also applies to particular causes, whether moral or physical; for it would be more for a man to be able to produce men and ants than to be able to produce only men, and it would be a greater power for a king to command even horses than to command only his people, as it has been claimed that the music of Orpheus could move even animals, in order to attribute all the more power to it.

It matters little whether my second demonstration, founded on our own existence, is considered as different from the first, or only as an explanation of it. But just as it is an effect of God to have created me, so it is also an effect of Him to have placed the idea of Him within me; and there is no effect that comes from Him by which His existence cannot be demonstrated. However, it seems to me that all these demonstrations, taken from effects, amount to a single one, and that they are not thorough unless these effects are evident to us (which is why I considered my own existence rather than that of the sky and the earth, of which I am not so certain), and unless we join to them the idea we have of God. For since my soul is finite, I can know that the order of causes is not infinite only insofar as I have in me this idea of the first cause; and even if it be admitted that there is a first cause which preserves me, I cannot say that it is God unless I truly have the idea of God. I implied this in my replies to the first objections, but only in a few words, in order not to despise the reasoning of others, who commonly admit that there is no infinite progression. I, however, do not admit this; on the contrary, I believe that there is such a progression in the division of the parts of matter, as will be seen in my philosophical treatise which is now being printed.

I do not know that I have determined that God always does what He knows to be most perfect, and it does not seem to me that a finite mind can judge this. But I have tried to clear up the difficulty proposed concerning the cause of errors by assuming that God created the world extremely perfect, because the difficulty vanishes if we assume the contrary.

I am greatly obliged to you for pointing out to me the passages in Saint Augustine which may serve to authorize my opinions; some of my other friends have also done so, and it gives me great satisfaction to know that my thoughts are in agreement with those of such a holy and excellent personage. For I am not of the same character as those who wish their opinions to appear to be new; on the contrary, I adapt my opinions to those of others, as much as truth will allow me to do so.

I place no other difference between the soul and its ideas than between a piece of wax and the various shapes it can receive. And since receiving various shapes is not, strictly speaking, an action, but a passion in the wax, it seems to me that it is also a passion in the soul to receive this or that idea, and that only its volitions are actions; and also that its ideas are placed in it partly by objects which affect the senses, partly by impressions that are in the brain, and partly by preceding dispositions in the soul itself, and by the movements of its will—just as a piece of wax receives its shapes partly from other bodies which press upon it, partly from the shapes or other qualities which are already in it, such as being more or less heavy or soft, etc., and partly also from its movements when, having been agitated, it has in itself the power to continue moving.

As for the difficulty of learning the sciences which is in us, and that of clearly representing to ourselves the ideas which are naturally known to us, it comes from the false prejudices of our childhood, and from the other causes of our errors, which I have tried to explain at rather great length in the treatise that is now being printed.

As for memory, I think that the memory of material things depends on the traces that remain in the brain after some image has been imprinted on it, and that the memory of intellectual things depends on other traces which remain in thought itself. But the latter are of a very different kind from the former, and I could not explain them by any example drawn from corporeal things which would not be quite different from them, whereas the traces in the brain make it capable of moving the soul in the same way as it had moved it previously, and thus of making it remember something, such as the creases in a piece of paper or cloth make it more capable of being folded in the same way again than if it had never been folded in that way before.

The moral error which occurs when we justifiably believe something that it false because it has been told to us by a worthy man, etc., contains no privation when we affirm it only in order to regulate the actions of our life, as something it is possible for us to know better; and thus it is not, strictly speaking, an error. But it would be an error if we affirmed it as a truth of physics, because the testimony of a worthy man is not sufficient for that.

As for free will, I have not seen what Father Petau has written about it, but from the way you explain your opinion on the subject, it does not seem to me that my own opinion is very different. First of all, I beg you to note that I have not said that man is indifferent only when he lacks knowledge, but that he is more indifferent as he knows fewer reasons which impel him to make one choice rather than another, and it does not seem to me that this can be denied by anyone. And I am in agreement with you when you say that we can suspend our judgment; but I have tried to explain the means whereby we can suspend it. For it seems to me that it is certain that "from a great light in the understanding follows a great inclination in the will," so that when we see very clearly that something is proper to us, it is very difficult, and even, I believe, impossible, while this thought remains present to us, to arrest the course of our desire. But because the nature of the soul is such that it is attentive to a single thing only, so to speak, for a moment at a time, as soon as our attention turns away from the reasons which make us know that a certain thing is proper to us, so that we remember only that it has appeared to be desirable to us, we can represent to our mind some other reason which makes us doubt it, and thus we suspend our judgment, or even perhaps form a contrary judgment. Thus, since you do not place freedom precisely in indifference, but in a real and positive power of determining oneself, there is only a difference of name between our opinions, for I admit that this power is in the will. But because I do not see that it is any different when it is accompanied by indifference, which you admit to be an imperfection, from what it is when it is not accompanied by it, or that there is anything in the understanding except light, as in that of the blessed who are confirmed in grace, I apply the word "free" to anything that is voluntary, and you want to restrict that word to the power of determining oneself which is accompanied by indifference. But, with regard to words, I desire nothing so much as to follow usage and example.

As for animals without reason, it is obvious that they are not free, because they do not have that positive power of determining themselves; it is in them a pure negation, of not being forced or constrained.

Nothing has prevented me from speaking of our freedom to pursue good or evil, except that I wished to avoid theological controversy as much as possible, and to restrain myself within the limits of natural philosophy. But I admit to you that there is indifference in everything where there is occasion to sin, and I do not believe that, in order to do evil, we need to see clearly that what we are doing is wrong: it is sufficient to see it confusedly, or merely to remember that we have once judged it to be wrong, without seeing it in any way, that is, without being attentive to the reasons which prove it. For if we saw it clearly, it would be impossible for us to sin while we were seeing it in that way; that is why it is said that "every sinner sins through ignorance." And it does not detract from our merit if, seeing very clearly what we ought to do, we do it unfailingly and without any indifference, as Jesus Christ did in this life. For since man cannot always be perfectly attentive to the things he ought to do, it is a good action to have this kind of attention to them, and to make sure, by means of it, that our will follows the light of our understanding so closely that it is never indifferent at all. Furthermore, I have not written that divine grace prevents indifference, but only that it makes us more inclined to one choice rather than another, and that it thus diminishes indifference, although it does not diminish freedom. From this it follows, it seems to me, that this freedom does not consist in indifference.

As for the difficulty of conceiving how it was free and indifferent to God to cause it not to be true that the three angles of a triangle are equal to two right angles, or that, in general, contradictories cannot be together, it is easy to resolve it if we consider that the power of God can have no limits, and that our mind is finite and has been created in such a way that it can conceive as possible those things which God has willed to be truly possible, but not in such a way that it can also conceive as possible those things which God could have made possible, but which he nevertheless willed to make impossible. For the first consideration shows us that God could not have been determined to make it true that contradictories cannot be together, and that consequently He could have done the contrary; and the second consideration assures us that, even though this is true, we must not try to understand it, because our nature is not capable of doing so. And although God has willed that certain truths be necessary, this does not mean that He necessarily willed them to be so, for willing them to be necessary is quite different from necessarily willing it, or being under a necessity to will it. I admit that there are contradictions so obvious that we cannot represent them to our mind without judging them to be entirely impossible, such as the one you suggest: "That God could have caused His creatures not to be dependent on Him." But we do not have to represent them to ourselves in order to know the vastness of His power, and we must not conceive any preference or priority between His understanding and His will, for the idea we have of Him teaches us that there is in Him only a single action, entirely simple and entirely pure. Saint Augustine expresses this very well when he writes, "Because you see these things, they are," etc., because, in God, seeing and willing are the same thing.

I distinguish lines from surfaces, and points from lines, as one mode from another; but I distinguish body from the surfaces, lines and points which modify it, as a substance from its modes. And there is no doubt that a certain mode which belongs to bread remains in the Eucharist, since its external aspect, which is a mode, remains in it. As for the extension of Jesus Christ in this Eucharist, I have not explained it, because I was not obliged to do so, and because I abstain as much as possible from discussing questions of theology; indeed, the Council of Trent has said that it is in the Eucharist "in that mode of existence which we can scarcely express in words." I have purposely inserted these words at the end of my replies to the fourth objections in order to exempt myself from explaining it. But I venture to say that if men were a little more accustomed than they are to my manner of philosophizing, it would be possible to make them understand a means of explaining this mystery which would silence the enemies of our religion, and which they could not contradict.

There is a great difference between *abstraction* and *exclusion*. If I said merely that the idea I have of my soul represents it to me as not being dependent on my body or identical with it, this would be only an abstraction, and I could draw from it only a negative argument which would conclude badly. But I say that this idea represents my soul to me as a substance which can exist even if everything pertaining to body is excluded from it; from this I draw a positive argument and conclude that my soul can exist without my body. And this exclusion of extension is seen very clearly in the nature of the soul from the fact that we cannot conceive half of a thinking thing, as you have quite rightly pointed out.

I would not like to make you take the trouble to send me

what you have written about my *Meditations*, because I hope that I shall soon go to France, where, if I may, I shall have the honor of seeing you. Meanwhile, I beg you to believe me, etc.

చిల్లో

To the Marquis of Newcastle (?)
March or April, 1648

Although I am extremely grateful for the benefits I have received from your favor, when I was in Paris as well as since then, as I have learned from Monsieur de Martigny, who has informed me that, without your help, he would have been unable to do anything in dispatching the pension certificate which he has just sent to me, I shall nevertheless express my heartfelt thanks to you here. Normally only those who wish to be ungrateful make use of this coin, in order to pay with words for the genuine benefits they have received. But I humbly beg you to judge it good that I should tell you that I cannot doubt that you will henceforth have great good will toward me, not for any merit I may claim to have, but because you have already done more for me than most of the relatives or friends I have ever had, so that you may rightly consider me to be one of your creatures. And in examining all the causes of friendship, I find none so powerful or pressing as this one. I take the liberty of writing this to you in order that, when you know that I make this reflection, you will also be unable to doubt that I have a very special zeal for your service. I shall add only this, that the philosophy I cultivate is not so barbarous or savage as to reject the function of the passions; on the contrary, it is in it alone that I place all the sweetness and felicity of this life. And although there are many of these passions whose excesses are vicious, there are others which I judge to be better as they are more excessive. I place gratitude among these latter, as well as among the virtues. That is why I would not believe myself able to be either virtuous or happy if I did not have a passionate desire to show you concretely, at every opportunity, that I am not lacking in gratitde. And since you now offer me no other opportunity than that of fulfilling your two requests, I shall make every effort to do so, although one of your questions concerns a matter which is far removed from my usual speculations.

First, then, I shall tell you that I hold that there is in all created matter a certain amount of movement which never increases or decreases, and thus that when one body makes another move, it loses as much of its movement as it gives. If, for example, a stone falls to the ground, I believe that it stops because it shakes the earth and thus transfers its movement to it. But if the earth it moves contains a thousand times more matter than the stone, in transferring its movement to it the stone transfers only a thousandth of its velocity. And if two unequal bodies each receive the same amount of movement, this movement does not give as much velocity to the larger as to the smaller; we may therefore say that the more matter a body contains, the more natural inertia it has. To this we may add that a large body can better transfer its movement to other bodies than can a small one, and that it can be moved less by them, so that there is one kind of inertia which depends on the amount of matter, and another kind which depends on the extent of its surfaces.

As for your other question, you yourself, it seems to me, have given a very good answer concerning the quality of the knowledge of God in beatitude, for you distinguish it from the knowledge we now have of Him by saying that it will be intuitive. However, if this term does not satisfy you, and if you believe that this intuitive knowledge of God is the same as our present knowledge of Him, or that it is different only with regard to the number of things known, rather than with regard to the manner of knowing, that is where, in my opinion, you have strayed from the right path. Intuitive knowledge is an illumination of the mind by which it sees, in the light of God, those things which it pleases Him to reveal to it by a direct impression of divine light upon our understanding, which in this is not to be considered as an agent, but only as receiving the radiation of the Divinity. Now all the non-miraculous knowledge we can have of God in this life descends from the reasoning and progress of our discourse, which deduces it from the principles of faith, which is obscure, or else it comes from the natural ideas and notions that are in us, and which, however clear they may be, are only crude and confused on such a lofty subject. Therefore, all the knowledge we have or acquire by way of our reason has, first of all, the obscurity of the principles from which it is drawn, and, furthermore, the uncertainty which we experience in all our reasoning.

Now compare these two kinds of knowledge and see

whether this confused and doubtful perception, which costs us a great deal of effort and which we enjoy only for a few moments at a time after we have acquired it, has anything in common with a light that is pure, constant, bright, certain, effortless and always present.

Is it possible to doubt that our mind will be able to receive such direct illumination and knowledge when it is detached from the body, or when the glorified body is no longer a hindrance to it, if we consider that, even in our present body, the senses give us direct knowledge of corporeal and sensible things, and that our soul already has a few pieces of such knowledge of the beneficence of its Creator, without which it would not be capable of reasoning? I confess that these illuminations are somewhat obscured by the mixture of the body, but they still give us primary, gratuitous and certain knowledge which our mind accepts with greater confidence than it places in the reports of our eyes. Will you not admit to me that you are less certain of the presence of the objects you see than of the truth of this proposition: "*I think, therefore I am*"? Now this knowledge is neither a result of your reasoning nor something you have learned from your teachers; your mind sees it, feels it and handles it; and although your imagination, which inopportunely mingles itself with your thoughts, diminishes its clarity by trying to clothe it in its shapes, it is nevertheless a proof of the ability of our soul to receive intuitive knowledge from God.

I seem to discern that you have drawn grounds for doubt from your opinion that intuitive knowledge of God is that in which we know God by Himself. And on this foundation you have built the following reasoning: "I know that God is one because I know that He is a necessary being; now this form of knowing makes use only of God Himself; therefore I know that God is one, by Himself, and conseqeuntly I know intuitively that God is one."

I do not think any extensive examination is required in order to destroy this argument. It should be clear to you that knowing God by Himself, that is, by an immediate illumination of the Divinity on our mind, as is understood by the term "intuitive knowledge," is quite different from making use of God Himself in order to make an induction from one attribute to another, or, to speak more precisely, making use of the natural (and therefore rather obscure, at least in comparison with the other kind) knowledge of one attribute of God in order to form an argument which will establish

another attribute of God. Confess, then, that in this life you
do not see in God, and by His light, that He is one, but that
you conclude it from a proposition you have made about Him,
and that you reach this conclusion by the force of argument,
which is a machine that is often defective. You can see the
power you have over me, for you have made me pass beyond
the limits of philosophizing which I have laid down for
myself, in order to show you how much I am, etc.

BIBLIOGRAPHY

WORKS BY RENÉ DESCARTES

The standard edition is *Oeuvres de Descartes*, edited by Charles Adam and Paul Tannery, 13 vols., Paris, 1897-1913.

The Philosophical Works of Descartes, translated by E. S. Haldane and G. R. T. Ross, 2 vols., Cambridge Univ. Press, 1911. Corrected edition, 1931. Reprinted by Dover, 1955. Volume I contains *Rules for the Direction of the Mind, Discourse on Method, Meditations on First Philosophy, The Principles of Philosophy* (incomplete), *The Search after Truth, The Passions of the Soul, Notes Directed against a Certain Programme.* Vol. II contains the *Objections* urged against the Meditations and the *Replies* by Descartes. *The Principles of Philosophy*, Amsterdam, 1644, is Descartes' most comprehensive work, but the writing is not as lively as in the *Discourse* or the *Meditations*; it is more like a text-book.

BIOGRAPHY

Baillet, Adrien. *La Vie de M. Descartes*, Paris, 1691. The first biography of Descartes. All others draw heavily on this one.

Adam, Charles. *Vie & Oeuvres de Descartes, étude historique*, Paris, 1910. This is a supplement to the Adam & Tannery edition, and is printed in Vol. 12. The same author has a briefer version, *Descartes, sa vie, son oeuvre*, Paris, 1937.

A GOOD GENERAL HISTORY OF PHILOSOPHY

Copleston, Frederick, S.J. *A History of Philosophy*, Vol. IV, The Newman Press, Westminster, Maryland, 1959. Contains five chapters on Descartes and one on Cartesianism; good bibliographies.

COMPREHENSIVE COMMENTARIES

Balz, A. G. A. *Descartes and the Modern Mind*. New Haven, Yale Univ. Press, 1952.

Gibson, A. Boyce. *The Philosophy of Descartes.* London, Methuen & Co., Ltd., 1932.

Smith, N. K. *New Studies in the Philosophy of Descartes.* London, Macmillan & Co. Ltd., 1952. Includes a translation of Descartes' *Threefold Dream,* and other material from Baillet's biography.

CRITICAL DISCUSSIONS OF
SPECIAL ASPECTS OF DESCARTES' THOUGHT

His religious thought:

Gouhier, Henri. *La Pensée Religieuse de Descartes.* Paris, 1924.

Gilson, Étienne. *La Liberté chez Descartes et la Théologie.* Paris, 1913.

Maritain, Jacques. *The Dream of Descartes.* New York, Philosophical Library, 1944. Leaves no doubt in the reader's mind that Descartes is not his favorite philosopher.

His scientific work:

Scott, J. F. *The Scientific Works of René Descartes.* London, Taylor and Francis, Ltd., 1952. The best commentary in English on Descartes' scientific writings.

Milhaud, Gaston. *Descartes, Savant.* Paris, 1921.

BOOKS DEALING WITH THE RELATION
OF DESCARTES' THOUGHT TO OTHERS'

Brunschvicg, Leon. *Descartes et Pascal, Lecteurs de Montaigne.* New York, Brentano's, 1944.

Butterfield, H. *The Origins of Modern Science, 1300-1800.* New York, The Macmillan Co., 1956. First ed. London, 1949. There is also a paperback reprint. This is a worth-while discussion of the scientific background of the entire period; takes up Copernicus, Harvey, Bacon, Descartes, Galileo, Newton and many others.

Crombie, A. C. *Augustine to Galileo, The History of Science, 400-1650.* Cambridge, Harvard Univ. Press, 1953. A good source book; stresses scientific and technological developments; contains good bibliographies and interesting plates.

Gilson, Étienne. *Le Role de la Pensée Médiévale dans la formation du systeme cartésien,* Paris, Librairie Philosophique, J. Vrin, 1930. A valuable book for its historical materials and insights.

Whitehead, Alfred North. *Science and the Modern World.* Lowell Lectures, 1925. New York, The Macmillan Co., 1927. A classic, and delightfully written. Whitehead calls the seventeenth the Century of Genius, and he discusses from that period Francis Bacon, Harvey, Kepler, Galileo, Descartes, Pascal, Huyghens, Boyle, Newton, Locke, Spinoza, Leibniz. His discussions of these figures are brief but illuminating. Most of the book is Whitehead. It is available in paperback.

The etching of Descartes on the cover
of this Bantam Classic is from the
picture collection of the New York
Public Library

BANTAM CLASSICS

are chosen from the whole span of
living literature. They comprise
a balanced selection of the best novels,
poems, plays and stories by writers
whose works and thoughts have made
an indelible impact on Western culture.

BANTAM CLASSICS

NOVELS

BRAVE NEW WORLD Aldous Huxley.................FC85 50¢
THE IDIOT Fyodor Dostoevsky.........................SC4 75¢
LORD JIM Joseph Conrad..............................FC7 50¢
OF MICE AND MEN John Steinbeck....................AC12 35¢
THE DAY OF THE LOCUST Nathanael West........AC14 35¢
HERMAN MELVILLE FOUR SHORT NOVELS....FC16 50¢
BARCHESTER TOWERS Anthony Trollope............FC21 50¢
CRIME AND PUNISHMENT Fyodor Dostoevsky......FC30 50¢
ALL THE KING'S MEN Robert Penn Warren.........HC123 60¢
MADAME BOVARY Gustave Flaubert.................AC35 35¢
   (Translated by Lowell Bair—Introduction by Malcolm Cowley)
LIFE ON THE MISSISSIPPI Mark Twain.............FC39 50¢
THE RED AND THE BLACK Marie-Henri Beyle de Stendhal SC40 75¢
   (Translated by Lowell Bair—Introduction by Clifton Fadiman)
THE AGE OF REASON Jean-Paul Sartre..............SC43 75¢
THE REPRIEVE Jean-Paul Sartre.....................SC69 75¢
ANNA KARENINA Leo Tolstoy........................NC62 95¢
   (Translated by Joel Carmichael—Introduction by Malcolm Cowley)
THE CHARTERHOUSE OF PARMA Stendhal........SC67 75¢
   (Translated by Lowell Bair—Introduction by Harry Levin)
THE ILIAD Homer...................................FC72 50¢
   (Translated by Alston H. Chase and William G. Perry, Jr.)
WHAT MAKES SAMMY RUN? Budd Schulberg......FC99 50¢
REFLECTIONS IN A GOLDEN EYE Carson McCullers.FC100 50¢
   (Introduction by Tennessee Williams)
TYPEE Herman Melville.............................FC96 50¢
   (Introduction by Clifton Fadiman)
EYELESS IN GAZA Aldous Huxley...................SC93 75¢
HENRY ESMOND William Makepeace Thackeray........FC90 50¢
   (Introduction by Lionel Stevenson)
THE AENEID Vergil.................................HC108 60¢
   (Edited with an Introduction by Moses Hadas)
SWEET THURSDAY John Steinbeck...................FC103 50¢
THE HEART IS A LONELY HUNTER Carson McCullers SC102 75¢

PHILOSOPHY

ESSENTIAL WORKS OF STOICISM..............FC121 50¢
   (Edited by Moses Hadas)
ESSENTIAL WORKS OF DESCARTES...........HC110 60¢
   (Translated by Lowell Bair)
ESSENTIAL WORKS OF JOHN STUART MILL...SC111 75¢
   (Edited by Max Lerner)

(continued on next page)

DRAMA

TEN PLAYS BY EURIPIDES........................SC78 75¢
   (Translated by Moses Hadas and John Harvey McLean—Introduction by
   Moses Hadas)
THREE PLAYS Thornton Wilder......................HC98 60¢
MAN AND SUPERMAN George Bernard Shaw..........FC52 50¢
   (Introduction by Brooks Atkinson)
FOUR GREAT ELIZABETHAN PLAYS............FC53 50¢
   (Introduction by John Gassner)
SEVEN PLAYS BY AUGUST STRINDBERG.......SC70 75¢
   (Introduction by John Gassner)
FIVE PLAYS BY OSCAR WILDE.................FC80 50¢
   (Introduction by Hesketh Pearson)
FIVE PLAYS BY GERHART HAUPTMANN.......HC107 60¢
   (Introduction by John Gassner)

RD-4-2385

COLLECTIONS

TALES OF ANCIENT INDIA......................FC60 50¢
   (Translated, with an Introduction, by J. A. B. Van Buitenen)
FANCIES AND GOODNIGHTS John Collier...........SC91 75¢
   (Introduction by Moses Hadas)
HENRY JAMES: FIFTEEN SHORT STORIES.......SC84 75¢
   (Introduction by Morton D. Zabel)
75 SHORT MASTERPIECES: STORIES FROM THE WORLD'S
LITERATURE (Edited by Roger B. Goodman).........HC106 60¢
THE DARING YOUNG MAN ON THE FLYING TRAPEZE
   William Saroyan.........................FC105 50¢
FIFTY GREAT POETS...........................NC104 95¢
   (Edited by Milton Crane)
FIVE SHORT NOVELS Ivan Turgenev.................SC92 75¢
   (Translated and with an Introduction by Franklin Reeve)

NON-FICTION

ONLY YESTERDAY Frederick Lewis Allen.............FC15 50¢
RATS, LICE AND HISTORY Hans Zinsser............FC55 50¢
BEYOND THE PLEASURE PRINCIPLE Sigmund Freud FC49 50¢
   (Translated by James Strachey—Introduction and Notes by
   Dr. Gregory Zilboorg)
GROUP PSYCHOLOGY AND THE ANALYSIS
OF THE EGO Sigmund Freud.........................FC58 50¢
   (Translated by James Strachey—Introduction by Dr. Franz Alexander)
THE PELOPONNESIAN WAR Thucydides............SC71 75¢
   (Translated by Benjamin Jowett—Introductions by Hanson Baldwin &
   Moses Hadas)
THE BIG CHANGE Frederick Lewis Allen...............FC79 50¢
POINTS OF VIEW W. Somerset Maugham.................FC82 50¢
MY LIFE AND HARD TIMES James Thurber ....FC88 50¢
   (Introduction by John K. Hutchens)

Look for Bantam Classics at local newsstands and bookstores. If your
dealer does not carry these books, they may be ordered by sending the
price of the book plus 10¢ postage and handling charge for each copy
to: Dept. BC; Bantam Books, Inc.; 657 W. Chicago Ave.; Chicago 10,
Ill. (On orders for 5 or more books there is no postage charge.) Sorry
no C.O.D.'s. Send check or money order. No currency, please. Allow
three weeks for delivery.

BC-2-61